W9-BNM-752

Some comments from our readers...

"I have to praise you and your company on the fine products you turn out. I have twelve of the *Teach Yourself VISUALLY* and *Simplified* books in my house. They were instrumental in helping me pass a difficult computer course. Thank you for creating books that are easy to follow."

—*Gordon Justin (Brielle, NJ)*

"I commend your efforts and your success. I teach in an outreach program for the Dr. Eugene Clark Library in Lockhart, TX. Your *Teach Yourself VISUALLY* books are incredible and I use them in my computer classes. All my students love them!"

—*Michele Schalin (Lockhart, TX)*

"Thank you so much for helping people like me learn about computers. The Maran family is just what the doctor ordered. Thank you, thank you, thank you."

—*Carol Moten (New Kensington, PA)*

"I would like to take this time to compliment maranGraphics on creating such great books. Thank you for making it clear. Keep up the good work."

—*Kirk Santoro (Burbank, CA)*

"I write to extend my thanks and appreciation for your books. They are clear, easy to follow, and straight to the point. Keep up the good work!

—*Seward Kollie (Dakar, Senegal)*

"What fantastic teaching books you have produced! Congratulations to you and your staff. You deserve the Nobel prize in Education in the Software category. Thanks for helping me to understand computers."

—*Bruno Tonon (Melbourne, Australia)*

"Over time, I have bought a number of your 'Read Less – Learn More' books. For me, they are THE way to learn anything easily."

—*José A. Mazón (Cuba, NY)*

"I was introduced to maranGraphics about four years ago and YOU ARE THE GREATEST THING THAT EVER HAPPENED TO INTRODUCTORY COMPUTER BOOKS!"

—*Glenn Nettleton (Huntsville, AL)*

"Compliments To The Chef!! Your books are extraordinary! Or, simply put, Extra-Ordinary, meaning way above the rest! THANK YOU THANK YOU THANK YOU! for creating these.

—*Christine J. Manfrin (Castle Rock, CO)*

"I'm a grandma who was pushed by an 11-year-old grandson to join the computer age. I found myself hopelessly confused and frustrated until I discovered the Visual series. I'm no expert by any means now, but I'm a lot further along than I would have been otherwise. Thank you!"

—*Carol Louthain (Logansport, IN)*

"Thank you, thank you, thank you....for making it so easy for me to break into this high-tech world. I now own four of your books. I recommend them to anyone who is a beginner like myself. Now....if you could just do one for programming VCRs, it would make my day!"

—*Gay O'Donnell (Calgary, Alberta, Canada)*

"You're marvelous! I am greatly in your debt."

—*Patrick Baird (Lacey, WA)*

maranGraphics is a family-run business located near Toronto, Canada.

At **maranGraphics**, we believe in producing great computer books — one book at a time.

maranGraphics has been producing high-technology products for over 25 years, which enables us to offer the computer book community a unique communication process.

Our computer books use an integrated communication process, which is very different from the approach used in other computer books. Each spread is, in essence, a flow chart — the text and screen shots are totally incorporated into the layout of the spread.

Introductory text and helpful tips complete the learning experience.

maranGraphics' approach encourages the left and right sides of the brain to work together — resulting in faster orientation and greater memory retention.

Above all, we are very proud of the handcrafted nature of our books. Our carefully-chosen writers are experts in their fields, and spend countless hours researching and organizing the content for each topic. Our artists rebuild every screen shot to provide the best clarity possible, making our

screen shots the most precise and easiest to read in the industry. We strive for perfection, and believe that the time spent handcrafting each element results in the best computer books money can buy.

Thank you for purchasing this book. We hope you enjoy it!

Sincerely,

Robert Maran
President
maranGraphics
Rob@maran.com
www.maran.com
www.hungryminds.com/visual

Teach Yourself VISUALLY™

Adobe®
Acrobat® 5 PDF

by Ted Padova

Visual

From
maranGraphics®

&

Hungry Minds™

Best-Selling Books • Digital Downloads • e-books • Answer Networks
e-Newsletters • Branded Web Sites • e-learning

New York, NY • Cleveland, OH • Indianapolis, IN

Teach Yourself VISUALLY™ Acrobat® 5 PDF

Published by
Hungry Minds, Inc.
909 Third Avenue
New York, NY 10022

Copyright © 2002 Hungry Minds, Inc.

Certain designs and illustrations Copyright © 1992-2002 maranGraphics, Inc., used with maranGraphics' permission. All rights reserved. No part of this book, including interior design, cover design, and icons, may be reproduced or transmitted in any form, by any means (electronic, photocopying, recording, or otherwise) without the prior written permission of the publisher.

maranGraphics, Inc.
5755 Coopers Avenue
Mississauga, Ontario, Canada
L4Z 1R9

Library of Congress Control Number: 2002100175

ISBN: 0-7645-3667-2

Printed in the United States of America

10 9 8 7 6 5 4 3 2 1

1K/RQ/QV/QS/IN

Distributed in the United States by Hungry Minds, Inc.

Distributed by CDG Books Canada Inc. for Canada; by Transworld Publishers Limited in the United Kingdom; by IDG Norge Books for Norway; by IDG Sweden Books for Sweden; by IDG Books Australia Publishing Corporation Pty. Ltd. for Australia and New Zealand; by TransQuest Publishers Pte Ltd. for Singapore, Malaysia, Thailand, Indonesia, and Hong Kong; by Gotop Information Inc. for Taiwan; by ICG Muse, Inc. for Japan; by Intersoft for South Africa; by Eyrolles for France; by International Thomson Publishing for Germany, Austria and Switzerland; by Distribuidora Cuspide for Argentina; by LR International for Brazil; by Galileo Libros for Chile; by Ediciones ZETA S.C.R. Ltda. for Peru; by WS Computer Publishing Corporation, Inc., for the Philippines; by Contemporanea de Ediciones for Venezuela; by Express Computer Distributors for the Caribbean and West Indies; by Micronesia Media Distributor, Inc. for Micronesia; by Chips Computadoras S.A. de C.V. for Mexico; by Editorial Norma de Panama S.A. for Panama; by American Bookshops for Finland.

For corporate orders, please call maranGraphics at 800-469-6616 or fax 905-890-9434.

For general information on Hungry Minds' products and services please contact our Customer Care Department within the U.S. at 800-762-2974, outside the U.S. at 317-572-3993 or fax 317-572-4002.

For sales inquiries and reseller information, including discounts, premium and bulk quantity sales, and foreign-language translations, please contact our Customer Care Department at 800-434-3422, fax 317-572-4002, or write to Hungry Minds, Inc., Attn: Customer Care Department, 10475 Crosspoint Boulevard, Indianapolis, IN 46256.

For information on licensing foreign or domestic rights, please contact our Sub-Rights Customer Care Department at 212-884-5000.

For information on using Hungry Minds' products and services in the classroom or for ordering examination copies, please contact our Educational Sales Department at 800-434-2086 or fax 317-572-4005.

For press review copies, author interviews, or other publicity information, please contact our Public Relations department at 317-572-3168 or fax 317-572-4168.

For authorization to photocopy items for corporate, personal, or educational use, please contact Copyright Clearance Center, 222 Rosewood Drive, Danvers, MA 01923, or fax 978-750-4470.

Screen shots displayed in this book are based on pre-released software and are subject to change.

Trademark Acknowledgments

Permissions

maranGraphics
Certain text and Illustrations by maranGraphics, Inc., used with maranGraphics' permission.

Hungry Minds™ is a trademark of Hungry Minds, Inc.

U.S. Corporate Sales	U.S. Trade Sales
Contact maranGraphics at (800) 469-6616 or Fax (905) 890-9434.	Contact Hungry Minds at (800) 434-3422 or fax (317) 572-4002.

CREDITS

Acquisitions, Editorial, and Media Development

Editorial Manager
Rev Mengle

Acquisitions Editor
Jen Dorsey

Product Development Supervisor
Lindsay Sandman

Development Editor
Ted Cains

Technical Editor
Sherri Schafer

Permissions Editor
Laura Moss

Special Help
Maureen K. Spears, Sarah Hellert,
Tim Borek, Jade Williams

Production

Book Design
maranGraphics®

Production Coordinator
Dale White

Layout
Beth Brooks, Melanie DesJardins,
LeAndra Johnson, Kristin McMullan, Heather Pope

Screen Artists
Mark Harris, Jill A. Proll

Illustrators
Ronda David-Burroughs, David E. Gregory,
Sean Johannesen, Russ Marini, Greg Maxson,
Steven Schaerer

Proofreader
Mary Lagu

Quality Control
John Bitter

Indexer
Liz Cunningham

ACKNOWLEDGMENTS

General and Administrative

Wiley Technology Publishing Group: Richard Swadley, Vice President and Executive Group Publisher; Bob Ipsen, Vice President and Executive Publisher; Barry Pruett, Vice President and Publisher; Joseph Wikert, Vice President and Publisher; Mary Bednarek, Editorial Director; Mary C. Corder, Editorial Director; Andy Cummings, Editorial Director.

Wiley Production for Branded Press: Debbie Stailey, Production Director

ABOUT THE AUTHOR

Ted Padova has authored, co-authored, and contributed to more than a dozen publications on Adobe Acrobat, Adobe Photoshop, and digital imaging. Recent books include the top selling *Acrobat PDF Bible* (Hungry Minds, Inc.) and the first book to be published exclusively on Acrobat PDF forms, *Creating Acrobat PDF Forms*. He has owned and operated a digital imaging service bureau and custom photo finishing lab since 1990; taught university classes in Acrobat, Photoshop, and digital imaging for the University of California since 1986; and has served as a national and international conference speaker on Adobe Acrobat, PDF forms, and imaging programs. He has a graduate degree in clinical counseling and currently uses those skills providing therapy to graphic designers suffering from post-catatonic conditions after picking up match prints at service bureaus.

AUTHOR'S ACKNOWLEDGMENTS

Much gratitude and appreciation goes to the following people who collectively contributed to producing this publication: Jen Dorsey, my Acquisitions Editor; Rev Mengle, Managing Editor; Ted Cains, Development Editor; Laura Moss, Permissions Editor. And to all the background production folks at maranGraphics and Hungry Minds, Inc. for contributing to the production of this book and the *Teach Yourself VISUALLY* series.

Special thanks goes to Sherry Schafer of Schafer Design for her outstanding job as my Technical Editor. Barbara Obermeier — just because she's always in the background helping through each project, and the many readers of my *Acrobat PDF Bible* who asked for a more simplified work on Adobe Acrobat.

Посвящается Милочке

TABLE OF CONTENTS

Chapter 1

GET STARTED WITH ADOBE ACROBAT

Introducing Adobe Acrobat 4

Explore the Acrobat Document Window 6

Know the Acrobat Tools 8

Open Acrobat Distiller or Catalog 9

Understanding PDF .10

Open a PDF Document 11

Open a PDF in a Web Browser 12

Save a Copy from Acrobat Reader 14

Save a File from Acrobat 15

Organize Tools 16

Examine the Environment 18

Set Preferences 20

Using Adobe Online Services 21

Chapter 2

VIEW PDF FILES

Set the Page View .24

Navigate Documents 26

Using Bookmarks .27

View Thumbnails 28

Jump to a Page 29

Zoom a View 30

Tile Views 32

Activate Links 33

Using Context Menus 34

Rotate Pages 35

Control the Opening View 36

Chapter 3

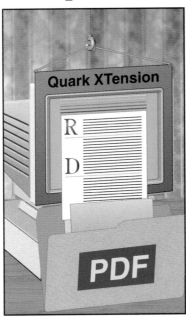

Understanding PDF Creation Options 40

Convert Image Files to PDF 42

Convert HTML Files to PDF 44

Convert Text Files to PDF 45

Using PDF Maker with Microsoft Word 46

Export Styles from Microsoft Word 48

Using PDF Maker with Microsoft Excel 50

Using PDF Maker with Microsoft PowerPoint 51

Export PDFs from Adobe Photoshop 52

Export PDFs from Adobe PageMaker 54

Export PDFs from QuarkXPress 56

Export PDFs from Adobe FrameMaker 58

Export PDFs from Adobe Illustrator 60

Export PDFs from CorelDraw 62

Capture Web Pages .64

Chapter 4

Print PostScript Files .68

Launch Acrobat Distiller 70

Set Acrobat Distiller Preferences 72

Using the Create Adobe PDF Option (Macintosh) . . .73

Adjust Job Options 74

Distill a PostScript File 78

Monitor Font Locations 80

Create Watched Folders 82

Repurpose PDF Documents 84

Correct Font Problems 86

Convert EPS to PDF .88

Secure PDFs with Acrobat Distiller 90

TABLE OF CONTENTS

Chapter 5

WORK WITH LINKS

Understanding Links .94
Create a Bookmark .96
Using Bookmark Properties 98
Create an Article Thread 100
Create Link Buttons 102
Create Links from Text 104
Create a World Wide Web Link 106
Import a Sound .107
Link to a Movie .108
Create a Form Field Link Button 110
Duplicate Field Buttons 114
Create a Destination 116
Link to a Destination 118

Chapter 6

CREATE COMMENTS

Understanding Comments 122
Set Comment Preferences 124
Create a Note Comment 126
Set Comment Properties 128
Create a Free Text Note 130
Create a File Attachment 131
Create an Audio Comment 132
Using the Stamp Tool 134
Create Custom Stamps 136
Create Comments with Graphic Markup Tools . . .140
Using the Text Markup Tools 141
Filter Comments .142
Create Comment Summaries 144
Select a Network Folder for Online Comments . . .146
Work with Online Comments 148
Spell Check Comments and Form Fields 150

Chapter 7

EDIT PAGES IN ACROBAT

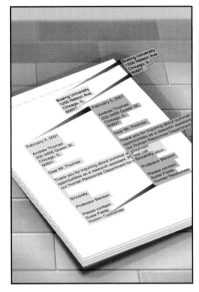

Understanding PDF Page Editing 154

Copy and Paste Pages 156

Extract Pages 158

Replace Pages 159

Insert Pages 160

Edit an Image 162

Edit an Object 164

Using the TouchUp Text Tool 166

Copy Text 168

Using RTF-Formatted Files 170

Export Table-Formatted Text 171

Crop Pages 172

Add a Text Block .174

Create URL Links from Text 175

Chapter 8

PRINT PDFS

Understanding Printing Devices and Terms 178

Using the Page Setup Dialog Box 180

Set Printing Controls 182

Control Print Security 184

Print a Soft-Proof Color Separation 186

View a Soft-Proof Separation On-Screen 188

Print Proofs for Commercial Printers 190

Chapter 9

CREATE SEARCH INDEXES

Launch Acrobat Catalog and Set Preferences 194

Create a Search Index 196

Restrict Word Options 198

Rebuild or Purge an Index 199

Examine Document Summaries 200

Create a Search Key Using the
Document Summary 202

TABLE OF CONTENTS

Chapter 10

USING ACROBAT SEARCH

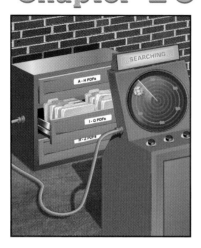

Load a Search Index .206
Using the Adobe Acrobat Search Dialog Box . . .208
Set Search Preferences 210
Search Document Summary Information 212
Understanding Keywords, Expressions,
    and Boolean Operators 214
Using Keywords, Expressions,
    and Boolean Operators 216
View Document Information 218
Understand Relative Referencing 219
Search Table Keys 220
Relocate a Search Index File 221

Chapter 11

CREATE ACROBAT FORMS

Understanding Acrobat Forms 224
Understanding Field Properties 226
Create Text Fields 228
Create Table Arrays 230
Create Radio Buttons 232
Create Check Boxes 234
Create Combo Boxes 236
Set Tab Order 238
Align Form Fields 240
Resize Form Fields 241
Export and Import Form Field Data 242
Save Populated PDF Forms 244

Chapter 12

CREATE JAVASCRIPTS

Understanding Acrobat JavaScript 248
Create an Application Beep 250
Import an Image .252
Navigate Pages with JavaScript 254

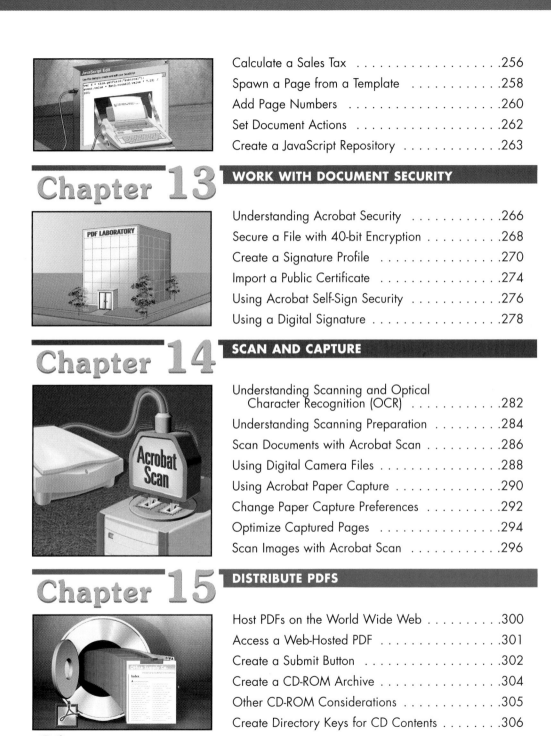

Calculate a Sales Tax 256

Spawn a Page from a Template 258

Add Page Numbers 260

Set Document Actions 262

Create a JavaScript Repository 263

Chapter 13

WORK WITH DOCUMENT SECURITY

Understanding Acrobat Security 266

Secure a File with 40-bit Encryption 268

Create a Signature Profile 270

Import a Public Certificate 274

Using Acrobat Self-Sign Security 276

Using a Digital Signature 278

Chapter 14

SCAN AND CAPTURE

Understanding Scanning and Optical
    Character Recognition (OCR) 282

Understanding Scanning Preparation 284

Scan Documents with Acrobat Scan 286

Using Digital Camera Files 288

Using Acrobat Paper Capture 290

Change Paper Capture Preferences 292

Optimize Captured Pages 294

Scan Images with Acrobat Scan 296

Chapter 15

DISTRIBUTE PDFS

Host PDFs on the World Wide Web 300

Access a Web-Hosted PDF 301

Create a Submit Button 302

Create a CD-ROM Archive 304

Other CD-ROM Considerations 305

Create Directory Keys for CD Contents 306

Glossary

. 308

HOW TO USE THIS TEACH YOURSELF VISUALLY BOOK

Teach Yourself VISUALLY Acrobat 5 PDF contains straightforward sections that you can use to learn the basics of Adobe Acrobat. This book is designed to help a reader receive quick access to any area of question. You can simply look up a subject within the Table of Contents or Index and go immediately to the section of concern. A *section* is a set of self-contained units that walks you through a computer operation step-by-step. That is, with rare exception, all the information you need regarding an area of interest is contained within a section.

WHO THIS BOOK IS FOR

This book is highly recommended for the visual learner who wants to learn the basics of Acrobat, and who may or may not have prior experience using Acrobat viewers or working with PDF documents.

CHAPTER ORGANIZATION

Each task contains an introduction, a set of screen shots, and, if the task goes beyond 1 page, a set of tips. The introduction tells why you want to perform the task, the advantages and disadvantages of performing the task, and references to other related tasks in the book. The screens, located on the bottom half of each page, show a series of steps that you must complete to perform a given section. The tip portion of the section gives you an opportunity to further understand the task at hand, to learn about other related tasks in other areas of the book, or to apply alternative methods.

A chapter may also contain an illustrated group of pages that gives you background information that you need to understand the sections in a chapter.

GENERAL ORGANIZATION

The first chapter, "Get Started with Adobe Acrobat," shows you how to view and navigate PDF files, organize tools and move around the Acrobat environment. The differences among the Acrobat viewers and using Adobe online services are also demonstrated.

Chapter 2, "View PDF Files," shows you how to set opening views, and how to use bookmarks and thumbnails to further assist you in navigating through PDF files.

Chapter 3, "Create PDF Files," shows you how to convert many different document files to the Portable Document Format (PDF). You learn to use Acrobat tools and authoring applications for conversion methods to PDF.

PDF Creation is extended in Chapter 4, "Using Acrobat Distiller," to show you how to print PostScript files and have them converted with the Acrobat Distiller software. Controlling the Distiller Job Options and learning what they do are covered in detail.

Chapter 5, "Work with Links," shows you how to create interactivity in Acrobat PDFs through tools like the link tool and actions associated with links. Linking to sounds, movies and other PDF documents shows you how Acrobat can be used for many different purposes.

Chapter 6, "Create Comments," shows you how to add many different kinds of comment notes. You learn how to *mark up* a PDF for collaboration and how to use comments on networks and Web servers for workgroup collaboration.

Chapter 7, "Edit Pages in Acrobat," shows you how to edit and refine PDF documents. You learn how to extract PDF data, change the contents of the PDF file, and change content on individual PDF pages.

Chapter 8, "Print PDFs," shows you how to print your PDF files to desktop printers and how to prepare files for commercial print shops.

Chapter 9, "Create Search Indexes," shows you how to create index files from a collection of PDF documents. Once an index file is created, it can be loaded in Acrobat and used with Acrobat Search to find words among many different PDF documents.

Chapter 10, "Using Acrobat Search," shows you how to search PDF documents. From the search index files you create in Chapter 9, you learn how to invoke sophisticated searches to find information fast.

Chapter 11, "Create Acrobat Forms," shows you how to create interactive forms in Adobe Acrobat. The various form field types and how to manage form fields are covered in this chapter.

Chapter 12 "Create JavaScripts," extends the Acrobat forms introduced in Chapter 11 to show you how to add interactivity to Acrobat forms. Even if you have never programmed JavaScript, this chapter helps you understand basic fundamentals you can easily duplicate on your own forms.

Chapter 13, "Work with Document Security," shows you how to secure PDF documents to protect them against unauthorized viewing or changing content. You learn to use Acrobat Standard Security and also use Acrobat Self-Sign Security for securing files among workgroups.

Chapter 14, "Scan and Capture," shows you how to use other Acrobat features for scanning documents and converting scanned documents to recognizable text.

Chapter 15, "Distribute PDFs," shows you how to host PDF documents on the World Wide Web and copy collections of PDF documents to CD-ROMs.

MOUSE CONVENTIONS

This book uses the following conventions to describe the actions you perform when using the mouse:

CLICK

Press and release the left mouse button (Windows) or the mouse button (Macintosh). You use a click to select an item on the screen.

DOUBLE-CLICK

Quickly press and release the left mouse button twice. You double-click to open a document or start a program.

RIGHT-CLICK (WINDOWS)

Press and release the right mouse button. You use a right-click to display a shortcut menu, a list of commands specifically related to the selected item.

CONTROL-CLICK (MACINTOSH)

Press the Control key down and click the mouse button to emulate the same features as the Windows users when pressing the right mouse button. The same shortcut menus mentioned above open on the Macintosh with a Control-click.

CLICK AND DRAG, AND RELEASE THE MOUSE

Position the mouse pointer over an item on the screen and then press and hold down the left mouse button. Still holding down the button, move the mouse to where you want to place the item and then release the button. Dragging and dropping makes it easy to move an item to a new location.

PLATFORM CONVENTIONS

Although this book contains a Windows bias, you can also perform the same steps on a Mac. When there is a difference between the platforms' keyboard or menu conventions, this book lists the PC convention first, followed by the Mac convention. Please note that at the time of this writing, some program features were not available for both platforms. If a feature is platform-specific, the headline will indicate either (Windows only) or (Mac only).

This book assumes that you are using Windows 98, 2000, or XP or a Mac with OS 9.x installed on your computer. Other OS versions may give different results than those stated in this book.

OTHER CONVENTIONS

A number of typographic and layout styles have been used to distinguish different types of information.

Bold indicates what you must click in a menu or dialog box.

Italics indicates a new term being introduced.

Numbered steps indicate that you must perform these steps in order to successfully perform the task.

Bulleted steps give you alternative methods, explain various options, or present what a program will do in response to the numbered steps.

Notes give you additional information to help you complete a task. The purpose of a note is three-fold: It can explain special conditions that may occur during the course of the task, warn you of potentially dangerous situations, or refer you to tasks in the same, or a different chapter. References to tasks within the chapter are indicated by the phrase "See the section..." followed by the name of the task. References to other chapters are indicated by "See Chapter..." followed by the chapter number.

Icons in the steps indicate a button that you must click to perform a section.

CHAPTER 1

Get Started with Adobe Acrobat

Are you ready to start using Adobe Acrobat? In this chapter, you learn what Acrobat is and some basic concepts about the Acrobat environment.

Introducing Adobe Acrobat 4

Explore the Acrobat
  Document Window..........................6

Know the Acrobat Tools 8

Open Acrobat Distiller or Catalog 9

Understanding PDF 10

Open a PDF Document 11

Open a PDF in a Web Browser 12

Save a Copy from Acrobat Reader......14

Save a File from Acrobat 15

Organize Tools 16

Examine the Environment 18

Set Preferences...............................20

Using Adobe Online Services 21

INTRODUCING ADOBE ACROBAT

Adobe Acrobat is a complex suite of programs that provides users the ability to create and author PDF files for distribution in print, on the Internet, and on CD-ROM. The Acrobat Portable Document Format (PDF) has become a standard viewing file format for many industries, serving almost any digital purpose.

Print Files

Most service centers, magazine and newspaper publishers, and individual users printing to desktop printers create, share, and use PDF documents for professional and personal document printing needs.

Distribute on the World Wide Web

Because any end user can acquire the free Adobe Acrobat Reader software, anyone owning a Macintosh, Windows, or UNIX computer can view PDF files. When PDF documents are hosted on Web servers, users can use a Web browser, in conjunction with an Acrobat viewer, to view documents with complete document integrity.

Replicate CD-ROMs

You can copy any collection of files to CD-ROMs and distribute them to users. For large volumes or simply to make a copy of a company's annual report or product brochure, replicating CD-ROMs is a cost-effective method for distributing information. Once again, with the free Acrobat Reader software, end users can view any PDF files distributed on CD-ROMs.

Create Smart Forms

You can create forms with Adobe Acrobat for distribution on the Web, CD-ROMs, or on a company's network server. You can even create forms with fields in which end users with the free Reader software can type information and print the form.

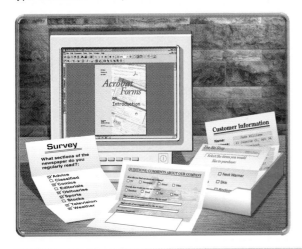

Create Search Indexes

For a collection of PDF files hosted locally on your computer, a company network server, or PDFs copied to a CD-ROM, you can create a search index to help users find information quickly.

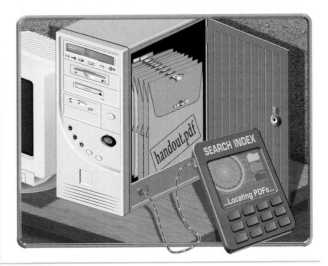

Add HyperText Links

You can bookmark, create Article Threads, or link pages from text or buttons to provide end users with easy hyperlinking through a single PDF file or multiple PDFs. You can link to sounds, movies, and application files created in any authoring program.

Create Comments

You can annotate PDF documents with many different Comment tools designed to assist you in providing feedback on documents shared in workgroups. You can share your comments with office workers and colleagues on network servers or the Internet.

EXPLORE THE ACROBAT DOCUMENT WINDOW

Acrobat provides many different ways for viewing, navigating, and authoring PDF files. Take some time to become familiar with the on-screen elements.

Command Bar

The Command Bar includes both rows of tools. You can drag individual toolbars away from the Command Bar and position them anywhere in the document window for easy access.

Navigation Pane

Contains by default four palettes (Bookmarks, Thumbnails, Comments, and Signatures). Click the Palette tab to open the Navigation Pane and display the palette contents.

Status Bar

Allows you to check the page number or navigate to a page, view the page size, and display the page view from selections made in the Status Bar.

Title Bar

The Title Bar is the topmost area where text appears. After Adobe Acrobat, the name of the current open file is displayed in parentheses.

Document Pane

Displays PDF documents when opened in an Acrobat viewer.

Menu Bar

The Menu Bar is similar to menu bars in other applications, and displays the Acrobat viewer menus. When selected, a menu drops down where you can choose commands.

Scroll Bars

Enables you to scroll around a window when the display is zoomed by clicking the arrows or elevator bars.

Navigate with the Mouse

Drag the mouse on the desktop surface to move around the Document Pane or make selections from menus or palettes. The cursor changes as you select different tools in the Command Bar. To make a menu or tool selection, click the mouse button (the left button in Windows) and release it when the cursor appears over the desired selection.

Navigate with the Keyboard

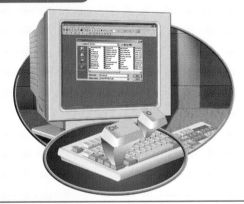

You can use the keyboard to make menu selections, activate tools, or invoke many different actions. For example, press the Page Down key or the Right Arrow key to navigate forward in an open PDF document with multiple pages. You can use keyboard shortcuts for menu actions. For example, hold the `Ctrl` (Windows) or ⌘ (Macintosh) key down and press the `O` key to open a file.

Open Companion Programs

You can launch other programs from within Acrobat. To open Adobe Acrobat Distiller or Adobe Acrobat Catalog, click the Tools menu and then click Distiller or Catalog from the menu choices. When applications such as Distiller or Catalog are running concurrent with Acrobat, click the Features button (`X`). On the Macintosh, click the Close button (🔲) to close Acrobat catalog. To close the Acrobat Distiller application, click **File**, then click **Quit**. Distiller or Catalog closes and returns you to the Acrobat window.

Adobe Acrobat contains several different programs. The free Acrobat Reader software is limited in capability. However, when you purchase the full version of Adobe Acrobat, you receive the Acrobat authoring application, which enables you to edit PDF files with more tools than those provided by Reader.

KNOW THE ACROBAT TOOLS

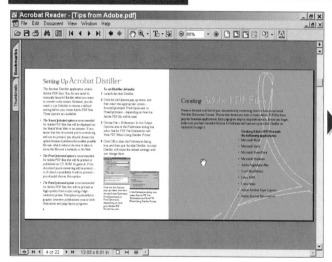

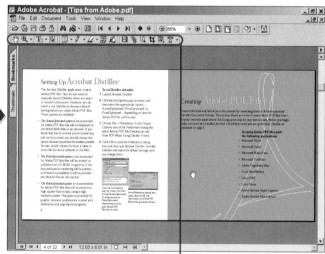

■ The Acrobat Reader window.

■ The Acrobat Window.

■ Notice that more tools are available in Acrobat than in Reader.

OPEN ACROBAT DISTILLER OR CATALOG

Acrobat offers more tools in the form of companion applications. You can launch Acrobat Distiller and Acrobat Catalog from within Acrobat.

OPEN ACROBAT DISTILLER OR CATALOG

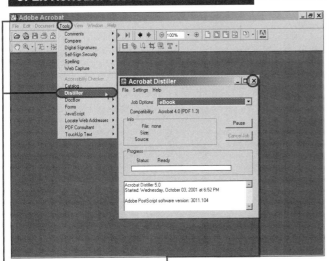
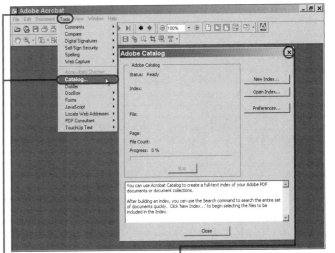

OPEN ACROBAT DISTILLER

■1 Click **Tools**.

■2 Click **Distiller**.

■ The Acrobat Distiller application window appears.

■ You can also double-click the application icon from the Desktop view.

■3 To close Distiller, click ⊠ (Windows), or click **File**, **Quit** (Macintosh).

Note: For more on Distiller, see Chapter 4.

OPEN ACROBAT CATALOG

■1 Click **Tools**.

■2 Click **Catalog**.

■ The Acrobat Catalog window appears.

■3 To close Catalog, click ⊠ (Windows), or ▣ (Macintosh).

Note: For more on Catalog, see Chapter 9.

UNDERSTANDING PDF

The Portable Document Format (PDF) was designed as a common format for exchanging files between computers running different operating systems. You can embed text and graphics in a PDF file to preserve exactly how the document should look. PDFs are displayed in Acrobat viewers, such as Reader, Acrobat Approval, or Acrobat.

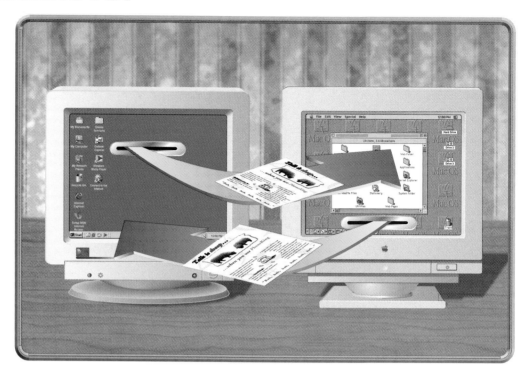

UNDERSTANDING PDF

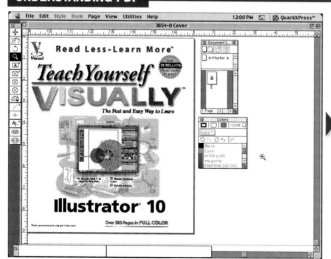

■ A document as viewed in QuarkXpress on a Macintosh computer.

■ When converted to a PDF file and opened in Acrobat on Windows, the document appears identical to the original.

When a document is converted to PDF, you can open it in an Acrobat viewer. You open PDF files the same way in all viewers.

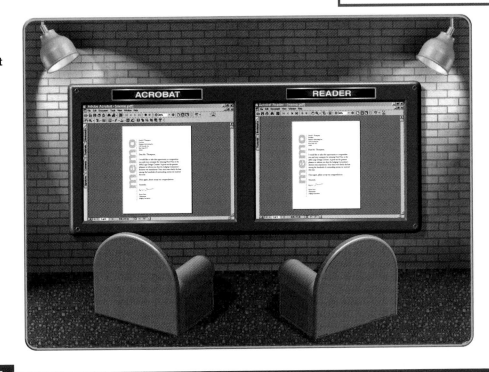

OPEN A PDF DOCUMENT

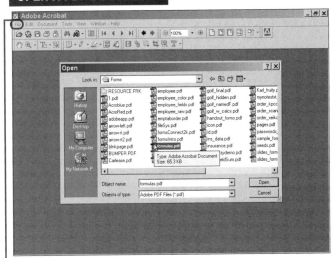

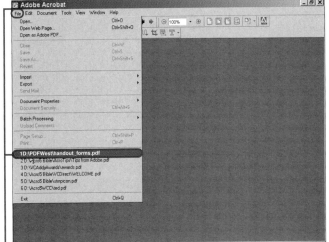

OPEN A PDF DOCUMENT IN ACROBAT

■1 Click **File**.

■2 Click **Open**.

■ The Open dialog box appears.

OPEN A RECENTLY VIEWED PDF

■1 Click **File**.

■2 Click the filename for the recently viewed file.

■ You can also click 📂 to display the Open dialog box.

■ The designated file opens in the Document Pane.

Note: You can also use the keyboard shortcut Ctrl + O *(Windows) or* ⌘ + O *(Macintosh) to open the dialog box.*

OPEN A PDF IN A WEB BROWSER

You can view PDF files in a Web browser, such as Microsoft Internet Explorer or Netscape Navigator. Acrobat, Acrobat Approval, or Acrobat Reader must be installed on your computer to view a PDF inside the browser window.

OPEN A PDF IN A WEB BROWSER

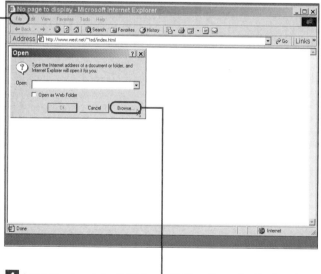

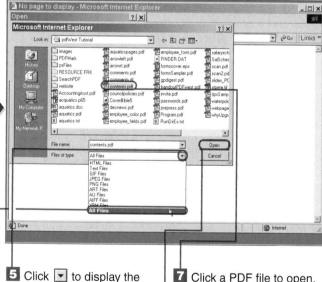

1 Launch your default Web browser.

2 Click **File**.

3 Click **Open** (in Internet Explorer) or **Open File** (in Netscape Navigator).

■ The Open (in Explorer) or Open Page (in Navigator) dialog box appears.

4 Click **Browse** (Explorer) or **Choose File** (Navigator).

5 Click ▼ to display the file types.

6 Click **All Files** from the drop-down menu.

7 Click a PDF file to open.

8 Click **Open**.

Can I open a PDF file on the World Wide Web?

You can open a file from a Web server by navigating to the URL (for example, www.mycompany.com/file.pdf) where the PDF resides. The destination URL includes the PDF filename, and the PDF is viewed in the browser window. Notice the Acrobat tools appearing inside the browser window. You can use these tools when viewing PDFs in a browser.

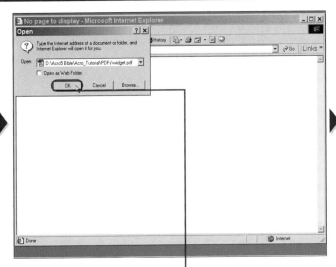

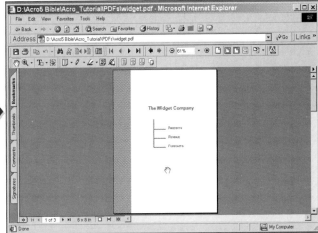

■ The Open dialog box (Explorer) or Open Page dialog box (Navigator) appears.

9 Click **OK**.

■ The PDF document opens in the Web browser window.

Note: Viewing PDFs in a Web browser window is commonly referred to as inline viewing.

SAVE A COPY FROM ACROBAT READER

You can create a duplicate copy of a PDF file with Acrobat Reader. You can save files viewed as inline PDFs in a Web browser to a local hard drive or a network server.

SAVE A COPY FROM ACROBAT READER

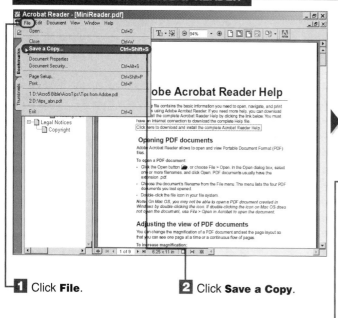

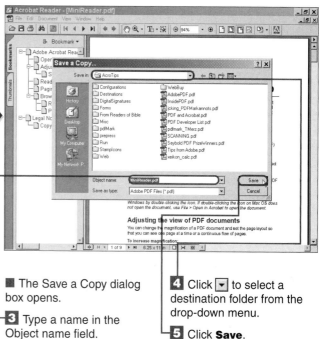

1 Click **File**.

2 Click **Save a Copy**.

■ The Save a Copy dialog box opens.

3 Type a name in the Object name field.

4 Click ▼ to select a destination folder from the drop-down menu.

5 Click **Save**.

Note: You can also click 🖫 in the Acrobat toolbar to open the Save a Copy dialog box.

SAVE A FILE FROM ACROBAT

Acrobat is the editing application in the Adobe Acrobat suite of software. After making edits to PDF files in Acrobat, you can save the changes. When you click Save As from the File menu, Acrobat rewrites the entire PDF to disk. By rewriting the file, you can often reduce the file size.

SAVE A FILE FROM ACROBAT

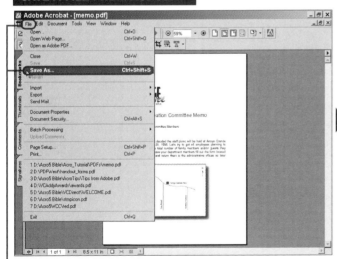

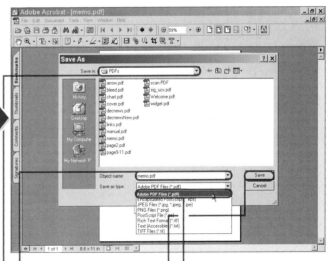

1 Click **File**.

2 Click **Save As**.

Note: If no edits have been made in the PDF, only the Save As option is available. Save becomes active after you make a change in the PDF.

■ The Save As dialog box opens.

3 Type a name in the Object name field.

4 Click ▼ to select a destination folder for the file from the drop-down menu.

5 Click ▼ to select **Adobe PDF Files (*.pdf)** from the Save as type drop-down menu.

Note: Acrobat can save documents in several different file formats.

6 Click **Save**.

ORGANIZE TOOLS

You can reorganize the Acrobat user interface to accommodate your personal needs. You can remove toolbars from the Command Bar and relocate them to the Document Pane for easy access.

ORGANIZE TOOLS

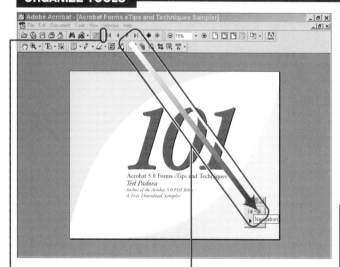

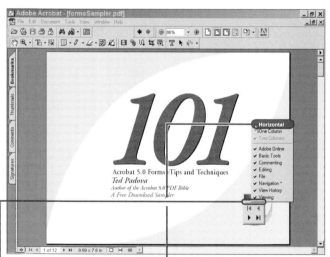

UNDOCK TOOLBARS FROM THE COMMAND BAR

1 Click the vertical line in the toolbar you wish to detach.

2 Hold the mouse button down and drag away from the Command Bar.

Note: You can move a toolbar only by clicking and dragging the vertical embossed line in a toolbar.

CHANGE TOOLBAR ORIENTATION

1 Position the cursor on the horizontal line in the detached toolbar.

2 Right-click the mouse button (**Control** +click on the Macintosh).

■ A context menu appears.

3 Click one of the menu selections.

■ Acrobat displays the tools accordingly.

Can I group palettes?

You can open several palettes by clicking the Window menu and subsequently clicking a palette name. When a palette is opened, you can dock it in the Navigation Pane by dragging the tab to the Navigation Pane and releasing the mouse button. To close a palette and hide it from view, drag the palette tab from the Navigation Pane and click ⊠. On the Macintosh, click ▢.

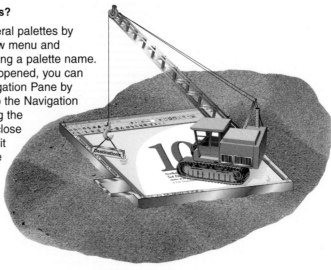

EXPAND AND COLLAPSE TOOLBARS

1 Click ▾ in a tool group.

■ A drop-down menu opens displaying additional tools.

2 Click **Expand This Button**.

■ The toolbar expands to reveal all tools in the tool group.

3 Click ◂ in an expanded toolbar.

■ The toolbar collapses.

EXAMINE THE ENVIRONMENT

In addition to tools and palettes, menu commands offer additional editing tasks in Acrobat. Take a moment to become familiar with the menus and note the various commands available to you.

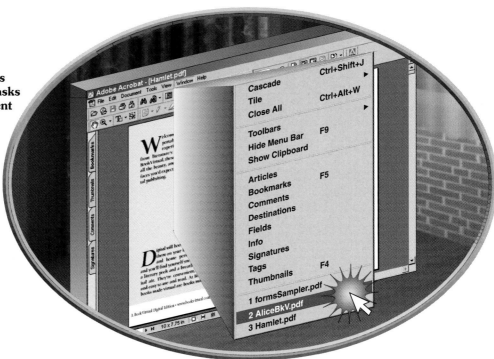

EXAMINE THE ENVIRONMENT

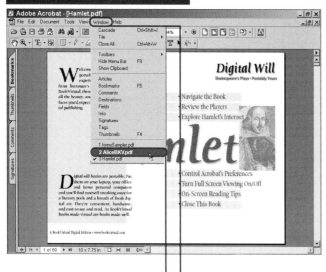

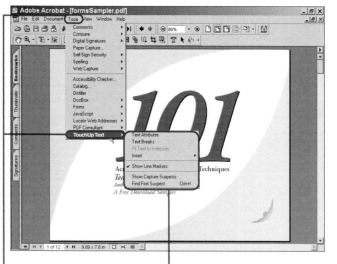

VIEW OPEN DOCUMENTS

1 Open several PDFs.

Note: See "Open a PDF Document" earlier in this chapter.

2 Click **Window**.

■ All open documents appear by name at the bottom of the menu.

VIEW SUBMENUS

1 Click **Tools**.

2 Click **TouchUp Text**.

■ A submenu opens.

3 To select a submenu, drag the mouse to the right, highlight the desired command, and release the mouse button.

How can I quickly access menu choices?

You can make menu and tool choices by using keyboard shortcuts. As you explore the menus, note various options for keystrokes on the right side of different commands. The key combinations activate the menu commands when you type them. For example:
`Ctrl` + `Shift` + `S` (`⌘` + `Shift` + `S` on the Macintosh) opens the Save As dialog box. As you use menu commands, try to remember frequently accessed menu choices.

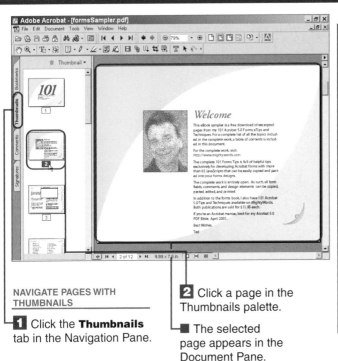

NAVIGATE PAGES WITH THUMBNAILS

1 Click the **Thumbnails** tab in the Navigation Pane.

2 Click a page in the Thumbnails palette.

■ The selected page appears in the Document Pane.

SELECT A HELP DOCUMENT

1 Click **Help**.

2 Click **Acrobat Help**.

■ A help file installed with Acrobat opens in the Document Pane. Browse the file to find help information on using Adobe Acrobat.

SET PREFERENCES

Preference settings add further control over your Acrobat environment. As you work with tools and menu commands, you may periodically want to change the General Preferences to suit your needs.

Preference Settings

SET PREFERENCES

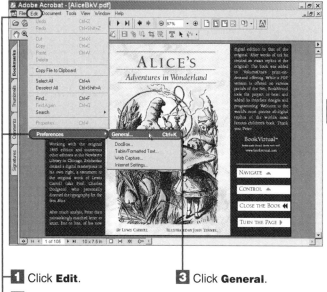

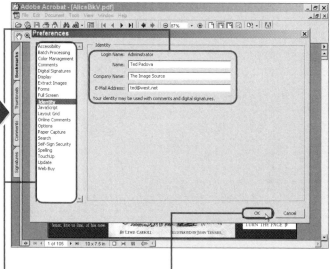

1 Click **Edit**.

2 Click **Preferences**.

3 Click **General**.

■ The General Preferences dialog box opens.

4 Click one of the preference categories.

5 Change the settings as appropriate.

■ In this example, the identifying information is used when you annotate a PDF with comments and when you create digital signatures.

6 Click **OK** to make the changes.

USING ADOBE ONLINE SERVICES

From time to time, you may need to update resources for Acrobat, or you may want to find valuable tips and techniques for working with the program. Adobe Systems has made these tasks easy by providing online information and resources. To perform the steps, you need to have an Internet connection.

USING ADOBE ONLINE SERVICES

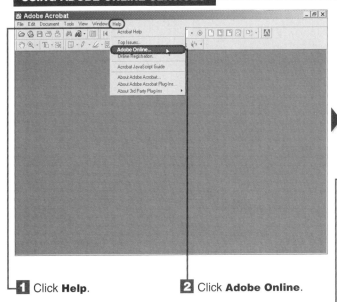

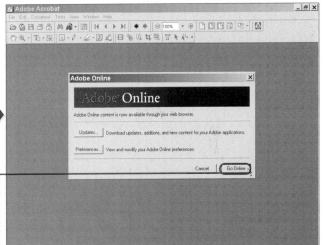

1 Click **Help**.

2 Click **Adobe Online**.

■ The Adobe Online dialog box opens. Be certain your Internet connection is active.

3 Click **Go Online**.

■ Your default Web browser launches and takes you to Adobe's Web site, where you can find out more about Acrobat.

*Note: To update resources, click **Updates** in the Adobe Online dialog box. A connection is made, and any new updates download to your computer.*

CHAPTER 2

Viewing PDF Files

Are you ready to start viewing and navigating through PDF documents? This chapter shows you how to move around PDF files and become familiar with many different viewing options.

Set the Page View 24

Navigate Documents 26

Using Bookmarks 27

View Thumbnails 28

Jump to a Page 29

Zoom a View....................................30

Tile Views 32

Activate Links..................................33

Using Context Menus 34

Rotate Pages 35

Control the Opening View.................36

SET THE PAGE VIEW

You commonly view and navigate PDF documents much like a Web browser. Acrobat determines the page view and size of the document in the Document Pane through the use of tools and settings. You can make adjustments for your own personal level of comfort when navigating through PDF documents and pages.

SET THE PAGE VIEW

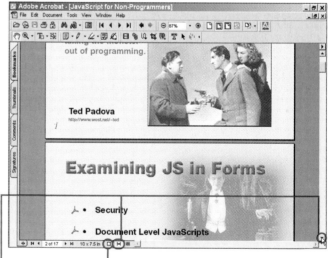

FIT IN WINDOW

1 Open a PDF file.

2 Click 🔲.

■ When files are opened, they may appear too large for comfortable viewing. Fit in Window enables you to view each page in its entirety.

Note: You can also use the keyboard shortcut **Ctrl** *+* **O** *(zero) in Windows or* **⌘** *+* **O** *on a Macintosh to set the view to* **Fit in Window**.

VIEW SINGLE PAGES

1 Scroll through the pages by clicking ▼ in the scroll box.

■ If pages are not snapping to a Single Page view, the view is in Continuous mode.

2 Click 🔲.

■ The view displays single pages.

Why do some files open in Single Page view and others in Continuous Page view?

Users who create PDF files can set the viewing parameters when saving a file in Acrobat. If you set the file to open as a Default view, then your default settings in the General Preferences dialog box prevail. To temporarily change the view from Continuous Page view to Single Page view, click the Single Page tool (☐) in the Status Bar after opening a document.

Can I control page views when viewing PDFs in Web browsers?

Because many of the Acrobat tools appear inside a browser window when you view PDFs inline, you can use the same tools for viewing single or continuous pages.

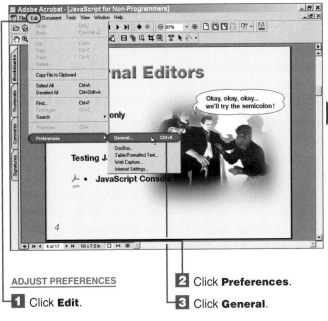

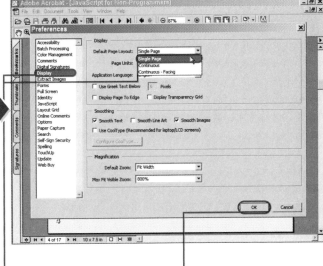

ADJUST PREFERENCES

1 Click **Edit**.

2 Click **Preferences**.

3 Click **General**.

■ The Preferences dialog box appears.

4 Click **Display**.

5 Click ▾ to select **Single** from the drop-down menu.

6 Click **OK**.

■ When PDF files are saved with default viewing options, all your PDFs appear in Single Page views.

NAVIGATE DOCUMENTS

You can use navigational tools to trace your viewing steps. Many of the navigation tools are intuitive, for example, click ▶ or ◀ to move forward or backward, respectively. A couple of navigational tools offer more viewing options that may not be apparent when you first use them.

NAVIGATE DOCUMENTS

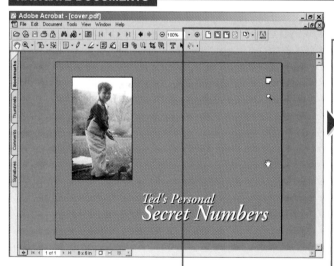

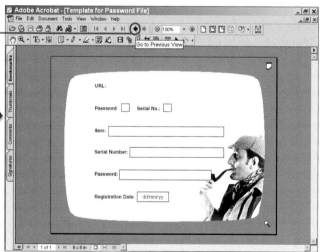

1 Open a PDF file.

2 Click ⊠ to close the file.

3 Open a second file.

4 Click ◀.

■ The last view from the closed file appears. Acrobat remembers your views and returns you to the last view even after you have closed the file.

USING BOOKMARKS

You can bookmark a page, a document, a zoom view, and many other items. For easy navigation through topical items, open the Bookmarks palette and click a bookmark name. The page view jumps to the page associated with the bookmark.

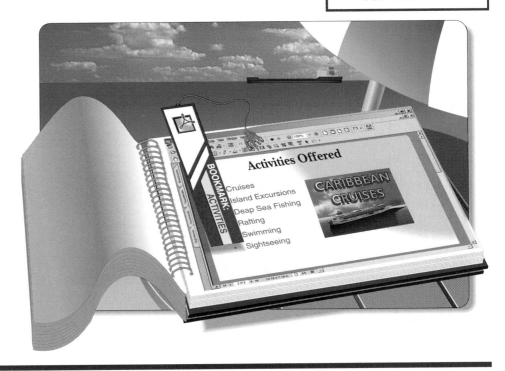

USING BOOKMARKS

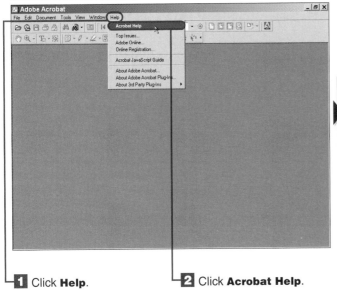

1 Click **Help**.

2 Click **Acrobat Help**.

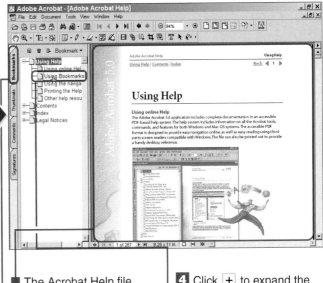

■ The Acrobat Help file opens in the Document Pane.

3 Click the **Bookmarks** tab in the Navigation Pane.

4 Click **+** to expand the listing.

5 Click **Using Bookmarks**.

■ The Acrobat Help file jumps to the page that explains bookmarks.

Thumbnails display a small, mini-view of each page in a PDF document. You can view many pages at a time by opening up the Thumbnails pane.

VIEW THUMBNAILS

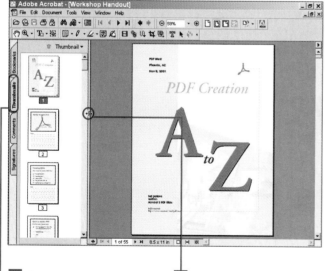

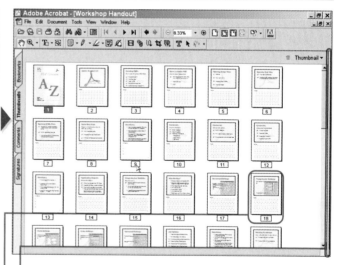

1 Open a multipage PDF file.

2 Click **Thumbnails**.

3 Click the vertical line on the far right of the Thumbnails palette.

■ The cursor changes to ↔.

4 Drag open to the right side of the monitor.

5 Click any page to open it in the Document Pane.

Note: To view a page behind the Thumbnails palette, drag the vertical line left to reduce the palette size.

JUMP TO A PAGE

You can jump quickly to a
certain page number in a large
document without using a
navigational link.

JUMP TO A PAGE

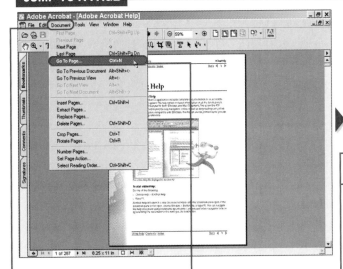

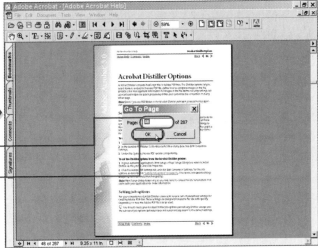

1 Click **Document**.

2 Click **Go To Page**.

■ The **Go To Page** dialog
box opens.

3 Enter a page number in
the **Go To Page** dialog box.

4 Click **OK**.

*Note: You can also type a page
number in the Status Bar where
(x of y) appears. X is the page
number, and Y is the total pages.*

■ The page entered in the
dialog box appears in the
Document Pane.

*Note: If you want to quickly
determine how many pages are
included in an open document,
glance at the Status Bar to see what
page you are viewing and the total
pages in the file.*

ZOOM A VIEW

Zooming in and out of pages is part of every Acrobat session. To quickly move around pages and between views, you want to master using the tools and keyboard shortcuts for changing views.

ZOOM A VIEW

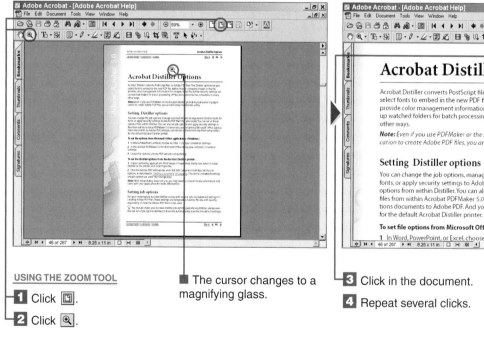

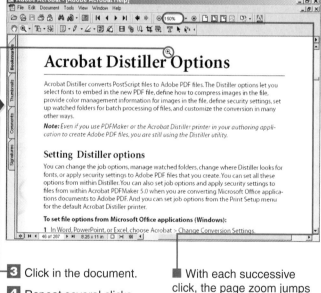

USING THE ZOOM TOOL

1 Click 🔲.

2 Click 🔍.

■ The cursor changes to a magnifying glass.

3 Click in the document.

4 Repeat several clicks.

■ With each successive click, the page zoom jumps 25 percent in size.

How do I change views from the keyboard?

To quickly change views, you can press the specific keystroke combinations in the following table.

Zoom In	Press Ctrl + + (Windows)
	Press ⌘ + + (Macintosh)
Zoom Out	Press Ctrl + - (Windows)
	Press ⌘ + - (Macintosh)
Access Zoom In Tool	Press Ctrl + Spacebar (Windows)
	Press ⌘ + Spacebar (Macintosh)
Access Zoom Out Tool	Press Ctrl + Alt + Spacebar (Windows)
	Press ⌘ + option + Spacebar (Macintosh)

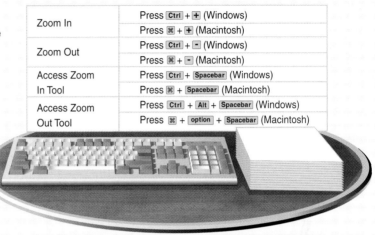

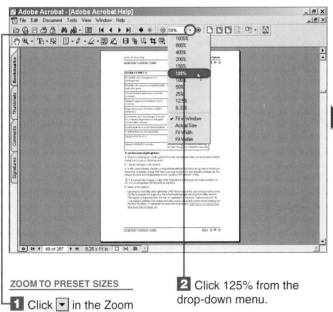

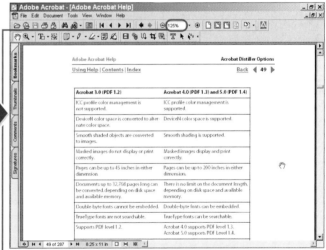

ZOOM TO PRESET SIZES

1 Click ▼ in the Zoom tool group.

2 Click 125% from the drop-down menu.

■ The zoom view jumps to 125 percent of the actual size.

■ Zooming in on a document with 🔍 jumps to the same presets listed in the Zoom tool group's drop-down menu. To quickly access 🔍, hold down the Ctrl key (Windows) or the option key (Macintosh). The cursor appears as ⊖.

TILE VIEWS

When one PDF document is in the Document Pane and a second file is open, the first file is normally hidden from view. At times, however, you may want to display two or more documents together in the Document Pane.

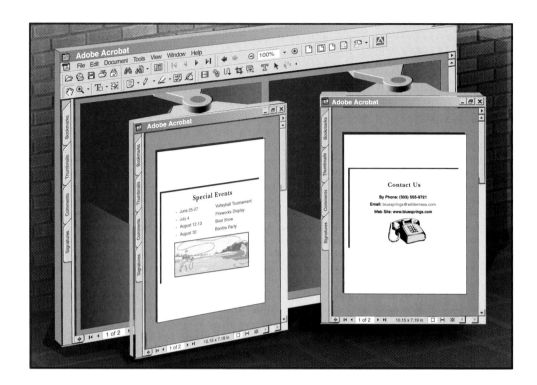

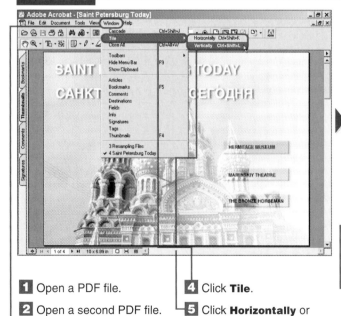

1 Open a PDF file.

2 Open a second PDF file.

3 Click **Window**.

4 Click **Tile**.

5 Click **Horizontally** or **Vertically**.

■ The Document Pane displays both files in individual separate windows. Whether the files are side-by-side or stacked depends on the orientation you chose in step **5**.

You can create links in PDF documents to pages and views, other PDF documents, and other action types associated with a link button. When the cursor approaches a link, Acrobat changes the cursor to inform you a link is available to click.

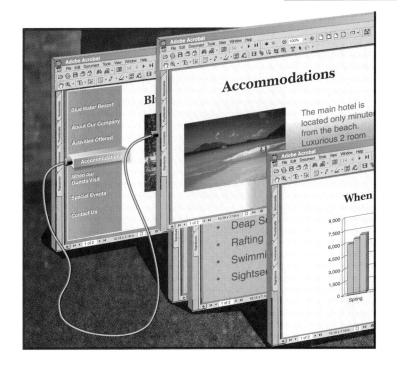

ACTIVATE LINKS

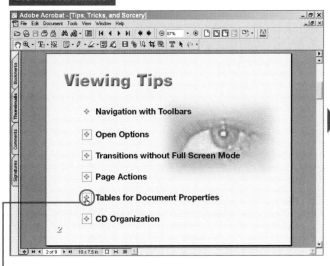

1 Open a PDF file with link buttons.

2 Place the cursor over a known link.

■ The cursor changes from 🖑 to 👆.

3 Click the mouse button.

■ The linked object appears. If the link is to another page, the new page view appears in the Document Pane.

Note: There are many different actions that can be associated with links. For more about link properties, see Chapter 5.

USING CONTEXT MENUS

Context menus offer many options in pop-up menus. When you select the Hand tool (), the options in the pop-up menu offer choices for page navigation. You can change the tool by clicking another button in the toolbar; the pop-up menu displays different options.

USING CONTEXT MENUS

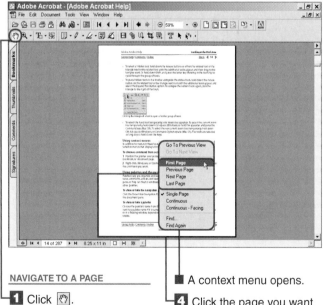

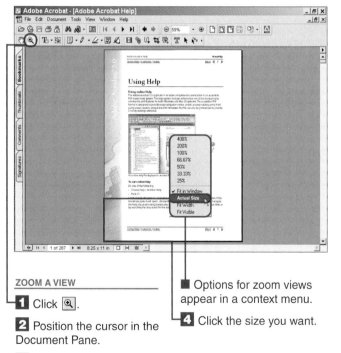

NAVIGATE TO A PAGE

1 Click .

2 Position the cursor in the Document Pane.

3 Right-click (Windows) or `Control` + click (Macintosh).

■ A context menu opens.

4 Click the page you want to go to.

■ Acrobat jumps to the page you specify.

ZOOM A VIEW

1 Click .

2 Position the cursor in the Document Pane.

3 Right-click (Windows) or `Control` + click (Macintosh).

■ Options for zoom views appear in a context menu.

4 Click the size you want.

ROTATE PAGES

Depending on how PDFs
are created, you may
occasionally find a page
or several pages rotated
in a document. With
Acrobat, you can rotate
a single page, a range of
pages, or all the pages
in a document.

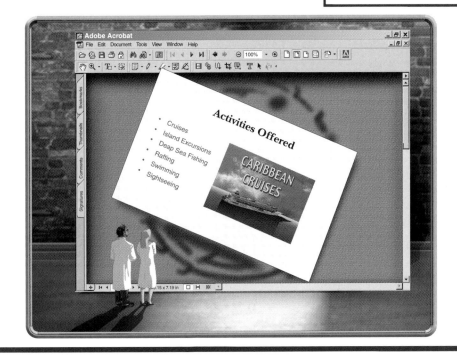

ROTATE PAGES

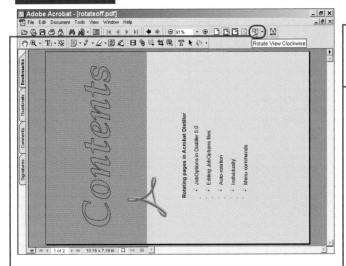

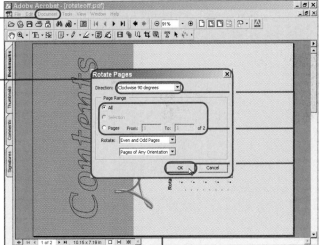

ROTATE A PAGE

1 Click 🖳.

■ The page viewed is rotated,
leaving the remaining pages
in the document undisturbed.

ROTATE MULTIPLE PAGES

1 Click **Document**.

2 Click **Rotate Pages**.

■ The Rotate Pages dialog
box appears.

3 Click 🔽 to select the
direction of rotation.

4 Click **All** or a specific
range of pages to rotate
(○ changes to ●).

5 Click **OK**.

CONTROL THE OPENING VIEW

If you open a PDF file in a fixed view, such as Fit in Window, you can set viewing options when you save a PDF file to disk.

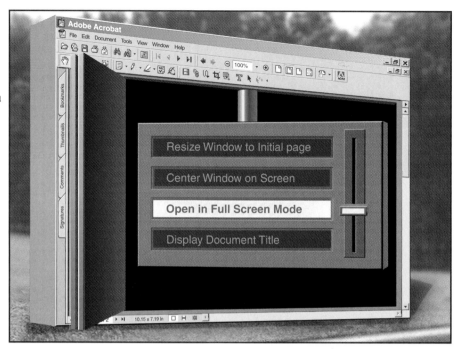

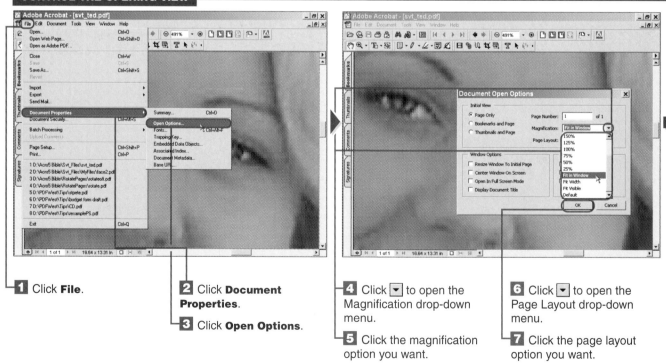

1 Click **File**.

2 Click **Document Properties**.

3 Click **Open Options**.

4 Click ▼ to open the Magnification drop-down menu.

5 Click the magnification option you want.

6 Click ▼ to open the Page Layout drop-down menu.

7 Click the page layout option you want.

What other viewing controls can I save with a PDF?

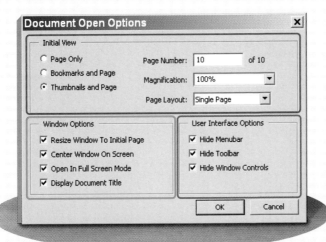

Initial View Options
The **Thumbnail** palette opens.

Window Options
The Acrobat window resizes to
the initial page size, centers,
opens in Full Screen Mode, and
displays the Title from the
Document Summary.

User Interface Options
The **Menubar**, **Toolbar**, and
Navigation Pane are hidden
when the file is opened.

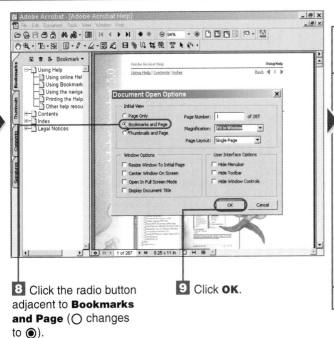

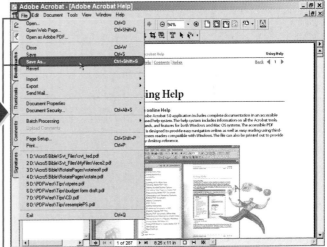

8 Click the radio button
adjacent to **Bookmarks
and Page** (○ changes
to ◉).

9 Click **OK**.

10 Click **File**.

11 Click **Save As**.

■ The Save As dialog box
appears.

12 Name and save a copy
to disk.

■ When the copy of the
saved file is opened, the
Bookmarks palette is
expanded and the document
snaps to the zoom view set in
the Open Options dialog box.

PDF

Photoshop

Allergy Newsletter
August 2002
Health: Allergens in the Home
Allergens in the home take many
forms. When a person is
diagnosed with allergies, the
common sources named were
carpeting, pets, house plants,
animals, knick-knacks, draperies,
dust and mold.
Vacuuming twice a week
usually be one of the first courses of
action recommended. This means
vacuuming not only carpets, but using
a special nozzle attachment and
vacuuming upholstered furniture and
draperies. An air purifier will
always be suggested, and

Word

MAKE

CHAPTER 3

Create PDF Files

Are you ready to start creating PDF documents? In this chapter, you learn how to create PDF files from many different authoring applications.

Understanding PDF Creation Options 40

Convert Image Files to PDF 42

Convert HTML Files to PDF 44

Convert Text Files to PDF 45

Using PDF Maker with
   Microsoft Word 46

Export Styles from Microsoft Word 48

Using PDF Maker with
   Microsoft Excel 50

Using PDF Maker with
   Microsoft PowerPoint 51

Export PDFs from Adobe Photoshop 52

Export PDFs from Adobe PageMaker 54

Export PDFs from QuarkXPress..............56

Export PDFs from Adobe FrameMaker ..58

Export PDFs from Adobe Illustrator 60

Export PDFs from CorelDraw 62

Capture Web Pages 64

UNDERSTANDING PDF CREATION OPTIONS

Unlike other computer programs, you cannot create a PDF by starting a new document in Acrobat. Rather, PDFs are files that you create in some other program and convert to PDF.

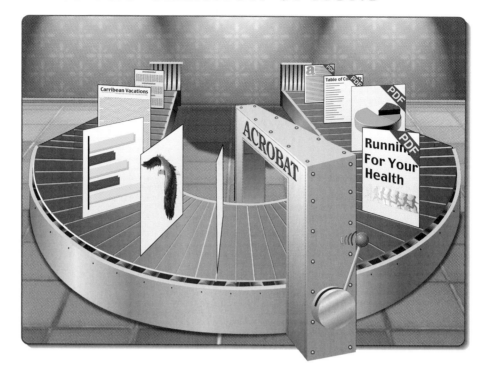

Open as Adobe PDF

Depending on what format was used to save a file, Acrobat can open some file types and convert them to PDF on-the-fly.

Export to PDF

You can export files directly to PDF from many professional programs, such as Microsoft Office applications, image-editing software, illustration software, and page layout software.

Save as PDF

Some programs can save to the PDF format and also open PDF files. In some cases, you can edit PDF files when you open them in other applications.

Convert Web Pages

Through a menu command, you can download and convert Web pages to PDF.

Distill PostScript Files

You can convert files printed to disk as PostScript files to PDF with Acrobat Distiller.

Convert EPS Files

Acrobat Distiller can also convert files saved in Encapsulated PostScript (EPS) format. Many illustration and drawing programs can save in EPS format. Once a file is saved as EPS, you can convert the file to PDF with Acrobat Distiller.

Scan Documents in Acrobat

Through a command for scanning images and text, files are scanned on a desktop scanner and converted on-the-fly to PDF.

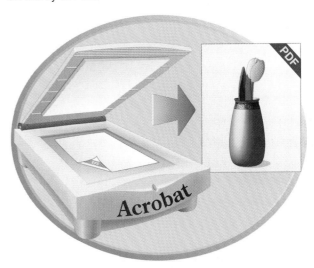

CONVERT IMAGE FILES TO PDF

You can open image files saved in several different formats in Adobe Acrobat and convert them to PDFs. When a file converts to PDF, you can then save it to a disk as a PDF. You can now open the file as any other PDF document.

OPEN AS ADOBE PDF

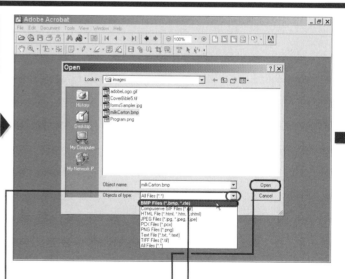

CONVERT IMAGE FILES TO PDF

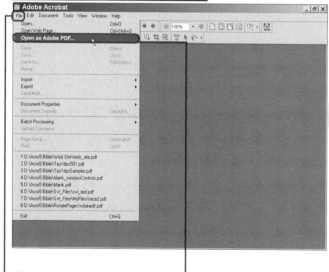

1 Click **File**.

2 Click **Open as Adobe PDF**.

■ The Open dialog box appears.

3 Click 🔽 to open the Objects of Type drop-down menu.

4 Click to select a format to which you want to convert.

5 Click **Open**.

*Note: If no files appear listed in the Open dialog box, click **All Files**. All the file types are listed in the dialog box.*

Can I open multiple files and convert them all to PDF?

To select a group of individual files to convert to PDF, click **Open as Adobe PDF**. When the Open dialog box appears, Ctrl +click (Windows) or Shift +click (Macintosh) to select several files.

How do I open several files and have them all appended to a single PDF?

You must first convert one image file to PDF and open it in the Document Pane. Then click **Open as Adobe PDF**. Select the files in the Open dialog box and click Open. Acrobat displays the Open dialog box prompting you to create new files or append the files to the open document.

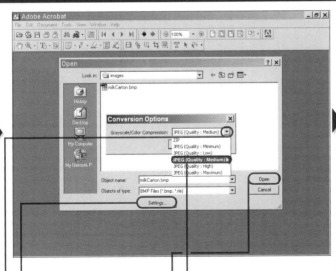

6 Click **Settings**.

■ The Conversion Options dialog box appears.

7 Click ▼ to open the Grayscale/Color Compression drop-down menu.

8 Click to select the desired compression amount.

■ You can select the amount of compression for all original image types except JPEG files.

9 Click **Open**.

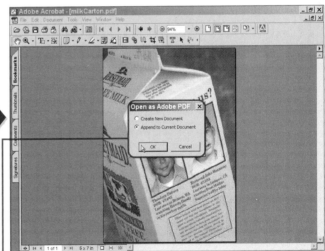

■ If a PDF file is open when you click Open, the Open as Adobe PDF dialog box will appear, asking you to create a new PDF document or append the file to the end of the open file. Click the appropriate choice and then click **OK**.

CONVERT HTML FILES TO PDF

You can convert HTML files located on local hard drives or network servers to PDF. You can convert an entire Web site by appending each HTML file to a single PDF file.

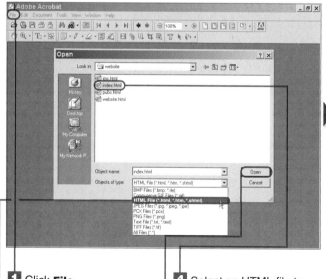

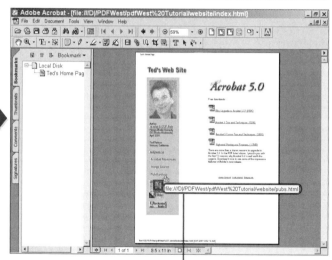

1 Click **File**.

2 Click **Open as Adobe PDF**.

3 In the Open dialog box, click **HTML File** from the Objects of Type drop-down menu.

4 Select an HTML file to open.

5 Click **Open**.

■ The Web Capture Status dialog box opens, and the HTML file is converted to PDF.

■ To add more PDF pages to the open file, you can click on any link button in the HTML file. Acrobat finds the associated page and appends it to the open document.

CONVERT TEXT FILES TO PDF

You can convert text files to PDF with the Open as Adobe PDF command. Text files must be ASCII text only and not files saved from word processors as a native document file type. When saving files from word processors, be certain to save the file as Text Only when using Open as Adobe PDF.

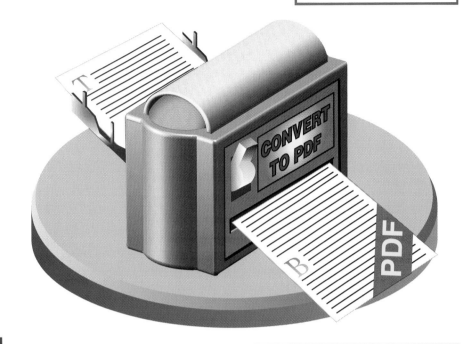

CONVERT TEXT FILES TO PDF

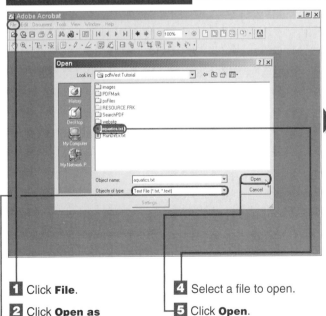

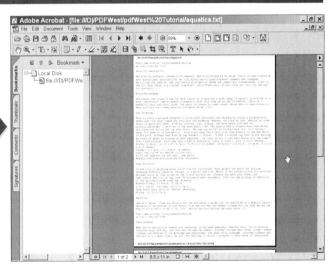

1 Click **File**.

2 Click **Open as Adobe PDF**.

3 In the Open dialog box, click **Text File** from the Objects of Type drop-down menu.

4 Select a file to open.

5 Click **Open**.

■ The plain text file is converted to PDF.

Note: All formatting is lost when converting text files to PDF. If you want to preserve formatting such as font color, you need to use another means of converting your files to PDF. See "Using PDF Maker with Microsoft Word," next in this chapter.

USING PDF MAKER WITH MICROSOFT WORD

The PDF format was designed to preserve document integrity and style. To preserve formatting from Microsoft Office applications, you can use the PDF Maker macro utility. When you install Acrobat, the macro is automatically installed in the appropriate Office applications folders. Remember to first install Microsoft Office, and then Adobe Acrobat.

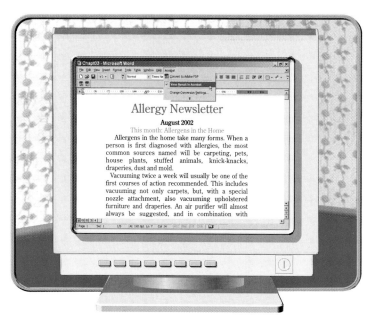

Before using the PDF Maker macro utility, define your conversion settings. Acrobat has four default Job Options. The eBook setting is good for creating e-books you want to download from Web sites, and the screen setting is good for viewing PDFs on a computer monitor. The Print settings is used for desktop printers, and the Press settings is used for professional printing devices of the highest quality. See Chapter 4 for more about Job Options.

USING PDF MAKER WITH MICROSOFT WORD

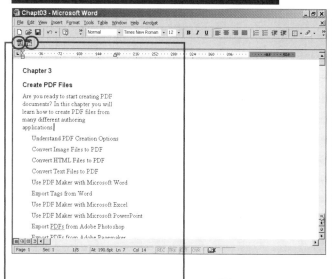

KNOW THE PDF MAKER TOOLS

■ After installing Acrobat, PDF Maker Tools appear in the Word toolbar and menu bar.

■ Click 🔳 to convert an open Word document to PDF.

■ Click 🔳 and your default e-mail application launches. The PDF created from the Word document is automatically attached to a new e-mail message.

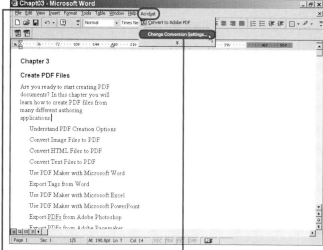

CHANGE CONVERSION SETTINGS

-1 Click **Acrobat**.

2 Click **Change Conversion Settings**.

What does the Embed Tags in the PDF option mean?

Tagged PDF files capture all the document structure from the original Word document. When you embed tags, you can make the files accessible for visually and motion challenged people who can have their PDF documents output from hardware devices that read aloud the PDF file. In addition, tagged PDFs enable you to export the PDF file back to a Word document with more reliable integrity for preserving tables, lists, and other document structure.

Allergy Newsletter

August 2002

This month: Allergens in the Home

Allergens in the home take many forms. When a person is first diagnosed with allergies, the most common sources named will be carpeting, pets, house plants, stuffed animals, knick-knacks, draperies, dust and mold.

Vacuuming twice a week will usually be one of the first courses of action recommended. This includes vacuuming not only carpets, but, with a special nozzle attachment, also vacuuming upholstered furniture and draperies. An air purifier will almost always be suggested, and in

Century Old Style 13pt.

Century Old Style 7pt.

Paragraph Justify Full Lines

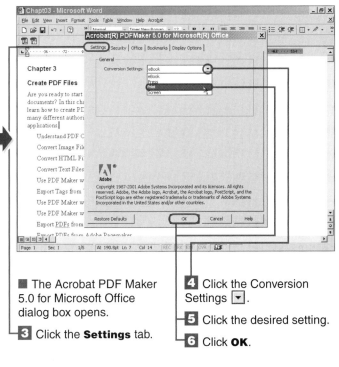

■ The Acrobat PDF Maker 5.0 for Microsoft Office dialog box opens.

3 Click the **Settings** tab.

4 Click the Conversion Settings ▾.

5 Click the desired setting.

6 Click **OK**.

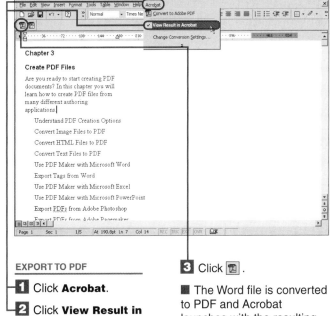

EXPORT TO PDF

1 Click **Acrobat**.

2 Click **View Result in Acrobat**.

3 Click 🔳 .

■ The Word file is converted to PDF and Acrobat launches with the resulting document displayed in the Document Pane.

EXPORT STYLES FROM MICROSOFT WORD

When you create a
document's structure in
Microsoft Word, such as
using style sheets for text
and paragraph formatting,
you can export the
document along with the
structure to a PDF file.

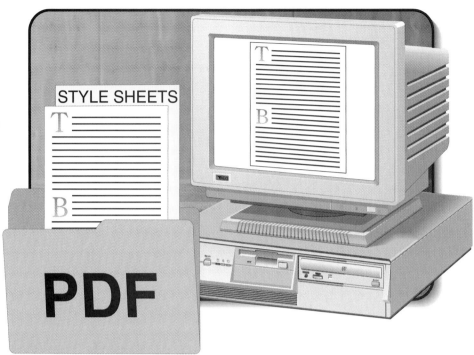

STYLE SHEETS

PDF

EXPORT STYLES FROM MICROSOFT WORD

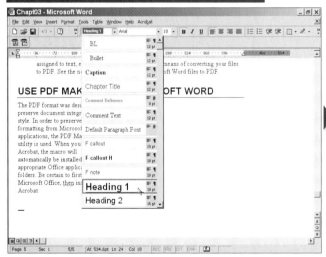

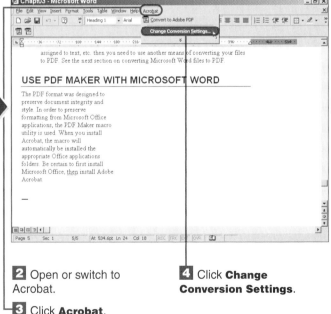

1 Create styles in your
Microsoft Word document for
different text elements.

2 Open or switch to
Acrobat.

3 Click **Acrobat**.

4 Click **Change
Conversion Settings**.

Can I have the bookmarks created in the PDF displayed when I open the document in Acrobat?

Some display options available in the Open Options dialog box can be predetermined in Word before exporting to PDF.

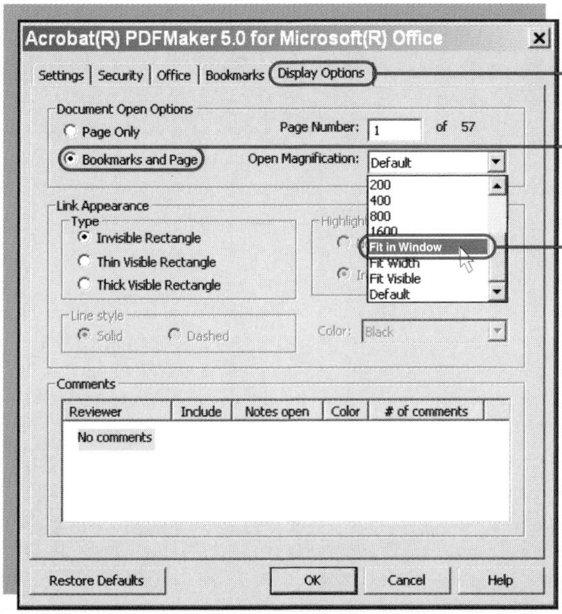

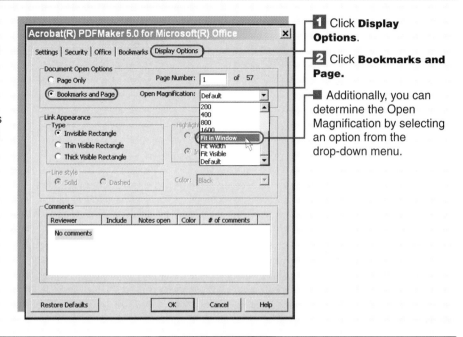

1 Click **Display Options**.

2 Click **Bookmarks and Page**.

■ Additionally, you can determine the Open Magnification by selecting an option from the drop-down menu.

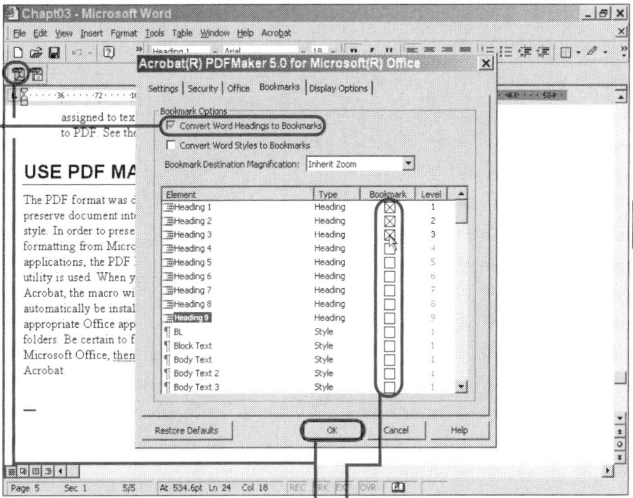

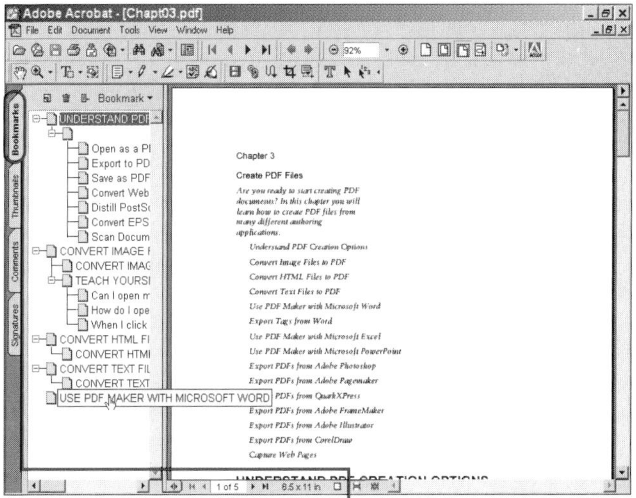

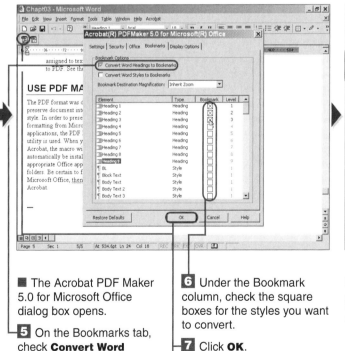

■ The Acrobat PDF Maker 5.0 for Microsoft Office dialog box opens.

5 On the Bookmarks tab, check **Convert Word Headings to Bookmarks** (☐ changes to ☑).

6 Under the Bookmark column, check the square boxes for the styles you want to convert.

7 Click **OK**.

8 Click ▣.

■ The file converts to PDF.

9 Open the PDF document in Acrobat.

*Note: If you click **View Result in Acrobat**, the PDF will automatically display in the Acrobat Document Pane.*

10 Click the **Bookmarks** tab.

■ All Word styles selected for conversion appear as bookmarks.

If you create financial documents and charts in Microsoft Excel, you can export the documents with the PDF Maker macro. You can create bookmarks from sheets in an Excel file. The bookmark name appears the same as the sheet name.

USING PDF MAKER WITH MICROSOFT EXCEL

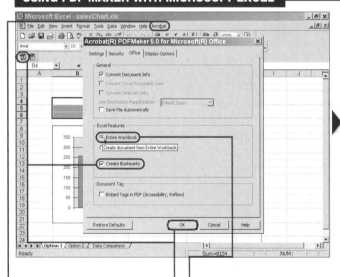

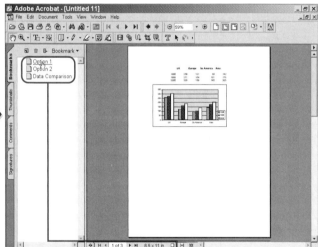

1 Open an Excel file with multiple sheets.

2 Click **Acrobat** and then click **Change Conversion Settings** from the drop-down menu.

■ The Acrobat PDF Maker 5.0 for Microsoft Office dialog box appears.

3 Click **Entire Workbook** (○ changes to ◉).

4 Check **Create Bookmarks** (☐ changes to ☑)

5 Click **OK**.

6 Click 🔲.

■ Acrobat converts the file to PDF.

7 Open the PDF file.

Note: If you click **View Result in Acrobat** in the Settings tab, the PDF will automatically display in the Acrobat Document Pane.

■ Each bookmark name was created from the sheet names in the Excel file.

USING PDF MAKER WITH MICROSOFT POWERPOINT

Microsoft PowerPoint is a standard among those who create slide presentations for seminars and speaking engagements. You can start a presentation in PowerPoint, convert to PDF, and add some of the features supported by Acrobat to enhance a slide show. The first step is converting the PowerPoint file to PDF.

USING PDF MAKER WITH MICROSOFT POWERPOINT

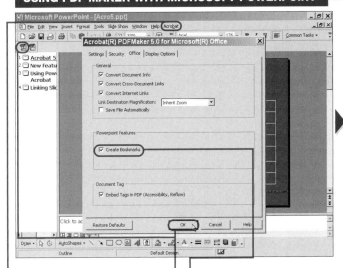

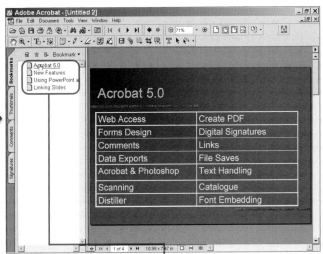

1 In PowerPoint, click **Acrobat** and then click **Change Conversion Settings** from the drop-down menu.

■ The Acrobat PDF Maker 5.0 for Microsoft Office dialog box appears.

2 Check **Create Bookmarks** (☐ changes to ☑).

■ Each slide in the PowerPoint presentation is bookmarked in the resulting PDF.

3 Click **OK**.

4 Click 🔁.

■ The file is converted to PDF.

5 Open the PDF in Acrobat.

*Note: If you click **View Result in Acrobat** in the Settings tab, the PDF will automatically display in the Acrobat Document Pane.*

■ Note that all slides are converted to bookmarks.

EXPORT PDFS FROM ADOBE PHOTOSHOP

Adobe Photoshop 6.0 and 7.0 support vector art and type preserved on layers. When a Photoshop file is exported to one of many different file formats, the art and type is rasterized into pixels. However, when exported to PDF, the vector art and type is preserved in the PDF. PDF is the only export format from Photoshop that preserves these elements.

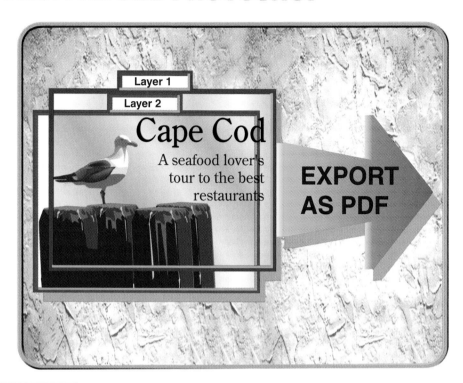

EXPORT PDFS FROM ADOBE PHOTOSHOP

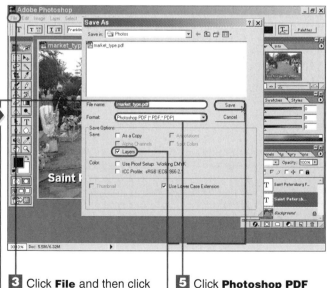

1 Open a Photoshop image.

2 If needed, click **T** and add a line of type to the image.

3 Click **File** and then click **Save As** from the drop-down menu.

■ The Save As dialog box appears.

4 Type in a filename.

5 Click **Photoshop PDF** from the Format drop-down menu.

6 Check **Layers** (☐ changes to ☑).

7 Click **Save**.

What is the advantage of preserving type in Photoshop PDFs?

One advantage you have with preserving type in PDF files is that the fonts are always printed at the optimum resolution of the printing device. Whereas Photoshop images are dependent on the resolution of the image and can suffer degradation without sufficient resolution, type carries no resolution and prints without any degradation.

Another distinct advantage in exporting text is that the text can be searched in an Acrobat file. Because Acrobat recognizes the text, when you click **Edit** and click **Find,** the Find dialog box opens. Type in the word to be searched and click the **Find** button. All text preserved from Photoshop files can be searched in the PDF.

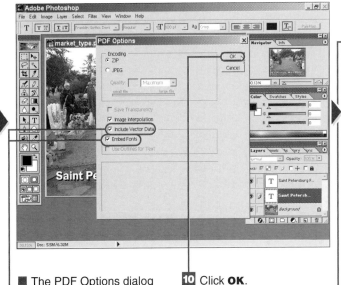

■ The PDF Options dialog box opens.

8 Check **Include Vector Data**.

9 Check **Embed Fonts**.

10 Click **OK**.

■ The file is saved as PDF.

11 Open the PDF in Acrobat.

12 Click T.

13 Click and drag across the text.

■ Notice the text has been preserved in the Photoshop file.

EXPORT PDFS FROM ADOBE PAGEMAKER

Layout programs like Adobe PageMaker incorporate text and graphics together to create formatted documents. Much better than word processors, page-layout software provides more flexibility in the design and creation of newsletters, brochures, pamphlets, and advertising. As with Microsoft Word, much of the PageMaker format style can be exported to PDF.

Export To PDF

EXPORT PDFS FROM ADOBE PAGEMAKER

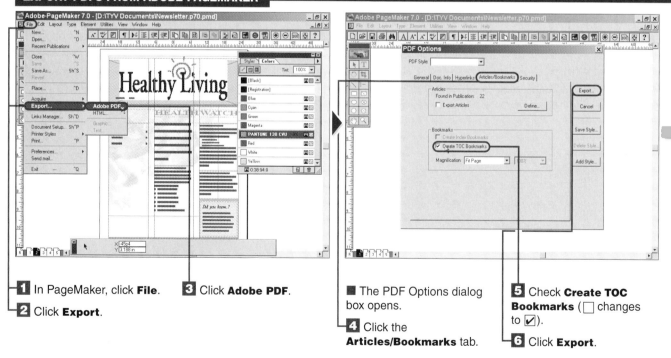

1 In PageMaker, click **File**.

2 Click **Export**.

3 Click **Adobe PDF**.

■ The PDF Options dialog box opens.

4 Click the **Articles/Bookmarks** tab.

5 Check **Create TOC Bookmarks** (☐ changes to ☑).

6 Click **Export**.

How do I create table of contents bookmarks in PageMaker?

A table of contents (TOC) needs to be properly created in PageMaker before the TOC is converted to bookmarks in the PDF document.

Each TOC item is selected in the PageMaker text, and the Paragraph Specifications dialog box must be opened by clicking **Type** and then **Paragraph.** In the Paragraph Specifications dialog box, click **Include in Table of Contents.**

To create a TOC, click **Edit** and then **Edit Story**, click **Utilities**, and then click **Create TOC.**

A TOC is created. When you close the Story Editor, PageMaker prompts you to place the story. Click **Place** and place the new text on a blank page. When the file is exported from PageMaker, the table of contents is converted to bookmarks.

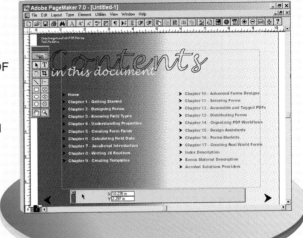

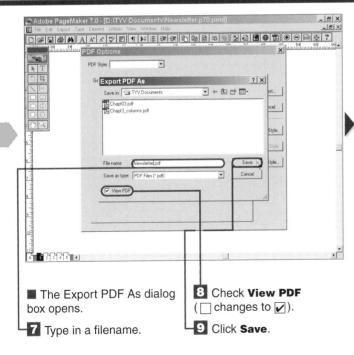

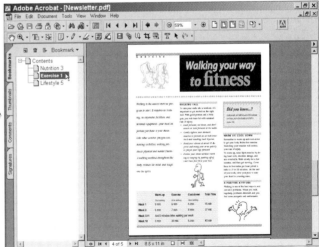

■ The Export PDF As dialog box opens.

7 Type in a filename.

8 Check **View PDF** (☐ changes to ☑).

9 Click **Save**.

■ The new PDF automatically opens in Acrobat.

■ PageMaker converts the document to PDF and, after a short wait, eventually opens the converted document in Acrobat.

EXPORT PDFS FROM QUARKXPRESS

QuarkXPress has long been a favorite among professional graphic designers and advertising agencies. In order to export to PDF from QuarkXPress, you need to download the free Quark XTension from www.quark.com. When the XTension is installed, you can export to PDF from QuarkXPress.

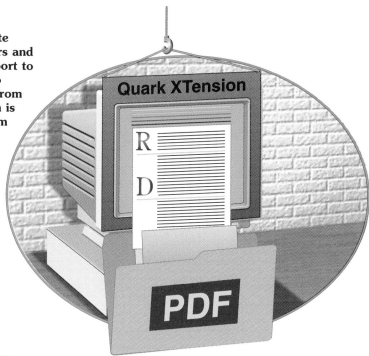

EXPORT PDFS FROM QUARKXPRESS

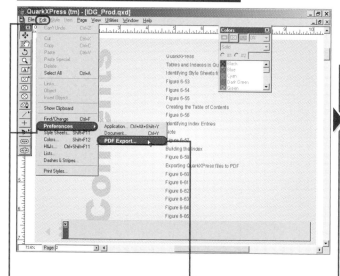

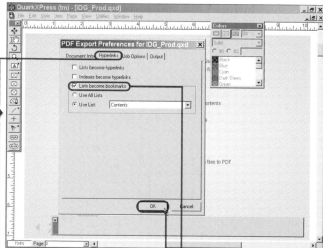

ADJUST PDF EXPORT PREFERENCES

1 In Quark, click **Edit**.

2 Click **Preferences**.

3 Click **PDF Export**.

■ The PDF Export Preferences dialog box opens. To convert TOC and Index entries to bookmarks, you must specify the items you want to convert.

4 Click the **Hyperlinks** tab.

5 Check **Lists become bookmarks** (☐ changes to ☑).

Note: For TOC and Index Entries, see the QuarkXPress user documentation for creating lists for Tables of Contents and Indexes.

6 Click **OK**.

Can I create a PDF from a QuarkXPress document without using the PDF Export XTension?

You can easily convert a QuarkXPress document by printing the file to the Acrobat Distiller printer driver.

When you install Adobe Acrobat, the Acrobat Distiller printer driver is installed.

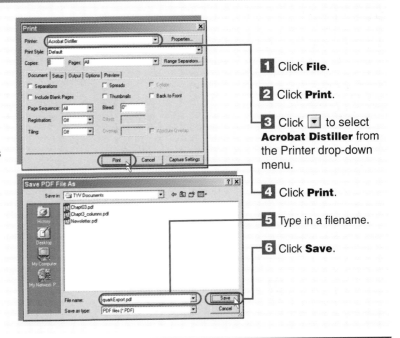

1 Click **File**.

2 Click **Print**.

3 Click ▼ to select **Acrobat Distiller** from the Printer drop-down menu.

4 Click **Print**.

5 Type in a filename.

6 Click **Save**.

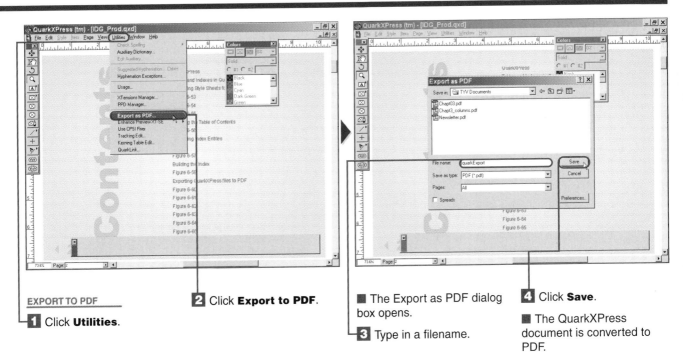

EXPORT TO PDF

1 Click **Utilities**.

2 Click **Export to PDF**.

■ The Export as PDF dialog box opens.

3 Type in a filename.

4 Click **Save**.

■ The QuarkXPress document is converted to PDF.

EXPORT PDFS FROM ADOBE FRAMEMAKER

Adobe FrameMaker has been a favorite tool for large document designers and those creating technical manuals. FrameMaker provides excellent PDF support and also handles exporting the document structure, including TOC and indexes.

EXPORT PDFS FROM ADOBE FRAMEMAKER

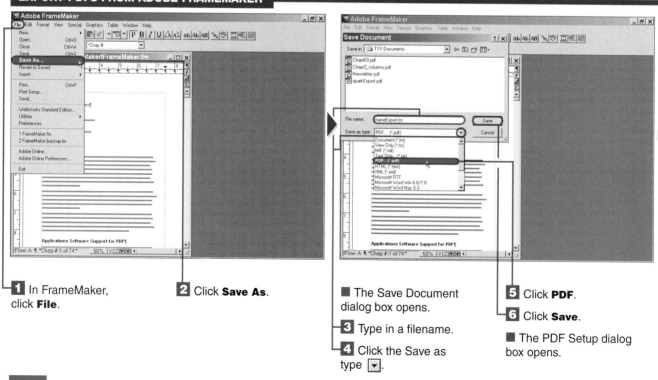

1 In FrameMaker, click **File**.

2 Click **Save As**.

■ The Save Document dialog box opens.

3 Type in a filename.

4 Click the Save as type ▼.

5 Click **PDF**.

6 Click **Save**.

■ The PDF Setup dialog box opens.

What is an article?

Article threads help users follow text through a document in a contiguous direction. If a story begins on page one and continues on page four, the user can click in the text on the first page and jump to the continuation of the story appearing on the fourth page.

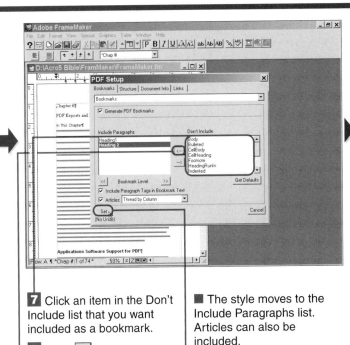

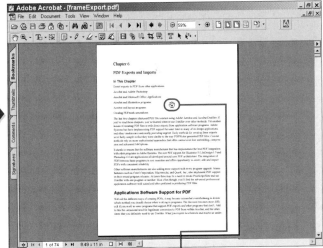

7 Click an item in the Don't Include list that you want included as a bookmark.

8 Click ⟵.

■ The style moves to the Include Paragraphs list. Articles can also be included.

9 Repeat steps **7** and **8** as needed.

10 Click **Set**.

■ The file converts to PDF and opens in Acrobat.

■ When you place the cursor on a page, the cursor icon changes to 🖑, indicating an article thread is present.

EXPORT PDFS FROM ADOBE ILLUSTRATOR

One of the strong features of exporting to PDF in Adobe Illustrator 9 or 10 is the ability to preserve transparency. When files are exported as EPS, transparent assignment of objects is lost and a simulated transparent effect is produced. When saved as PDF, all transparency is preserved.

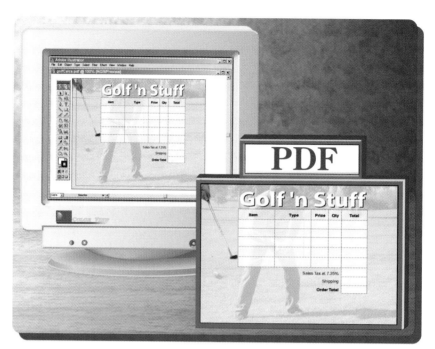

EXPORT PDFS FROM ADOBE ILLUSTRATOR

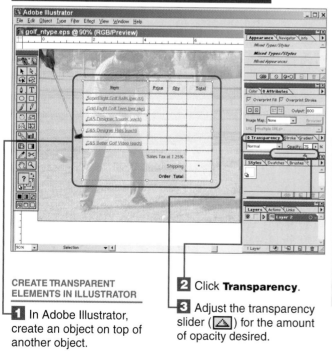

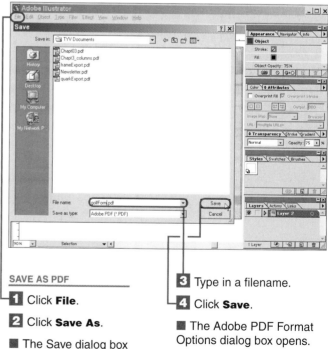

CREATE TRANSPARENT ELEMENTS IN ILLUSTRATOR

1 In Adobe Illustrator, create an object on top of another object.

2 Click **Transparency**.

3 Adjust the transparency slider ( ) for the amount of opacity desired.

SAVE AS PDF

1 Click **File**.

2 Click **Save As**.

■ The Save dialog box opens.

3 Type in a filename.

4 Click **Save**.

■ The Adobe PDF Format Options dialog box opens.

**Are there other ways
to Convert Illustrator
Files to PDF?**

When Illustrator files
are saved as EPS, they
can be distilled in
Acrobat Distiller. For
information about
Distiller, see Chapter 4.

In addition to distilling
EPS files, you can
convert native
Illustrator files to PDF.

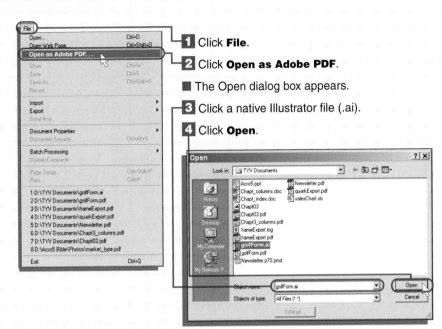

1 Click **File**.

2 Click **Open as Adobe PDF**.

■ The Open dialog box appears.

3 Click a native Illustrator file (.ai).

4 Click **Open**.

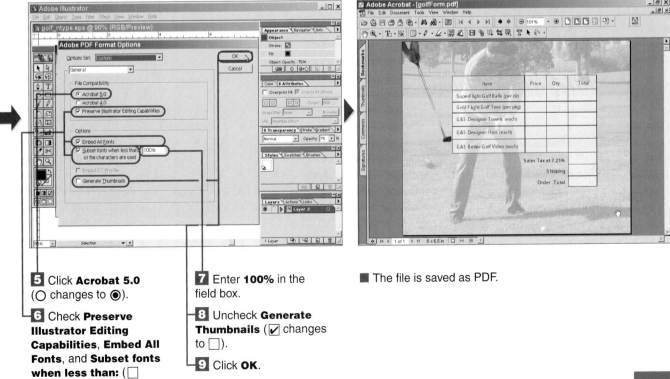

5 Click **Acrobat 5.0**
(○ changes to ◉).

6 Check **Preserve
Illustrator Editing
Capabilities**, **Embed All
Fonts**, and **Subset fonts
when less than:** (☐
changes to ☑).

7 Enter **100%** in the
field box.

8 Uncheck **Generate
Thumbnails** (☑ changes
to ☐).

9 Click **OK**.

■ The file is saved as PDF.

61

EXPORT PDFS FROM CORELDRAW

CorelDraw has long been the most popular illustration program among Windows users. Among other options for PDF exports, CorelDraw offers creation of Job Tickets in which production information about the file output and job requirements can be included in the PDF.

EXPORT PDFS FROM CORELDRAW

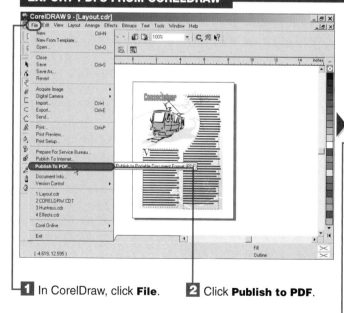

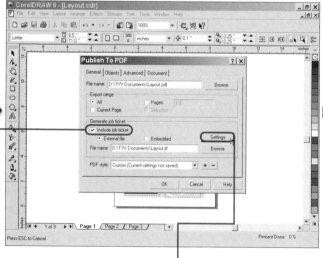

1 In CorelDraw, click **File**.

2 Click **Publish to PDF**.

■ The Publish to PDF dialog box opens.

3 To include a Job Ticket as an external file or embedded in the PDF, check **Include Job Ticket** (☐ changes to ✓).

4 Click **Settings**.

■ The Settings dialog box enables you to enter all the relevant information for job ticketing.

Why should I include a Job Ticket?

Job Tickets are often used with professional imaging centers and print shops. If you prepare a file for output at an imaging center, you can include all your billing and identifying information in a Job Ticket. Additionally, you can include the specifics about your job, such as the type of output, quantity of items, special trimming, cutting, and finishing.

Job Tickets from CorelDraw can be created as separate files that you can print and send to your service center.

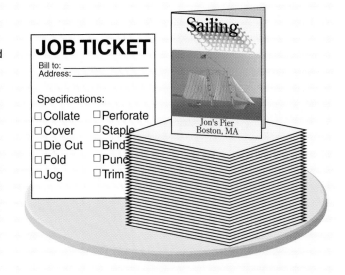

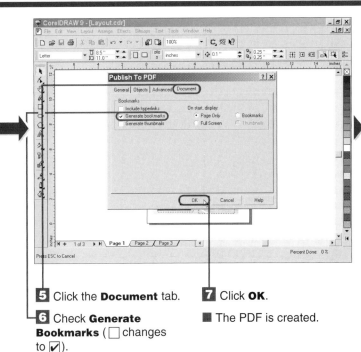

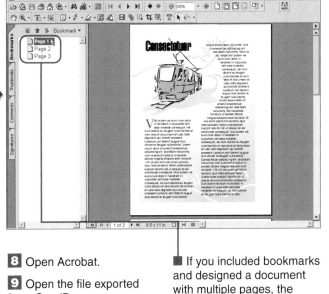

5 Click the **Document** tab.

6 Check **Generate Bookmarks** (☐ changes to ☑).

■ Bookmarks can be created from multiple-page CorelDraw files.

7 Click **OK**.

■ The PDF is created.

8 Open Acrobat.

9 Open the file exported from CorelDraw.

■ If you included bookmarks and designed a document with multiple pages, the bookmarks link to the respective pages.

CAPTURE WEB PAGES

You can also find Web pages on the World Wide Web and convert them to PDF directly in Acrobat. When Web pages are converted to PDF, all the HTML links are preserved in the PDF file. Clicking a link returns you to the Web site and appends new pages to the converted PDF.

Acrobat allows you to select how many levels of the Web site that you may want to capture. If you select Get Entire Site, an extraordinary number of pages will convert. When you first download pages, try to download just a couple of levels and examine the pages before continuing to download more.

CAPTURE WEB PAGES

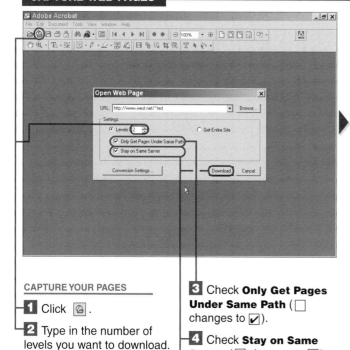

CAPTURE YOUR PAGES

1 Click 🖾 .

2 Type in the number of levels you want to download.

3 Check **Only Get Pages Under Same Path** (☐ changes to ☑).

4 Check **Stay on Same Server** (☐ changes to ☑).

5 Click **Download**.

■ The Download Status dialog box opens. As pages are downloaded, they are converted to PDF pages and appended to the document containing the first downloaded page.

Can I convert new pages linked to Web pages that I have converted to PDF?

If the link is to a page not yet downloaded, Web Capture reconnects to the URL and downloads the linked page. You can also manually add URLs:

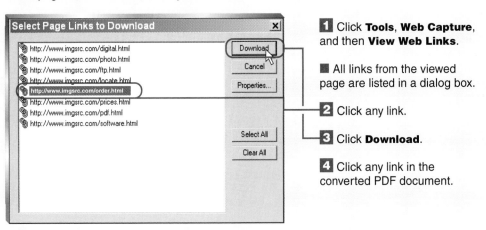

1 Click **Tools**, **Web Capture**, and then **View Web Links**.

■ All links from the viewed page are listed in a dialog box.

2 Click any link.

3 Click **Download**.

4 Click any link in the converted PDF document.

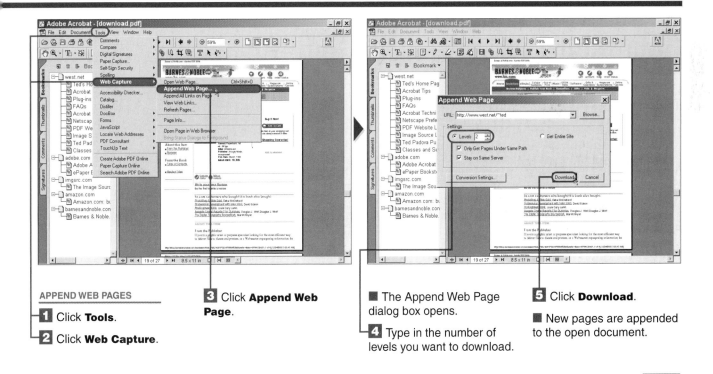

APPEND WEB PAGES

1 Click **Tools**.

2 Click **Web Capture**.

3 Click **Append Web Page**.

■ The Append Web Page dialog box opens.

4 Type in the number of levels you want to download.

5 Click **Download**.

■ New pages are appended to the open document.

CHAPTER 4

Using Acrobat Distiller

Are you ready for more PDF creation techniques? In this chapter, you learn how to work with PostScript and use the Acrobat Distiller program.

Print PostScript Files 68

Launch Acrobat Distiller......................70

Set Acrobat Distiller Preferences..........72

Using the Create Adobe
   PDF Option (Macintosh) 73

Adjust Job Options 74

Distill a PostScript File 78

Monitor Font Locations 80

Create Watched Folders 82

Repurpose PDF Documents 84

Correct Font Problems........................86

Convert EPS to PDF 88

Secure PDFs with Acrobat Distiller 90

PRINT POSTSCRIPT FILES

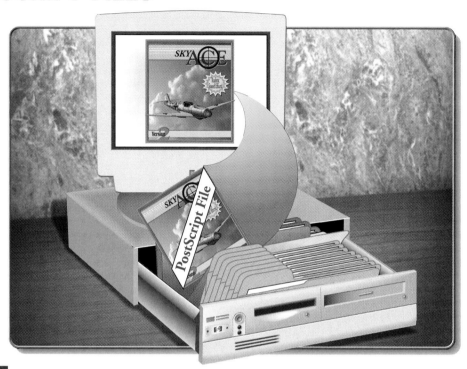

You use the Acrobat Distiller program to create PDF documents from PostScript or Encapsulated PostScript files. To use the Distiller program, you must first learn how to create a PostScript file. Regardless of the program you use, you can always convert a document to PDF by first printing it to disk as a PostScript file.

PRINT POSTSCRIPT FILES

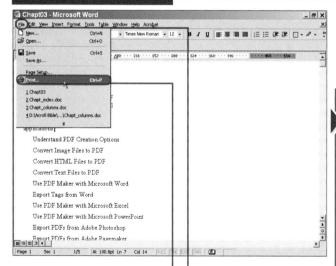

1 Create a document in any program.

■ This example uses Microsoft Word. The steps for other programs are similar.

2 Click **File**.

3 Click **Print**.

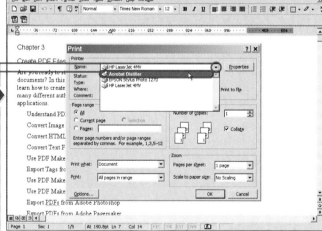

■ The Print dialog box or something similar appears.

4 Click ▾.

5 Click a PostScript printer.

Note: You must use a PostScript printer. In Windows, you can use the Acrobat Distiller printer. On a Macintosh, you can use the Adobe PS or LaserWriter printer.

**I have a document that uses a large page size. How do
I specify page sizes when printing with Acrobat Distiller?**

In any application, you can specify all print attributes
in Print dialog boxes just as you would when sending
a file to a printer. When
using the Acrobat Distiller
printer, follow these steps:

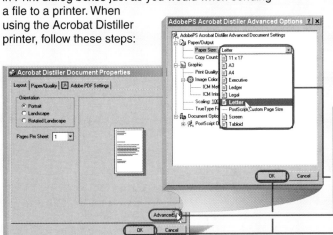

1 Click **Properties** in
the Print dialog box.

■ The Acrobat Distiller Document
Properties dialog box opens.

2 Click **Advanced**.

■ The AdobePS Acrobat Distiller
Advanced Options dialog box opens.

3 Click a fixed paper size or click
PostScript Custom Page Size and
enter values for width and height.

4 Click **OK** twice.

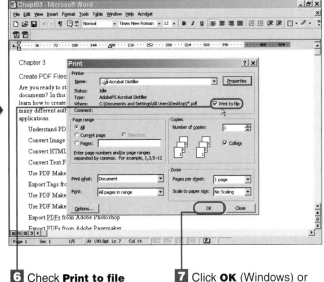

6 Check **Print to file**
(Windows) or select **File for
Destination** (Macintosh).

7 Click **OK** (Windows) or
Save (Macintosh).

■ The Print to File dialog
box opens.

8 Type in a name.

*Note: In Windows, many file names
default to .prn. Adobe commonly
uses .ps for a file extension. Either
extension works when using the file
with Acrobat Distiller.*

9 Click **OK**.

■ The file is saved to disk
and can later be used by
Acrobat Distiller to convert
the PostScript file to a PDF.

LAUNCH ACROBAT DISTILLER

Acrobat Distiller is a
separate program
installed with Adobe
Acrobat. You can
access the Distiller
application in several
ways.

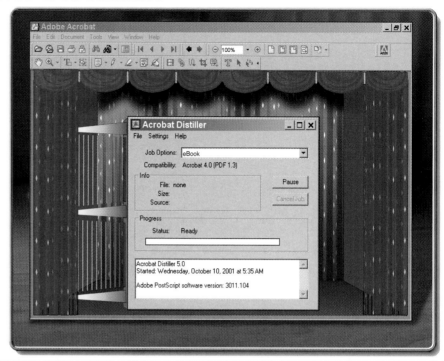

LAUNCH ACROBAT DISTILLER

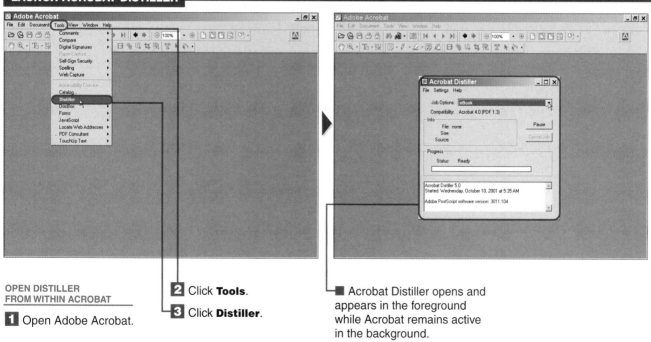

**OPEN DISTILLER
FROM WITHIN ACROBAT**

1 Open Adobe Acrobat.

2 Click **Tools**.

3 Click **Distiller**.

■ Acrobat Distiller opens and
appears in the foreground
while Acrobat remains active
in the background.

Can I double-click on a PostScript file to launch the Distiller application?

No. PostScript files are ASCII text files and often launch a text editor when double-clicked. You can have Distiller recognize a PostScript file by opening Distiller, clicking **File**, and then clicking **Open**; dragging the PostScript file on top of a Distiller shortcut/alias; or by dragging the PostScript file on top of the Distiller window.

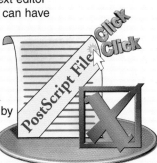

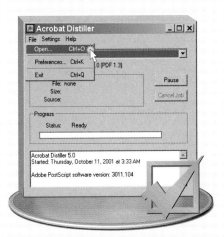

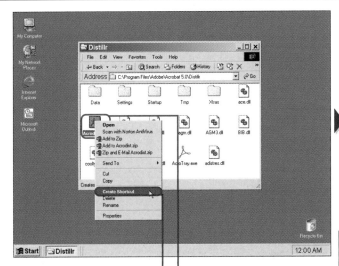

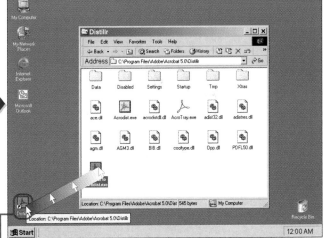

CREATE A SHORTCUT (ALIAS)

1 Locate the Acrobat Distiller application by opening the Programs folder.

2 Open the Adobe folder, then the Acrobat 5 folder, and then the Distiller folder.

3 Right-click the Acrodist.exe file (Windows) or click Acrobat Distiller 5.0 (Macintosh).

4 Click **Create Shortcut** (Windows) or click **File** and then click **Make Alias** (Macintosh).

■ A shortcut/alias is created inside the folder.

5 Drag the shortcut/alias to the Desktop.

■ If you choose to convert a PostScript file to PDF by using Acrobat Distiller, drag the PostScript file on top of the Distiller shortcut/alias.

SET ACROBAT DISTILLER PREFERENCES

Acrobat Distiller has no tools and limited menu commands. Because the program is used only for the purpose of converting PostScript and EPS files to PDF, you don't need tools or extensive menu commands. Before using the program, you may want to visit the preference settings.

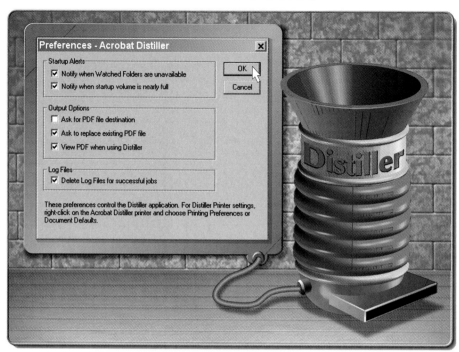

SET ACROBAT DISTILLER PREFERENCES

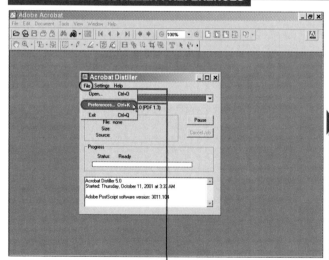

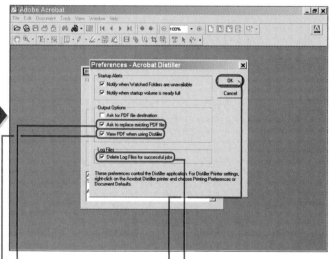

■ In Windows, you access menu commands by opening the menus in the application window. On a Macintosh, menu items are in the menu bar like all other applications.

1 Open Distiller from within Acrobat.

2 Click **File**.

3 Click **Preferences**.

■ The Preferences dialog box opens.

4 Check **Ask to replace existing PDF file** (Windows only) to be warned before overwriting an existing PDF.

5 Check **View PDF when using Distiller** (Windows only) to immediately display the PDF in Acrobat in Windows.

6 Check **Delete Log Files for successful jobs** to delete a text file that records any problems.

7 Click **OK**.

Acrobat on the Macintosh does not have the same preference settings as those found in Windows for immediate visiting of PDF files. You can however use another method to print a file to disk and have it distilled with Acrobat Distiller and immediately view the resultant PDF file. The Create Adobe PDF option in the printer driver offers this option.

USING THE CREATE ADOBE PDF OPTION (MACINTOSH)

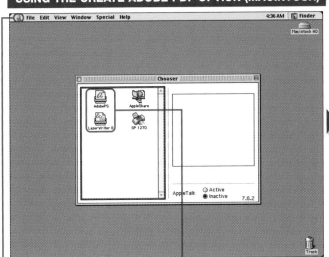

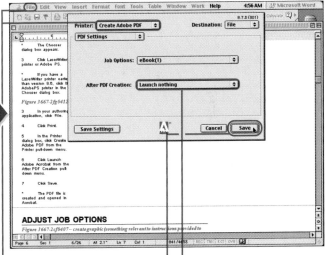

1 Click in the top left corner.

2 In the menu that appears, click **Chooser**.

■ The Chooser dialog box appears.

3 Click **LaserWriter** printer or **Adobe PS**.

■ If you have a LaserWriter printer earlier than Version 8.6, click the **AdobePS** printer in the Chooser dialog box.

4 In your authoring application, click **File**.

5 Click **Print**.

6 In the Printer dialog box, click the Printer 🔹 and click **Create Adobe PDF**.

7 Click the After PDF Creation 🔹 and click **Launch Adobe Acrobat**.

8 Click **Save**.

■ The PDF file is created and opened in Acrobat.

ADJUST JOB OPTIONS

Job Options are settings that are applied to the PDF creation process. Acrobat has four preset Job Options: eBook, for creating e-books to be downloaded from Web sites; Screen, for PDFs to be viewed on a computer monitor; Print, for desktop printers; and Press, for professional printing devices. You can also create custom Job Options sets.

There are many attributes that you can assign to the distillation process. You can change compatibility settings for earlier versions of Acrobat, compress file sizes significantly according to output needs, and choose whether to embed fonts. Without embedding, sharing files may create font substitution and render a different appearance for both screen and printed PDFs.

ADJUST JOB OPTIONS

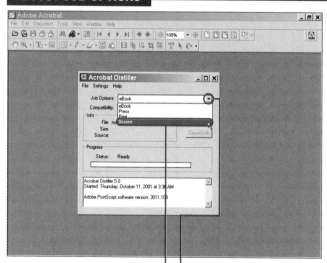

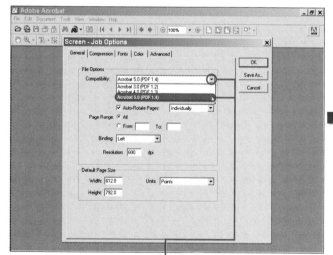

SELECT A JOB OPTION

■ When you install Acrobat, four preset Job Options sets are available. You select a Job Option set from a drop-down menu in the Distiller application window.

1 Click .

2 Click the desired option.

ADJUST COMPATIBILITY SETTINGS

1 Click **Settings** in the Distiller window.

2 Click **Job Options**.

■ The Screen-Job Options dialog box opens with the default Job Options settings.

3 Click the Compatibility ▼.

4 Click the desired compatibility.

Why are some fonts listed for Never Embed?

Acrobat installs fonts on your hard drive when you run the Acrobat installer. Among the fonts installed are the Base 14 fonts. These fonts are required for Acrobat to run properly. Because these fonts are installed with every Acrobat viewer, no one viewing a PDF needs these fonts embedded.

If I want to embed any of the Base 14 fonts, can I do so?

If, for some reason, you want to embed a Base 14 font, follow these steps:

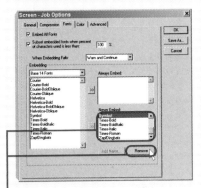

■1 Click the font in the Never Embed list.

■2 Click **Remove**.

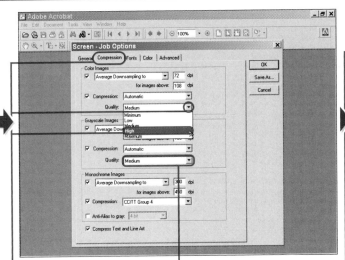

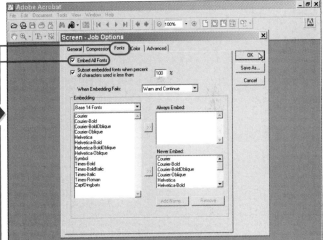

ADJUST COMPRESSION SETTINGS

■5 Click the **Compression** tab.

■6 Click the Quality ▼ under Color Images.

■7 Click the desired quality level.

■ **High** means less compression, resulting in a higher quality.

■8 Click the Quality ▼ under Grayscale Images to make the same adjustment as in step **7**.

EMBED FONTS

■9 Click the **Fonts** tab.

■10 Check **Embed All Fonts** (☐ changes to ☑).

■ When the file is distilled with Acrobat Distiller, all the fonts from the PostScript file are embedded in the PDF.

CONTINUED

ADJUST JOB OPTIONS

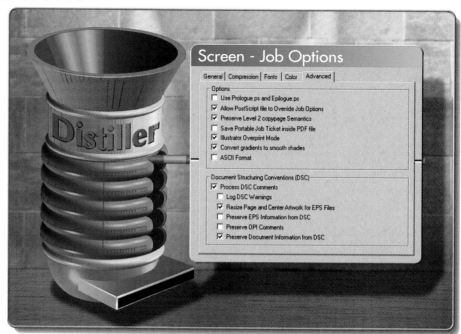

Acrobat has additional Job Options settings. You can adjust color settings to manage color profiles in PDFs. You can also adjust more advanced settings, save the Job Options set, and then share the set. Job Options settings are plain text files that you can copy from one computer to another and across platforms.

ADJUST JOB OPTIONS (CONTINUED)

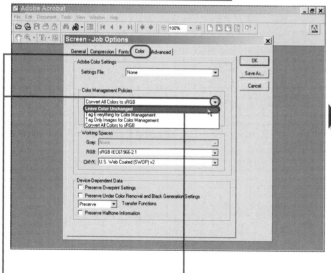

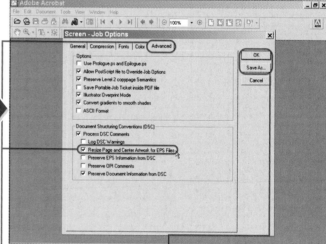

ADJUST COLOR SETTINGS

11 Click the **Color** tab.

12 Click the Color Management Policies ▼.

13 Unless you use a color-management system and want to tag files for color management or to convert colors, click **Leave Color Unchanged**.

ADJUST ADVANCED SETTINGS

14 Click the **Advanced** tab.

15 If unchecked, check **Resize Page and Center Artwork for EPS Files** (☐ changes to ☑).

■ This setting ensures that PDFs created from EPS files are produced at the page size that the original file was created.

16 Click **OK** to add a new Job Option.

I see many different settings in the Job Options. How can I know what they all mean?

Fortunately, the four preset Job Options suit most of your needs. If you need to create a custom set and want to learn more about the various options for the settings, look to the Acrobat Help file by clicking **Help** and then **Acrobat Help.**

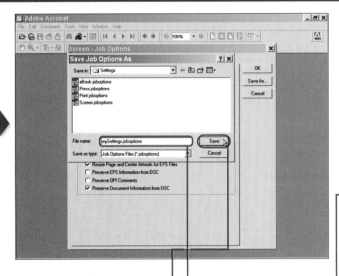

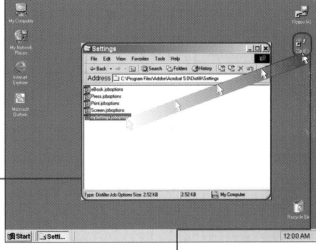

SAVE A JOB OPTIONS SET

■ The Save Job Options As dialog box opens. By default, Acrobat adds a number after the name of the set that the new set was based on, such as Screen(1).

17 If desired, type in a name for the new settings.

■ By default, the settings saves in the Settings folder inside your Distiller folder.

18 Click **Save**.

SHARE A JOB OPTIONS SET

1 Open the Settings folder.

■ The default path for the Settings folder is C:\Programs\Adobe\Acrobat 5.0\Distillr\Settings (Windows) or Macintosh HD: Acrobat 5.0: Distiller: Settings (Macintosh).

2 Drag the new settings to an external disk drive.

3 Copy the file to the same directory path on another computer.

■ When Distiller is launched, the new settings appear in the Job Options drop-down menu.

DISTILL A POSTSCRIPT FILE

After you get a handle on printing PostScript files and understand a little bit about Job Options settings, you can choose your Job Option setting and distill a PostScript file. Fortunately, this is an easy process.

DISTILL A POSTSCRIPT FILE

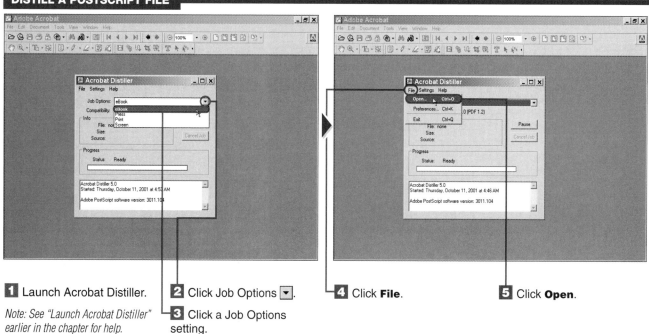

1 Launch Acrobat Distiller.

Note: See "Launch Acrobat Distiller" earlier in the chapter for help.

2 Click Job Options ▼.

3 Click a Job Options setting.

4 Click **File**.

5 Click **Open**.

I want to distill several files. Can I select multiple files in the Open dialog box?

You cannot select multiple files in the Open dialog box. If you want to distill multiple PostScript files, you need to use the drag-and-drop method for converting the files to PDFs. Just launch Acrobat Distiller from the Desktop, open the folder that contains the files you want to convert, and drag those files on top of the Distiller window. Or, you can drag mulitple files to the program icon or a shortcut/alias.

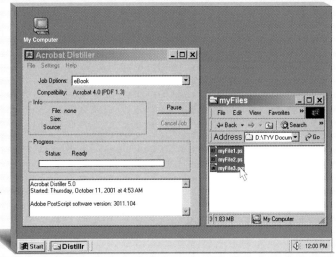

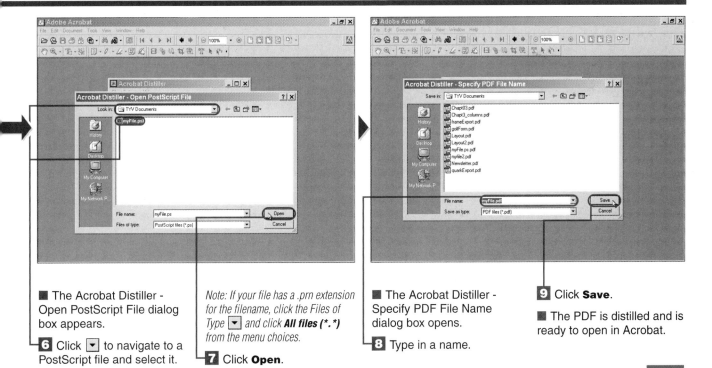

■ The Acrobat Distiller - Open PostScript File dialog box appears.

6 Click ⬛ to navigate to a PostScript file and select it.

*Note: If your file has a .prn extension for the filename, click the Files of Type ⬛ and click **All files (*.*)** from the menu choices.*

7 Click **Open**.

■ The Acrobat Distiller - Specify PDF File Name dialog box opens.

8 Type in a name.

9 Click **Save**.

■ The PDF is distilled and is ready to open in Acrobat.

MONITOR FONT LOCATIONS

Perhaps the single greatest problem in producing PDFs is ensuring proper font embedding. If fonts are not embedded in a PDF, the files may display and print differently than the original design. You can use Distiller to monitor the folders where fonts are located. When a font is not embedded in a PostScript file, Distiller seeks out used fonts in these folders and embeds the found fonts in the PDF.

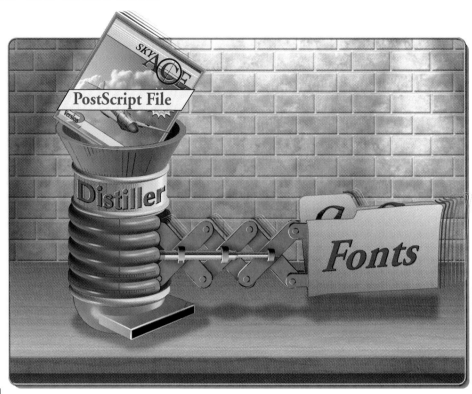

MONITOR FONT LOCATIONS

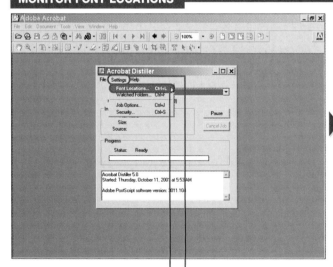

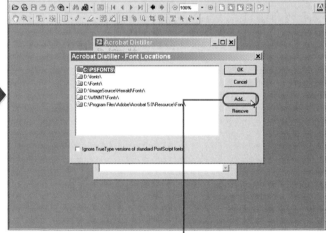

ADD A MONITORED FOLDER

1 Launch Acrobat Distiller.

Note: See "Launch Acrobat Distiller" earlier in the chapter for help.

2 Click **Settings**.

3 Click **Font Locations**.

■ The Acrobat Distiller – Font Locations dialog box opens.

4 Click **Add**.

How can I determine if fonts are embedded in a PDF?

To determine the font embedding status in a PDF examine the PDF's properties. Click **File** and then **Document Properties**. Click **Fonts** to view the Document Fonts dialog box. The list for Actual Font tells you whether a font has been embedded. If an item in the Actual Font list is embedded, it is noted in the list under the Actual Font heading. However, you must individually view each page to determine whether any given font is actually embedded.

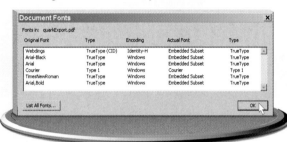

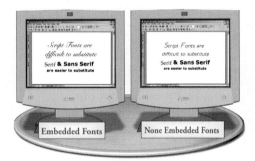
Why is font embedding important?

If fonts are embedded, the PDF displays and prints properly, even if the end user doesn't have the fonts installed on his or her computer. If fonts are not embedded in a PDF, Acrobat will substitute fonts if it cannot find them on the computer in an effort to simulate the document's original appearance. With some typefaces like script fonts, you will notice an obvious change from the original design.

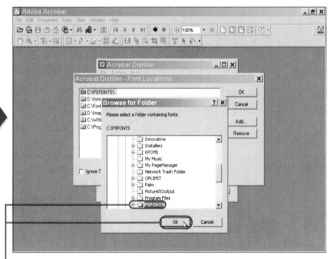

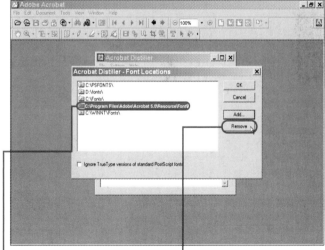

■ The Browse for Folder dialog box opens.

5 Select a folder on your hard drive where fonts are installed.

6 Click **OK**.

■ The folder is added to the monitored folders list. If Distiller cannot find a font in a PostScript file, it searches all folders for the fonts. When found, the font is embedded in the PDF.

DELETE A MONITORED FOLDER

1 Click **Settings**.

2 Click **Font Locations**.

3 Click the folder to delete.

4 Click **Remove**.

■ The folder is deleted from the list of folders monitored by Distiller.

CREATE WATCHED FOLDERS

If you work in a production workflow and have frequent need to create PDFs with different Job Options for different output requirements, you will want to use a Distiller Watched Folder. A Watched Folder makes it easy to create PDFs from PostScript files saved to disk that are later distilled by Acrobat Distiller.

CREATE WATCHED FOLDERS

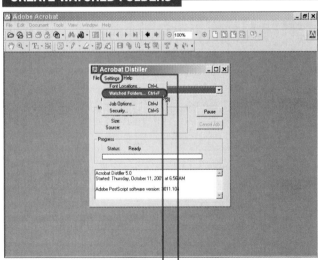

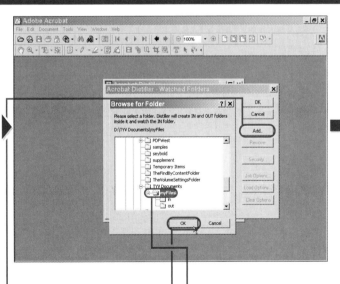

CREATE A WATCHED FOLDER

1 Launch Acrobat Distiller.

2 Click **Settings**.

3 Click **Watched Folders**.

■ The Acrobat Distiller – Watched Folders dialog box opens.

4 Click **Add**.

■ The Browse for Folder dialog box opens.

5 Select a folder on your hard drive as a Watched Folder.

Note: If you want to use a new folder, create a folder in your Desktop view before opening Acrobat Distiller.

6 Click **OK**.

Can I assign a Job Options set to a Watched Folder?

When you move a file to the In folder, the default Job Options are used. If you want to assign a specific Job Options set to override the default settings, you can load a set and assign it to a given Watched Folder. Open the Watched Folders dialog box and click **Load Options.** Select the Job Options to use and click **OK.** When files are distilled from the Watched Folder, the associated Job Options are used. You can create multiple Watched Folders and assign different Job Options to each folder. When a PostScript file is dropped into the In folder, the PDF is produced with the Job Options assigned to the folder.

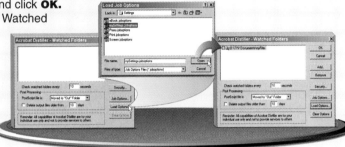

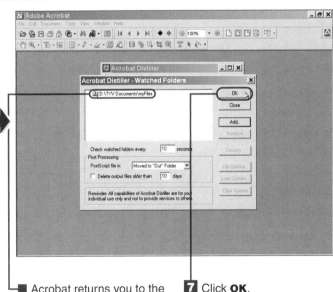

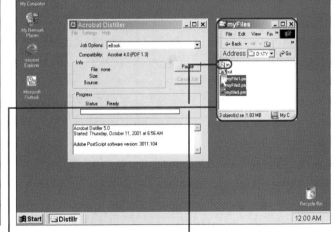

■ Acrobat returns you to the Acrobat Distiller – Watched Folders dialog box with the new Watched Folder listed.

7 Click **OK**.

DISTILL A FILE WITH A WATCHED FOLDER

1 With Distiller open, open the Watched Folder on your Desktop.

■ Acrobat creates two new folders inside your Watched Folder: the In folder and the Out folder.

2 Drag the file that you want to distill to the In folder.

■ Acrobat Distiller converts the PostScript file to PDF and moves the file to the Out folder.

REPURPOSE PDF DOCUMENTS

You can repurpose PDFs for other uses. For example, you may want to turn a PDF that was designed for commercial printing into one appropriate for Web use. In such case, the image sizes should be much smaller for Web displays than those developed for high-end printing. In this regard, you will want to repurpose a PDF document for a different output.

REPURPOSE PDF DOCUMENTS

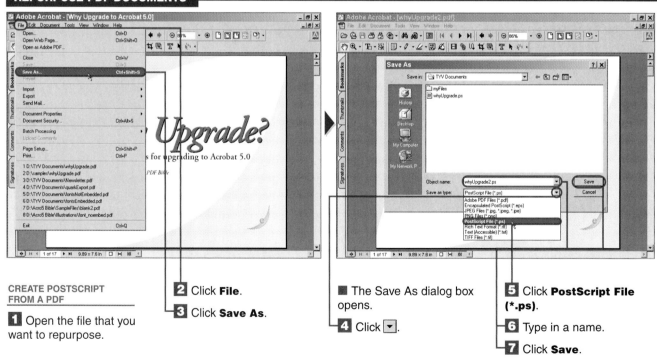

CREATE POSTSCRIPT FROM A PDF

1 Open the file that you want to repurpose.

2 Click **File**.

3 Click **Save As**.

■ The Save As dialog box opens.

4 Click ▼.

5 Click **PostScript File (*.ps)**.

6 Type in a name.

7 Click **Save**.

**Will the new PDF preserve my bookmarks from
the old PDF?**

The new PDF loses all content that you may have
added in Acrobat, such as bookmarks, links, form
fields, and comments. If
you want to preserve
these elements in the
new PDF, you need to
perform an additional
step. After creating a
new PDF, open the
original file and click
Document and then
Replace Pages.
Replace all pages in
the old file with the
new document pages.
Then click **File** and then **Save
As** to save the file with a new name. All
bookmarks, comments, and links are preserved.

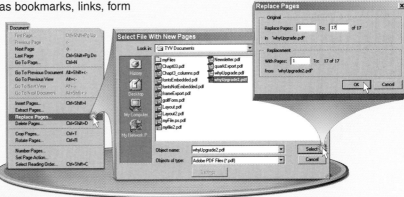

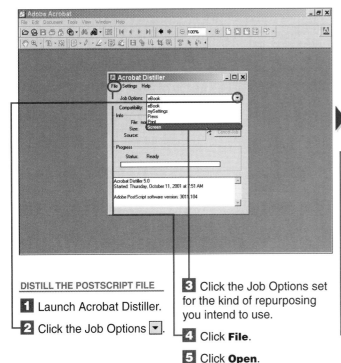

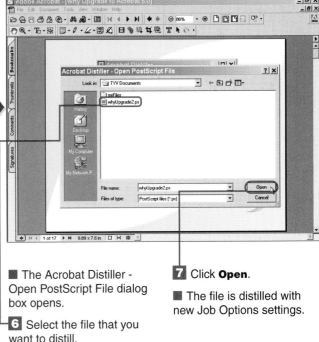

DISTILL THE POSTSCRIPT FILE

1 Launch Acrobat Distiller.

2 Click the Job Options ▼.

3 Click the Job Options set
for the kind of repurposing
you intend to use.

4 Click **File**.

5 Click **Open**.

■ The Acrobat Distiller -
Open PostScript File dialog
box opens.

6 Select the file that you
want to distill.

7 Click **Open**.

■ The file is distilled with
new Job Options settings.

CORRECT FONT PROBLEMS

At times, you may need to fix a problem with a PDF file when you do not have the original document. If problems with fonts occur and you need to fix them, then printing a PostScript file and redistilling the file can be an effective workaround. The process involves creating a folder where problem fonts are copied and instructing Distiller to monitor the folder.

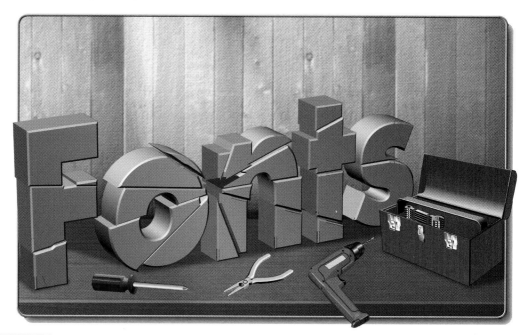

CORRECT FONT PROBLEMS

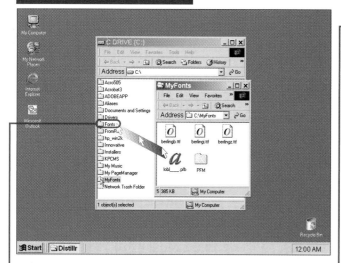

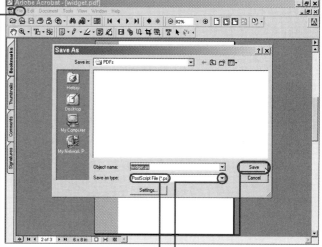

CREATE A FONT FOLDER TO MONITOR

1 Create a folder on your Desktop to monitor.

2 Copy your fonts to the folder.

Note: At times, fonts may become corrupted. If a problem persists with a given font, you may need to reinstall it. Create a separate folder and install a fresh copy to the folder.

SAVE THE PDF TO POSTSCRIPT

1 Open the PDF with the font problem in Acrobat.

2 Click **File**.

3 Click **Save As**.

4 Click the Save as type ▼.

5 Click **PostScript File (*.ps)** from the drop-down menu.

6 Click **Save**.

**Why are my
PostScript fonts
not embedding?**

You need to
exercise care to
properly install
PostScript fonts.
The most common
problem with these
fonts is not having
all the components
installed. PostScript
fonts require two
parts — the
screen font and
the printer font.

Windows

Macintosh

In Windows, make sure you have the
fonts installed with a .pfb extension. In
the folder where these fonts are
installed, you see a folder for .pfm
fonts. All PostScript fonts must have
both items installed.

On the Macintosh, notice a suitcase
icon and another icon with a similarly
abbreviated name. The suitcase is the
screen font, whereas the other icons
represent the printer fonts. Each
screen font needs a printer font to
display, print, and embed properly.

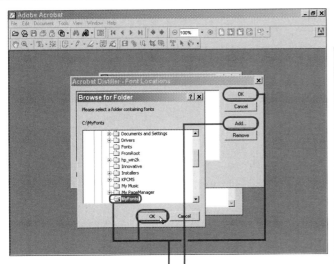

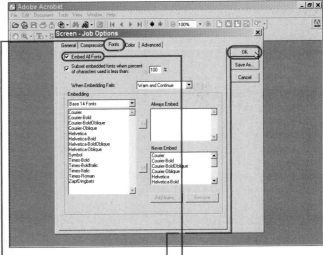

**MONITOR THE NEW
FONTS FOLDER**

1 In Acrobat Distiller, click
Settings and then click **Font
Locations**.

■ The Acrobat Distiller –
Font Locations dialog box
opens.

2 Click **Add**.

3 Select the new fonts
folder in the Browse for
Folder dialog box.

4 Click **OK** twice.

CHANGE JOB OPTIONS

1 Click **Settings**.

2 Click **Job Options**.

3 In the Screen – Job
Options dialog box that
appears, click the **Fonts** tab.

4 Check **Embed All Fonts**
(☐ changes to ☑).

5 Click **OK**.

6 Distill the PostScript file.

CONVERT EPS TO PDF

You may work with programs that do not export to PDF, but they can export to Encapsulated PostScript (EPS). Engineering and CAD programs often support exporting to EPS format. After you save a file as EPS, you can convert it to PDF with Acrobat Distiller.

CONVERT EPS TO PDF

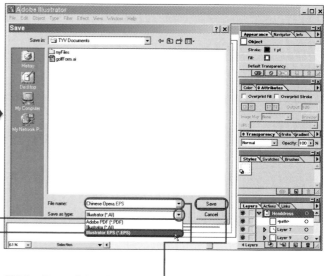

SAVE AS EPS

■ Any program that can save to EPS typically saves in the same manner. If the program you use does not use the Save As command for exporting to EPS, see the user documentation.

1 Click **File**.

2 Click **Save As**.

■ The Save dialog box opens.

3 Click ▼.

4 Click **Illustrator EPS (*.EPS)**.

Note: In this example, Adobe Illustrator is used. Save as type may display different names from different applications, but EPS should appear as part of the file type.

5 Type in a name.

6 Click **Save**.

Why do my PDFs appear to be offset and sometimes clipped at the edges?

If the PDFs you create from EPS files appear off center or sometimes lose data at the edges, your Distiller Job Options are not set properly.

If offsetting or clipping occurs, you need to make an adjustment in the Distiller Job Options. Click **Settings,** then **Job Options.** On the Advanced tab, check the box for Resize Page and Center Artwork for EPS Files.

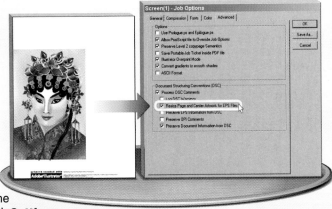

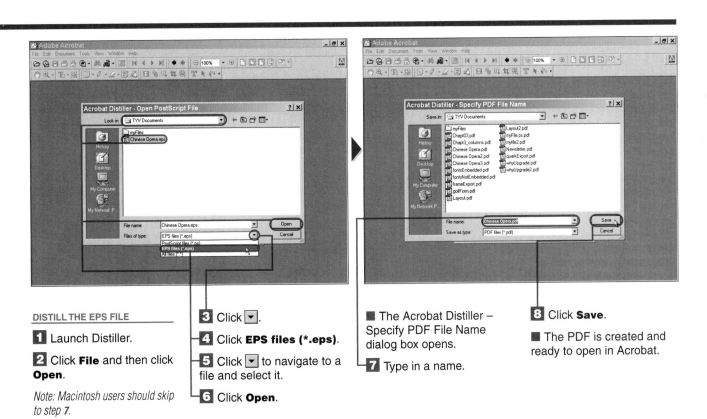

DISTILL THE EPS FILE

1 Launch Distiller.

2 Click **File** and then click **Open**.

Note: Macintosh users should skip to step 7.

■ An Open dialog box appears.

3 Click ▾.

4 Click **EPS files (*.eps)**.

5 Click ▾ to navigate to a file and select it.

6 Click **Open**.

■ The Acrobat Distiller – Specify PDF File Name dialog box opens.

7 Type in a name.

8 Click **Save**.

■ The PDF is created and ready to open in Acrobat.

SECURE PDFS WITH ACROBAT DISTILLER

Acrobat provides many options for securing PDF files. You can protect your PDF files from unauthorized viewing or from unauthorized editing. This task shows you how to secure a file when distilling. For more on security, see Chapter 13.

SECURE PDFS WITH ACROBAT DISTILLER

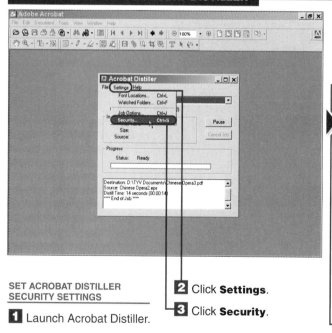

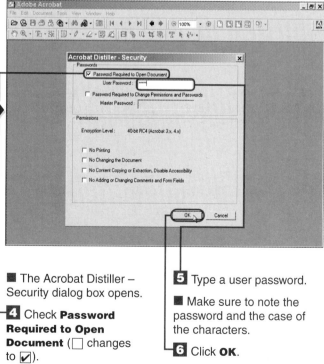

SET ACROBAT DISTILLER SECURITY SETTINGS

1 Launch Acrobat Distiller.

2 Click **Settings**.

3 Click **Security**.

■ The Acrobat Distiller – Security dialog box opens.

4 Check **Password Required to Open Document** (☐ changes to ☑).

5 Type a user password.

■ Make sure to note the password and the case of the characters.

6 Click **OK**.

What do the Document Assembly items mean?

Document Assembly items are related to the page editing tasks available in Acrobat. Features such as replacing pages, rotating pages, insertion of new pages and deleting pages are all related to Document Assembly. If you check the security settings and see the Document Assembly items disabled, you know you cannot insert, delete, or rotate pages or perform any other similar page-editing tasks.

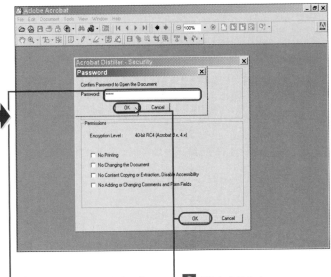

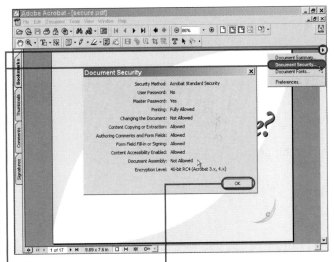

■ The Password dialog box opens.

7 Type the same characters to confirm your password.

8 Click **OK** twice.

■ The next file you distill will have the security settings applied to the PDF.

CHECK A DOCUMENT FOR SECURITY

1 Click ▶.

2 Click **Document Security** from the menu that appears to open the Document Security dialog box.

■ The dialog box summarizes the security applied to the document. In this example, security has been applied to prevent changing the document and to prevent document assembly.

3 Click **OK** when done.

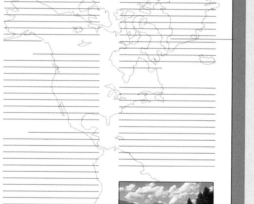

CHAPTER 5

Work With Links

Are you ready to create links and hypertext references in Acrobat? In this chapter you learn how to create hot links for navigating and viewing PDF files and imported documents.

Understanding Links 94

Create a Bookmark 96

Using Bookmark Properties 98

Create an Article Thread..................100

Create Link Buttons 102

Create Links from Text.....................104

Create a World Wide Web Link 106

Import a Sound 107

Link to a Movie 108

Create a Form Field Link Button 110

Duplicate Field Buttons 114

Create a Destination........................116

Link to a Destination 118

UNDERSTANDING LINKS

Acrobat shines at hyperlinking to pages, files, and actions to suit your information needs. You can create many different kinds of links, buttons, and actions in Acrobat.

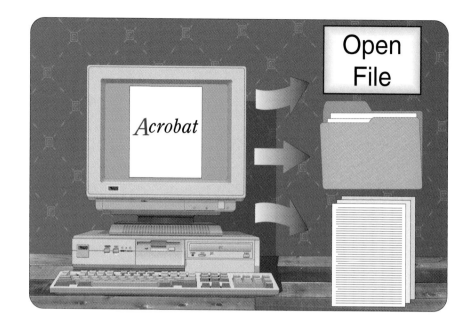

Bookmarks

Bookmark a page, and the bookmark appears in the Bookmarks palette. Click the bookmark, and it behaves like a link to a page and view.

Thumbnails

View thumbnails of your PDF pages in the Thumbnails palette. Click a thumbnail, and Acrobat jumps to the page.

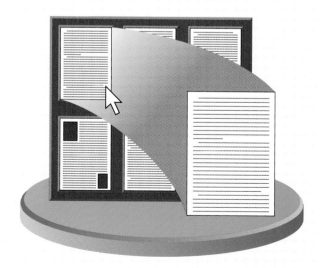

Article Threads

Article threads are also links. Drag a rectangle around a passage flowing across multiple pages, press the Enter key, and you create an article thread. Click inside the passage, and you can navigate through the article.

Links

Links are commonly created with the Link tool and behave like a button. Draw a rectangle, and you can define one of many different actions to associate with clicking the button.

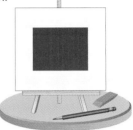

Form Fields

Form Fields can assume an appearance and behavior of a link button. You can import images for link button appearances by using the Form tool.

Destinations

Go to a view in a PDF and create a destination for the view. Destinations appear in a palette much like bookmarks. Click a destination, and you can jump to another page view.

Movie Clips

Movie clips are also links. Click a movie clip, and the linked movie file plays within the Acrobat Document Pane.

Actions

With links created from the bookmarks, links, and form fields, you can associate one of many different action types. You can execute any menu command, open a file, show or hide a form field, go to a view, execute a JavaScript, and more.

CREATE A BOOKMARK

Whereas an analog bookmark in a book on your desk is static, Acrobat bookmarks are dynamic. You can bookmark a page and a zoom view, or associate many different action types with a bookmark.

CREATE A BOOKMARK

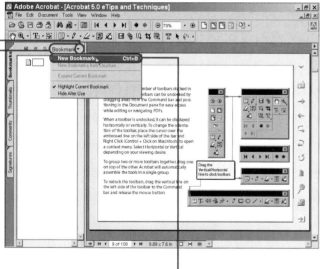

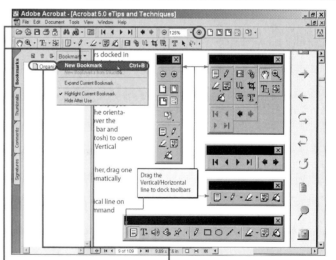

BOOKMARK A VIEW

1 Click **Bookmarks**.

2 Click ▼ in the Bookmarks Palette to open the drop-down menu.

3 Click **New Bookmark**.

4 Type a name for the bookmark.

■ The new bookmark is created for the current view.

BOOKMARK A ZOOM VIEW

1 Click ⊕ in the toolbar to zoom in and make the text as large as you want.

2 Click **New Bookmark** in the Bookmark palette.

3 Type a name for the bookmark.

■ The bookmark opens the current view at the size you chose.

Can I reorganize parent and child bookmarks together?

All child bookmarks are nested below the parent bookmarks. You can drag away any child bookmark to create a new parent, or you can drag a parent bookmark to a new location. All child bookmarks follow the parent bookmark to the new location.

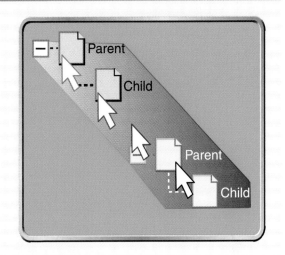

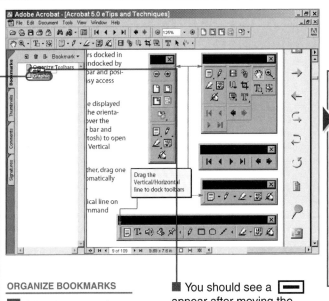

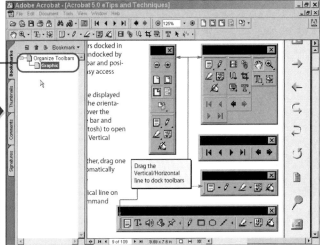

ORGANIZE BOOKMARKS

1 Click the second bookmark positioned below the first bookmark.

2 Drag up and right slightly.

■ You should see a ▭ appear after moving the bookmark.

3 Release the mouse button.

■ The bookmark appears like an indented line of text. The top bookmark is the parent bookmark, while the second indented bookmark is the child bookmark.

USING BOOKMARK PROPERTIES

In addition to bookmarking views, you can also associate many different actions with a bookmark. You access bookmark actions in the Bookmark Properties dialog box. These properties appear for bookmarks, links, and form fields.

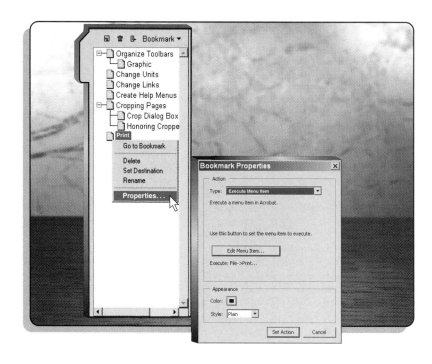

USING BOOKMARK PROPERTIES

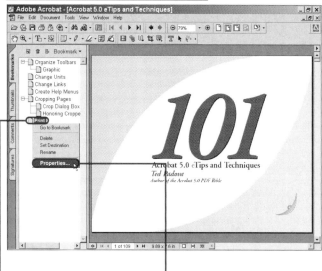

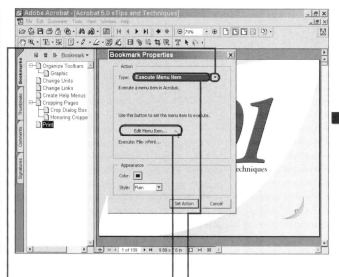

OPEN THE PROPERTIES DIALOG BOX

1 Create a new bookmark.

2 Type **Print** to name the bookmark.

3 Right-click (Windows) or **Control** +click (Macintosh) to open a context menu.

4 Click **Properties**.

*Note: You can also use the palette menu and click **Properties**.*

SELECT AN ACTION TYPE

■ The Bookmark Properties dialog box opens.

1 Click ▼ to open the drop-down menu.

2 Scroll the menu choices to the top and click **Execute Menu Item**.

3 Click **Edit Menu Item**.

After I create a bookmark, can I change the properties?

You can change and reassign properties for any
bookmark for views or different action types. To
change a bookmark property, follow these steps:

1 Click the bookmark in the Bookmark palette.

2 Open the Bookmark Properties dialog
box from a context menu or palette menu.

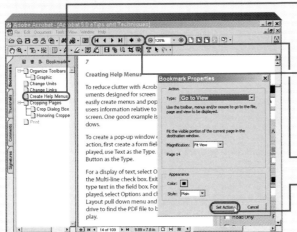

3 To change a view, click a
navigation tool from the toolbar.

*Note: All tools and menu commands are accessible
while the Bookmark Properties dialog box is open.*

4 Click ⊕ or ⊝ to set the desired zoom level.

5 Click **Set Action**.

■ The new properties are
established for the bookmark.

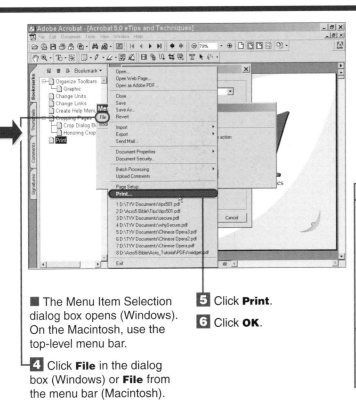

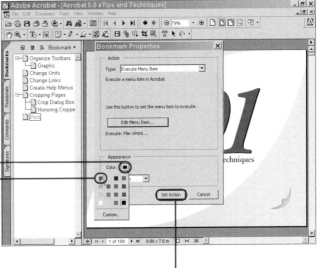

■ The Menu Item Selection
dialog box opens (Windows).
On the Macintosh, use the
top-level menu bar.

4 Click **File** in the dialog
box (Windows) or **File** from
the menu bar (Macintosh).

5 Click **Print**.

6 Click **OK**.

**ASSIGN A COLOR TO THE
BOOKMARK TEXT**

1 Click ▣.

■ A drop-down palette
opens.

2 Click ▤ for the color
choice.

3 Click **Set Action**.

■ The bookmark appears
with red text. When you click
the bookmark, the Print
dialog box opens.

CREATE AN ARTICLE THREAD

Article threads can help you design PDF documents for easy end-user viewing of passages of text. An article thread is like a button on top of a text passage. When you click the text passage, the button action takes you to the next view where the passage is continued.

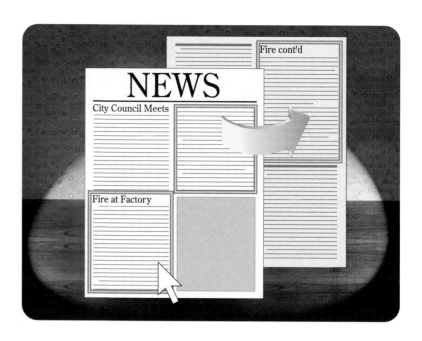

CREATE AN ARTICLE THREAD

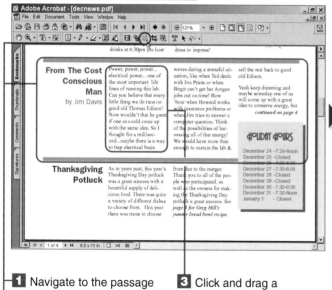

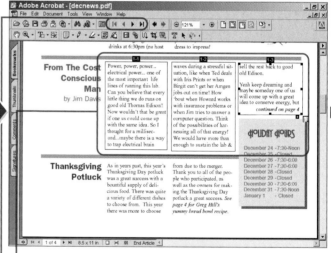

1 Navigate to the passage where you want to begin the article.

2 Click .

3 Click and drag a rectangle around the first column in your article.

4 Release the mouse button.

■ The first rectangle is drawn.

5 Continue drawing more rectangles around each column on the first page of your article thread.

6 Use |◄ ◄ ► ►| to move to the page where the article continues.

Note: Do not select any tool other than the navigation tools. You must keep selected in the toolbar to continue the thread.

Why does my view zoom in so high when I click in an article thread?

The zoom level for viewing article threads is determined in the General Preferences dialog box. To change the zoom level, you need to change the Max Fit Visible Zoom setting.

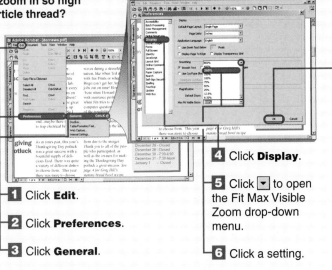

Note: You can also supply a custom zoom level by typing a number in the field box.

1 Click **Edit**.

2 Click **Preferences**.

3 Click **General**.

■ The General Preferences dialog box opens.

4 Click **Display**.

5 Click ▼ to open the Fit Max Visible Zoom drop-down menu.

6 Click a setting.

7 Click **OK**.

■ When you click an article thread, the zoom level is consistent with the preference setting.

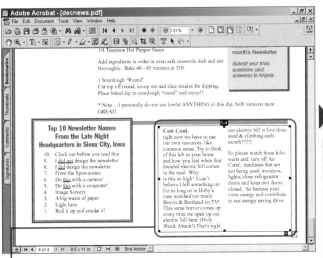

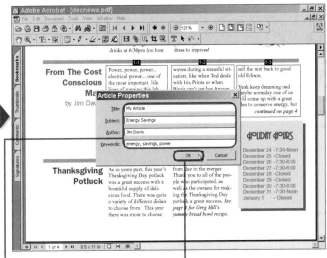

7 Finish drawing rectangles around columns on the continuation page.

8 Press **Enter** on the numeric keypad.

■ The Article Properties dialog box opens.

9 Supply the desired information in the field boxes.

10 Click **OK**.

■ The thread is complete. When the user places the cursor inside a column and clicks, Acrobat jumps to the top of the next column. Each click moves the view successively through the article.

101

CREATE LINK BUTTONS

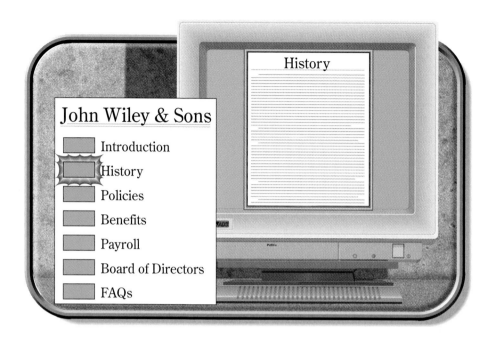

You use the Link button to create links that activate the same action types as those found with bookmark properties. You will often find it helpful to use the Link tool for navigation from button images and text in tables of contents.

CREATE LINK BUTTONS

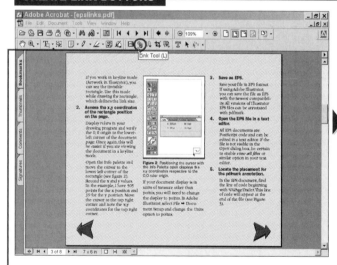

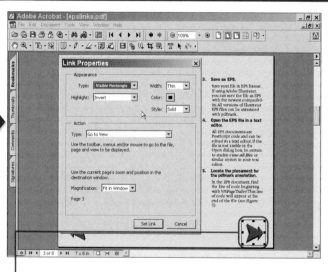

CREATE A LINK

1 Click 🖑.

Note: If any links have been created on the page in the Document Pane, they will appear as rectangle boxes when the Link tool is selected.

2 Click and drag a rectangle around the area where you want the Link buttons to appear.

3 Release the mouse button.

■ The Link Properties dialog box immediately opens.

After I finish creating a link, Acrobat changes my tool to the Hand tool. How can I keep the Link tool active to create more links?

Acrobat assumes you want to test your link after you create it. The Link button changes to the Hand button so that you can click the Link button and invoke the action. To keep the Link tool active, press the `Ctrl` key (Windows) or the `option` key (Macintosh) and then click the Link tool. Acrobat keeps the Link button active until you click the Hand tool.

What happens when I delete a page for the link destination?

The link becomes inoperative. To change the link destination, you need to edit the Link Properties. Just right-click (Windows) or `Control` + click (Macintosh) on the link and choose **Link Properties.** Click **Edit Destination,** change the destination, and click **Set Action.**

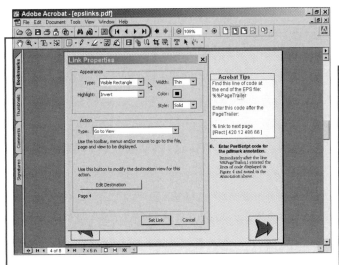

NAVIGATE TO A VIEW

1 With the Link Properties dialog box remaining open, use `|◀ ◀ ▶ ▶|` to move to the page and desired view.

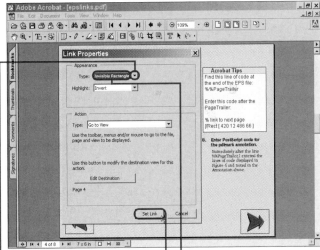

SELECT THE PROPERTIES

■ You can adjust the border size and color of the rectangle. If you have a graphic image on the PDF page, you can make the rectangle invisible.

1 Click the Type ▼ to open the drop-down menu.

2 Click **Invisible**.

3 Click **Set Link**.

■ Acrobat returns you to the page where the Link button was created. Place ᗡ over the link and click. Acrobat jumps to the linked view.

CREATE LINKS FROM TEXT

Often you may want to create a link from a table of contents (TOC) or an index. In such cases, the item from which the link is created may be a line of text. Fortunately, Acrobat makes it easy to create links from text.

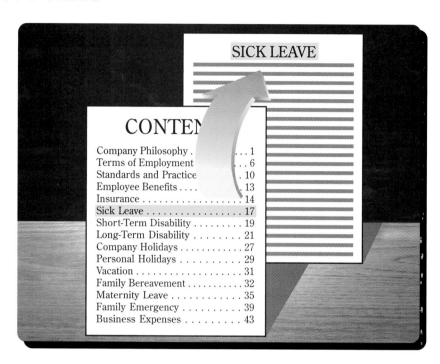

CONTEN[T]

Company Philosophy 1
Terms of Employment 6
Standards and Practice . . . 10
Employee Benefits 13
Insurance 14
Sick Leave 17
Short-Term Disability 19
Long-Term Disability 21
Company Holidays 27
Personal Holidays 29
Vacation 31
Family Bereavement 32
Maternity Leave 35
Family Emergency 39
Business Expenses 43

SICK LEAVE

CREATE LINKS FROM TEXT

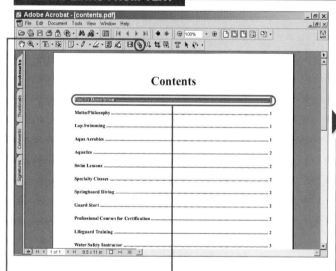

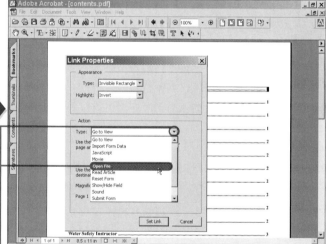

1 Open a PDF with a table of contents page.

2 Click 🔗.

3 Press **Ctrl** (Windows) or **option** (Macintosh).

■ While the Link tool is selected and the modifier key is pressed, the cursor appears as an I-beam (I).

4 Drag across the line of text to be the link button.

5 Release the mouse button.

■ The Link Properties dialog box opens.

6 Click the Type ▾.

7 Click **Open File**.

Note: If you previously set the Link Properties to display an invisible rectangle, it becomes a new default, and all subsequent links are created with the same properties. Leave the appearance at Invisible.

104

Why does the Save dialog box open when I create a link to open another file and then click the link?

When you click a link to open a second file, Acrobat closes the current file in the Document Pane and opens the second file. If you create a link and then click the link, Acrobat prompts you to save the changes in your document.

To keep both documents open, you can adjust a preference setting.

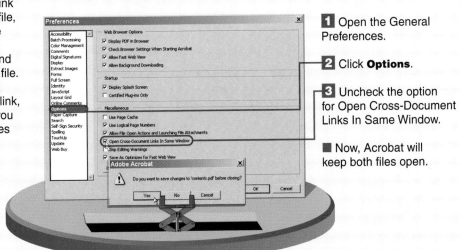

1 Open the General Preferences.

2 Click **Options**.

3 Uncheck the option for Open Cross-Document Links In Same Window.

■ Now, Acrobat will keep both files open.

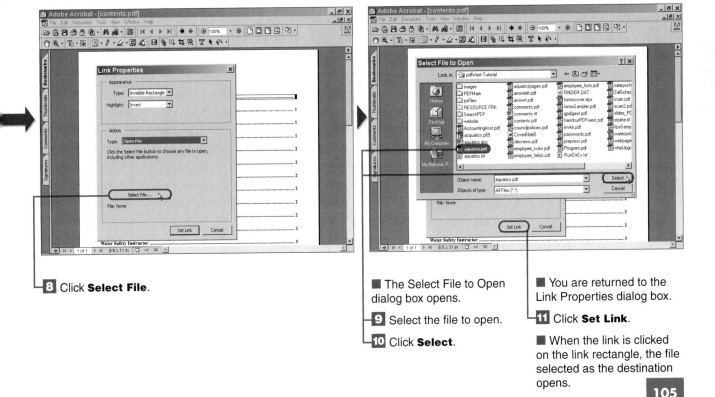

8 Click **Select File**.

■ The Select File to Open dialog box opens.

9 Select the file to open.

10 Click **Select**.

■ You are returned to the Link Properties dialog box.

11 Click **Set Link**.

■ When the link is clicked on the link rectangle, the file selected as the destination opens.

CREATE A WORLD WIDE WEB LINK

You can create links to URLs on the World Wide Web in an Acrobat PDF. When the link is clicked, Acrobat performs two steps. First, the default Web browser launches while Acrobat remains open. Second, the Web page for the link loads in the Web browser.

CREATE A WORLD WIDE WEB LINK

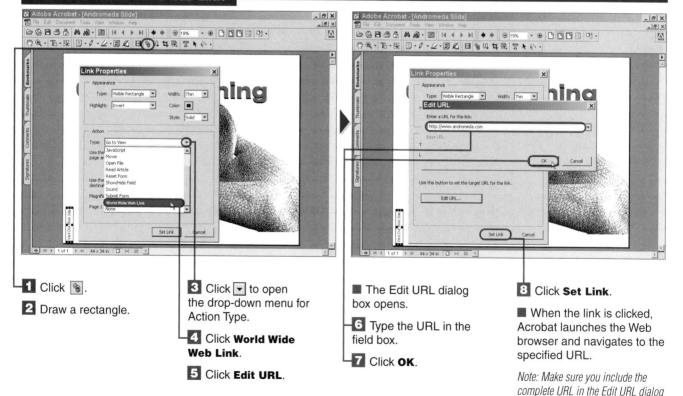

1 Click 🖑.

2 Draw a rectangle.

3 Click ▼ to open the drop-down menu for Action Type.

4 Click **World Wide Web Link**.

5 Click **Edit URL**.

■ The Edit URL dialog box opens.

6 Type the URL in the field box.

7 Click **OK**.

8 Click **Set Link**.

■ When the link is clicked, Acrobat launches the Web browser and navigates to the specified URL.

Note: Make sure you include the complete URL in the Edit URL dialog box, including the http://.

IMPORT A SOUND

You can import sounds in PDF files and have the sounds play by opening a page, or clicking a link button. Sounds are embedded in PDF files much like type or images. After importing a sound file in Acrobat, you can play the sound on any computer running Acrobat or Acrobat Reader.

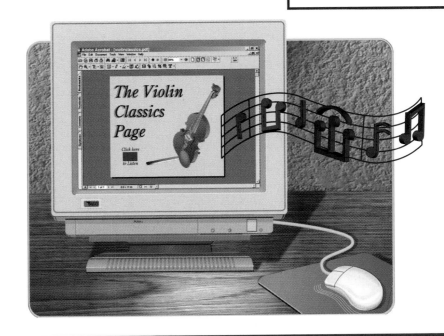

IMPORT A SOUND

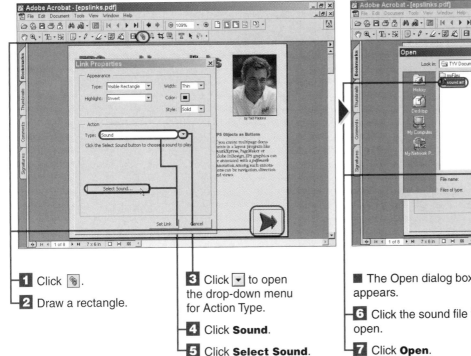

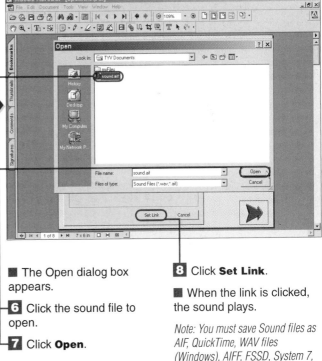

1 Click 📷.

2 Draw a rectangle.

3 Click ▼ to open the drop-down menu for Action Type.

4 Click **Sound**.

5 Click **Select Sound**.

■ The Open dialog box appears.

6 Click the sound file to open.

7 Click **Open**.

8 Click **Set Link**.

■ When the link is clicked, the sound plays.

Note: You must save Sound files as AIF, QuickTime, WAV files (Windows), AIFF, FSSD, System 7, or QuickTime files (Mac). Acrobat converts the imported file.

107

LINK TO A MOVIE

When you link to a movie, the movie frame becomes the link button. Movies are not embedded in PDFs like sound files. Whenever you transport the PDF to another computer, the movie file needs to accompany the PDF in order to play.

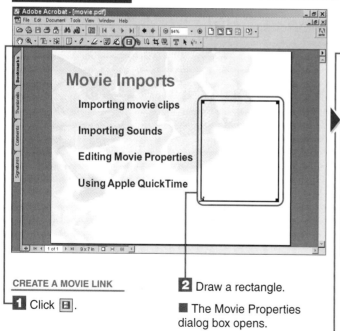

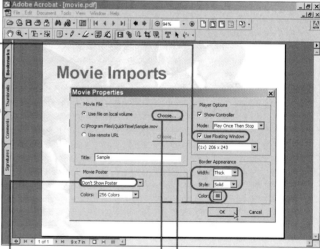

CREATE A MOVIE LINK

1 Click ▣.

2 Draw a rectangle.

■ The Movie Properties dialog box opens.

3 Under Movie Poster, click **Don't Show Poster** from the drop-down menu.

Note: The Movie Poster is the first frame in the file. By not showing the Poster, the movie frame first appears empty.

4 Check **Use Floating Window** (☐ changes to ☑).

5 Click ▼ to select border options for the player.

6 Click a color for the border.

7 Click **Choose**.

■ The Open dialog box appears.

Can I play movie clips from PDFs hosted on Web sites?

Like many other kind of link actions, you can play movies from PDFs on a Web site. You must have the movie clip on the Web site and identify the URL where the movie resides.

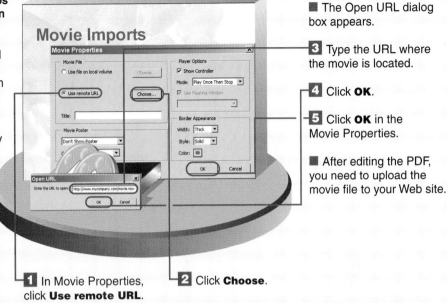

■ The Open URL dialog box appears.

3 Type the URL where the movie is located.

4 Click **OK**.

5 Click **OK** in the Movie Properties.

■ After editing the PDF, you need to upload the movie file to your Web site.

1 In Movie Properties, click **Use remote URL**.

2 Click **Choose**.

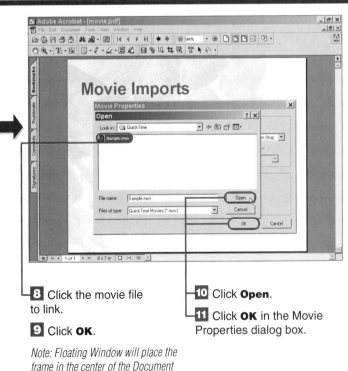

8 Click the movie file to link.

9 Click **OK**.

Note: Floating Window will place the frame in the center of the Document Pane.

10 Click **Open**.

11 Click **OK** in the Movie Properties dialog box.

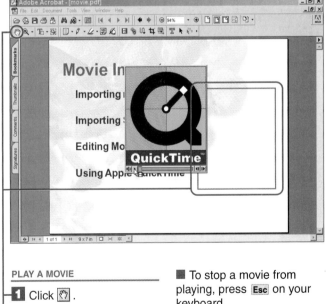

PLAY A MOVIE

1 Click 🖑.

2 Click the movie frame.

Note: When 🖑 is placed over a movie rectangle, the cursor changes to 🗄.

■ To stop a movie from playing, press Esc on your keyboard.

CREATE A FORM FIELD LINK BUTTON

Whereas links are limited to single appearances, you can use icons and images with form fields to create custom appearance buttons. Form fields offer many more options for creating link buttons than the Link tool.

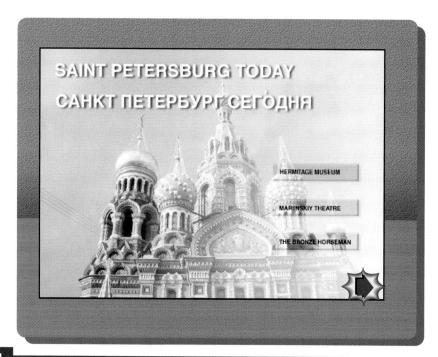

CREATE A FORM FIELD LINK BUTTON

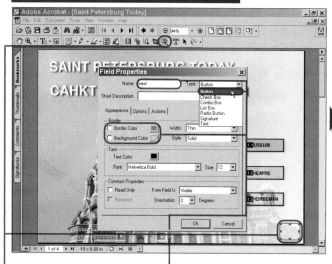

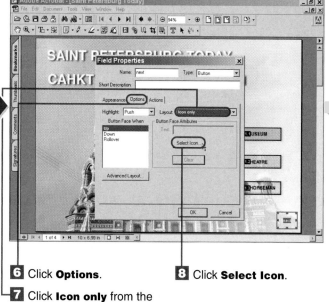

CREATE A LINK

1 Click 📋 tool.

2 Draw a rectangle.

■ The Field Properties dialog box opens.

3 Type in a name.

4 Click the type of field you want from the drop-down menu.

5 Click to select a border for the field (☐ changes to ☑).

6 Click **Options**.

7 Click **Icon only** from the Layout drop-down menu.

8 Click **Select Icon**.

What kinds of file types can I import for a button appearance?

You can import all the file types that you have available with the Open as Adobe PDF in the Select Appearance dialog box.

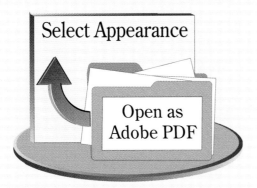

How can I easily create icons for using as button appearances?

If you do not have any illustrations handy, use type characters from a symbol font like Wingdings or Zapf Dingbats. Create text characters in an authoring program and convert to PDF. All the PDF files can be imported in the Button Appearance dialog box.

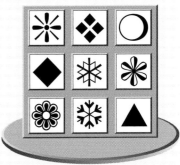

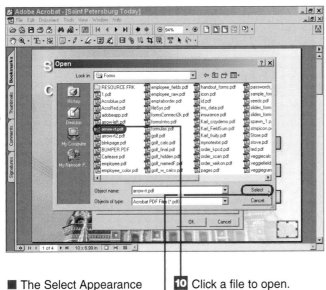

■ The Select Appearance dialog box opens.

9 Click **Browse**.

■ The Open dialog box appears.

10 Click a file to open.

11 Click **Select**.

■ The image to be used for the form field appearance is displayed in the Select Appearance dialog box.

12 Click **OK**.

CONTINUED

CREATE A FORM FIELD LINK BUTTON

Form field buttons use the same property settings as links. If you want to create navigation buttons, the Field Properties dialog box offers actions to enable page navigation.

CREATE A FORM FIELD LINK BUTTON (CONTINUED)

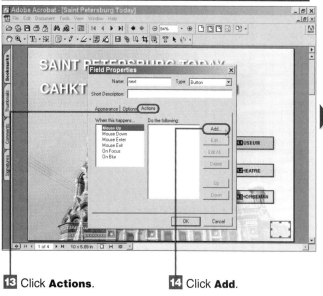

13 Click **Actions**.

14 Click **Add**.

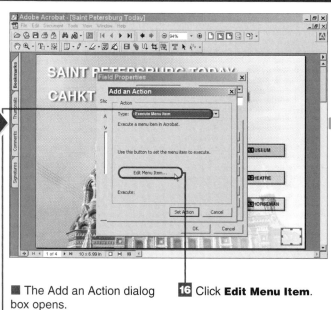

■ The Add an Action dialog box opens.

15 Click **Execute Menu Item** from the Type drop-down menu.

16 Click **Edit Menu Item**.

Can I create a link button to move backward in my PDF?

All the navigation items you have available with are available from menu commands.

If you want to create a button to move backward in a PDF file, use an icon that intuitively informs the user that the link moves backward.

When choosing the Execute Menu Item, click the **Previous Page** menu command.

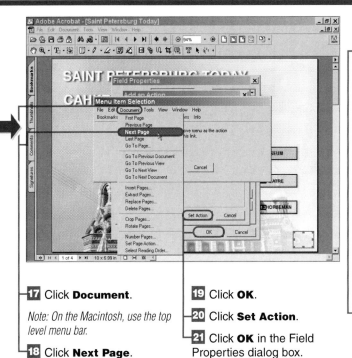

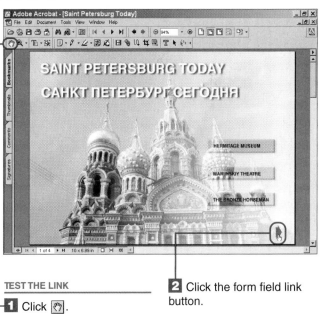

17 Click **Document**.

Note: On the Macintosh, use the top level menu bar.

18 Click **Next Page**.

19 Click **OK**.

20 Click **Set Action**.

21 Click **OK** in the Field Properties dialog box.

TEST THE LINK

1 Click .

■ When the Hand tool is positioned over the form field link button, the cursor changes to .

2 Click the form field link button.

■ When the link is clicked, the next page appears in the Document Pane.

DUPLICATE FIELD BUTTONS

Another great advantage in using form fields as opposed to links is the ability to duplicate or copy and paste form fields. Link rectangles cannot be duplicated or copied and pasted. However, you can duplicate form fields while retaining all the attributes of the button appearances and actions.

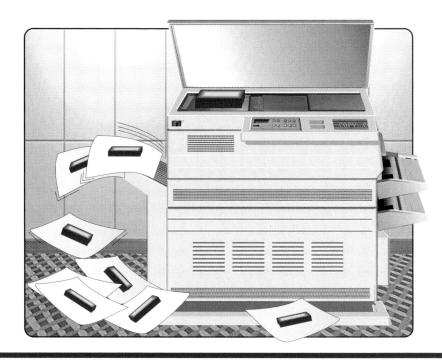

DUPLICATE FIELD BUTTONS

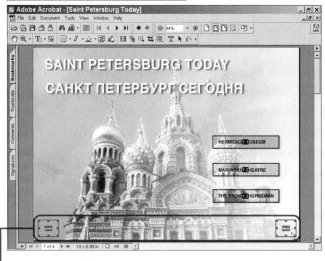

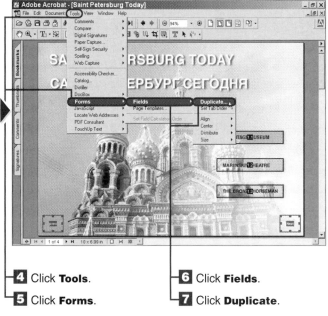

DUPLICATE FORM FIELDS

1 Create two form fields on a PDF page — one to move backward and one to move forward.

2 Click one form field with 🔁.

3 Shift +click the second field.

4 Click **Tools**.

5 Click **Forms**.

6 Click **Fields**.

7 Click **Duplicate**.

Are there any alternatives to using menu commands for duplicating fields?

Perhaps the best way to manage fields is to use a context menu. With the Form tool selected, right-click (Windows) or Control +click (Macintosh) to open a context menu. Click **Duplicate** from the menu options.

Why do all my fields disappear when I delete a field?

If you press the ◆Backspace / Delete key on your keyboard when a field is selected, Acrobat prompts you with a warning dialog box, if there are multiple fields with the same name. To delete a single field from one page while preserving the same field on the remaining pages, click **No** in the dialog box. To delete all occurrences of the field with the same name, click **Yes.**

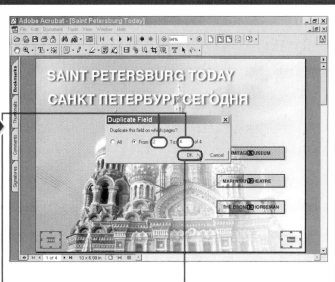

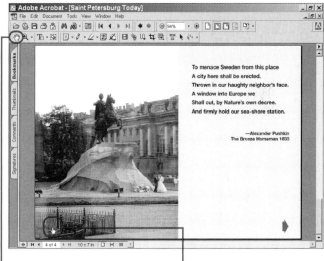

■ The Duplicate Field dialog box opens.

8 Type **2** in the first field box.

9 Type the last page number in the second field box.

10 Click **OK**.

■ The form fields are duplicated and appear on all pages from page 2 to the end of the document.

TEST THE FORM FIELD LINK BUTTONS

1 Click 🖑 .

2 Click the link buttons to move forward and back.

CREATE A DESTINATION

Destinations appear similar to bookmarks. They are created by choosing a view and linking to the view. With destinations, however, you access them in a palette and sort them according to the page order or alphabetically by name.

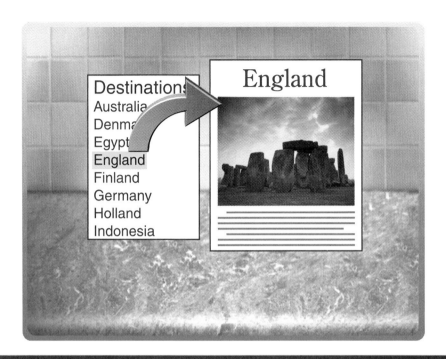

CREATE A DESTINATION

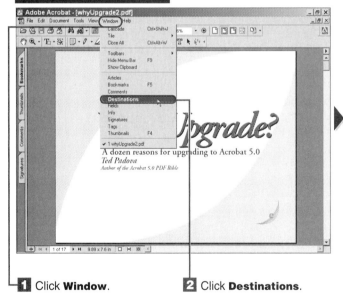

1 Click **Window**.

2 Click **Destinations**.

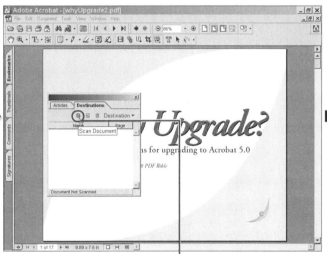

■ Before you can create or use destinations, the open PDF must be scanned for destinations.

3 Click **Scan Document** in the Destinations palette.

Note: After the document has been scanned, you can then proceed to create a destination.

Why do I need to scan a document for destinations?

Every time you open a PDF file, you need to scan the document for destinations. Acrobat will list existing destinations and before you can then create new ones. If destinations exist in a document, you can add more only after you scan the document.

Destinations

- Page 3, top left column.
- Page 15, entire page.
- Page 21, right column.
- Page 27, left column.
- Page 27, right column.
- Page 33, entire page.
- Page 35, last paragraph.
- Page 40, first three lines.
- Page 41, first paragraph.
- Page 46, entire page.
- Page 48, last paragraph.
- Page 49, left column.

How do I sort destinations?

You can sort destinations by Name or Page number. Click **Name** in the palette to sort alphabetically by destination name. Click **Page** to sort the destinations according to the page number where they appear.

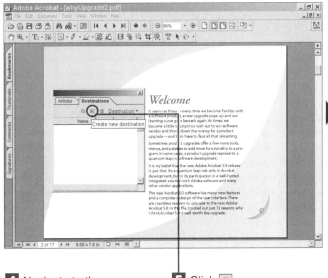

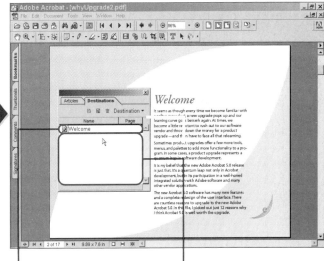

4 Navigate to the page where you want to create a destination.

5 Click 🔲 .

6 Type a name immediately after you create a destination.

7 Click anywhere below the name to deselect the text.

■ When you click the destination in the palette, Acrobat displays the page and view where the destination was created.

LINK TO A DESTINATION

If you create a link from one PDF file to another, the second file opens as the default first page in the document. However, the link or form tool will not open a page in the middle of a PDF. In this case, you need to link to a destination.

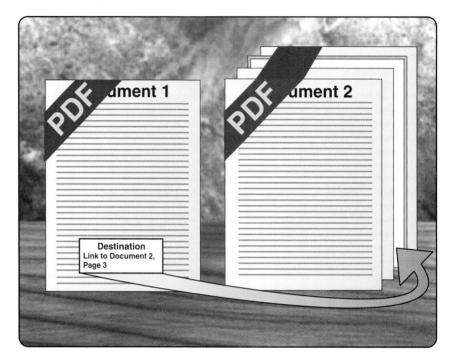

Destination
Link to Document 2, Page 3

LINK TO A DESTINATION

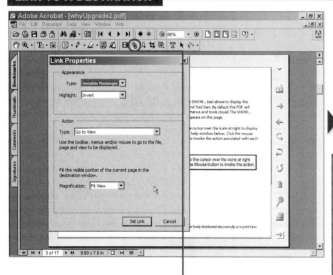

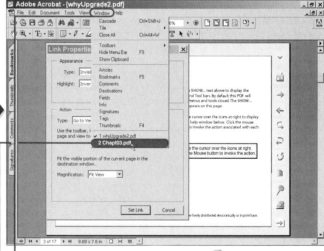

1 Open two documents — one for the link and one for the destination.

2 Click 🖉 to draw a link rectangle.

■ The Link Properties dialog box opens.

3 Click **Window**.

4 Click the second PDF filename at the bottom of the menu.

5 Navigate to a page in the middle of the document.

Note: The Link Properties dialog box remains open. Do not close it.

Can I bookmark a destination?

Bookmarks link only to pages in the document where they are created. Acrobat provides no means for bookmarking a page in a second document.

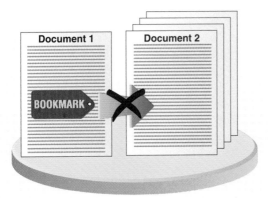

What happens if I delete a page where a destination has been created?

Unlike links that become inoperable, destinations behave differently. If you create a link to page 5 in a PDF and then subsequently delete page 5, the link takes you to the next page (in this case, the old page 6 now becomes page 5, and the destination is linked to the new page 5).

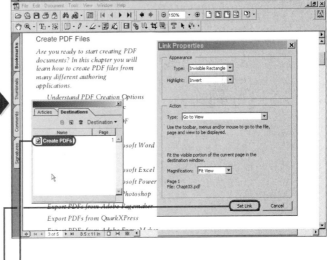

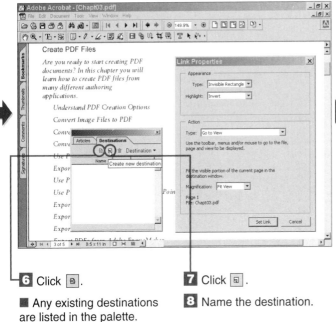

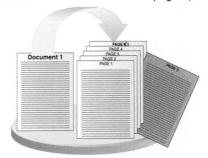

6 Click 🗐.

■ Any existing destinations are listed in the palette.

7 Click 🗐.

8 Name the destination.

9 Click the destination name to select it.

10 Click **Set Link** in the Link Properties dialog box.

■ When the link is clicked, the destination page opens.

When the company decided to relocate its move to St. Petersburg, Florida, several factors were key in the decision.

Among them were access to ports for shipping that would eliminate overland trucking expenses, which have steadily increased over the last few years.

~~Then again,~~ ~~T~~The warm, and for the most part, calm, ~~weather~~ would cut down on

I like the Intro - can you make it a paragraph longer? Other than that, great!

APPROVED WITH CORRECTIONS

Move this down to be third or fo reason.

Summary

CHAPTER 6

Create Comments

Are you ready to start working with annotations and markups? This chapter shows you how to create annotations for PDFs in the form of comments.

Understanding Comments 122

Set Comment Preferences 124

Create a Note Comment..................126

Set Comment Properties 128

Create a Free Text Note 130

Create a File Attachment................131

Create an Audio Comment 132

Using the Stamp Tool 134

Create Custom Stamps 136

Create Comments with
   Graphic Markup Tools 140

Using the Text Markup Tools 141

Filter Comments 142

Create Comment Summaries 144

Select a Network Folder for
   Online Comments.........................146

Work with Online Comments 148

Spell Check Comments and
   Form Fields 150

UNDERSTANDING COMMENTS

You can create comments with any one of many different comment tools. You can use these tools to markup and annotate PDF documents for collaboration among workgroups, either by sharing PDFs or commenting dynamically on networks or the Internet.

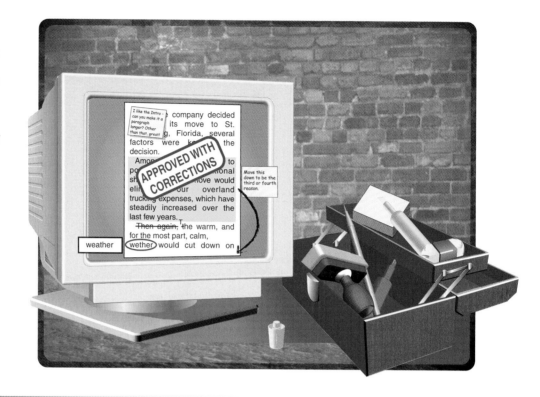

Note Comments

Note comments are the most common among the comment tools. Note comments are similar to sticky notes used in offices. Attach a note to a PDF much like you would stick a note on a piece of paper.

Free Text Note Comments

Free text comments enable you to create larger passages of text that can amplify messages. Whereas notes are limited in size and content, you can create free text comments as large as a PDF page.

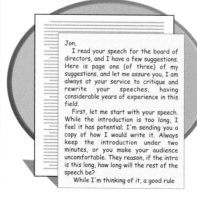

Audio Comments

Add sounds to your PDF documents for comment notes or instructional messages. Record a sound and import the sound by using the Audio Comment tool.

Stamp Comments

Common office stamps for marking up a document for approval, draft, confidential, or other types of messages can be made with the Stamp Comment tool.

File Attachments

Use the File Attachment tool to create a link to another file, such as a Microsoft Word document. The file is embedded in the PDF and can be extracted by users who have the authoring program installed on their computers.

Graphic Markups

Lines, boxes, circles, and geometric shapes can be drawn to mark up and annotate PDFs. With each markup, a note can be used to communicate a message about each markup.

Text Markups

While ~~you~~ a technician can ~~almost always~~ often diagnose **malfunctions** with a piece of equipment through training, intuition can ~~play~~ be an invaluable part of diagnostic work. Working backwards from a problem can often pinpoint the <u>exact</u> place of the **malfunction**.

Use a highlighter, strikethrough, or underline to correct or approve PDFs among people in your workgroup.

Online Comments

You can use all the comment tools to directly mark up PDF files, or you can log on to a server or Web-hosted document and make your comments online to be shared among coworkers.

SET COMMENT PREFERENCES

Preferences determine displays for comments in terms of author names, colors, and fonts. When you first create comments, you should visit the General Preferences and set the attributes for how you want your comments to display.

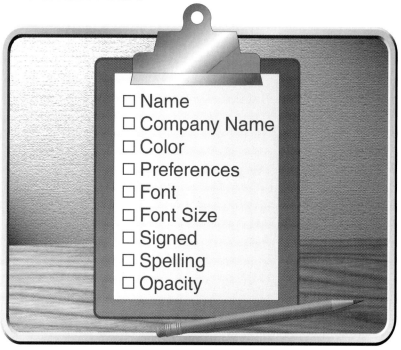

- ☐ Name
- ☐ Company Name
- ☐ Color
- ☐ Preferences
- ☐ Font
- ☐ Font Size
- ☐ Signed
- ☐ Spelling
- ☐ Opacity

SET COMMENT PREFERENCES

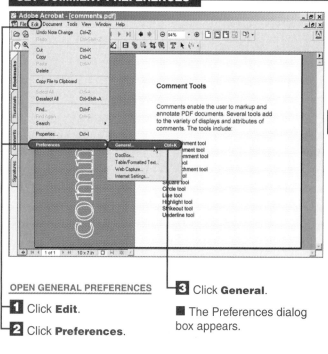

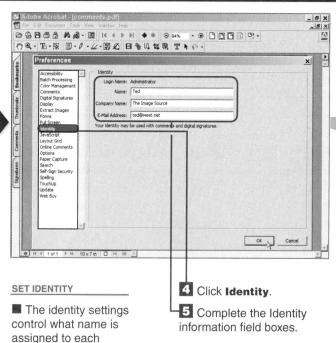

OPEN GENERAL PREFERENCES

1 Click **Edit**.

2 Click **Preferences**.

3 Click **General**.

■ The Preferences dialog box appears.

SET IDENTITY

■ The identity settings control what name is assigned to each comment you create.

4 Click **Identity**.

5 Complete the Identity information field boxes.

When I create a comment, why does the title bar of my comment note reflect my computer name — for example, Administrator (Windows) or MacintoshHD (Macintosh)?

You need to change the identity preferences to reflect the name you want to appear as the title of your comment notes. If your changes to the identity and the preferences do not apply to the comment note title bar, you may be using an earlier version of Acrobat 5.0. The initial release of Acrobat 5.0 had problems preserving this preference setting. To remedy the problem, visit www.adobe.com and download the most recent upgrade.

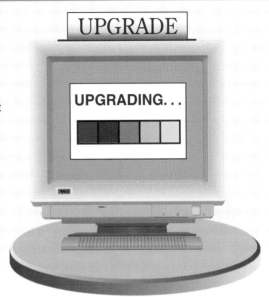

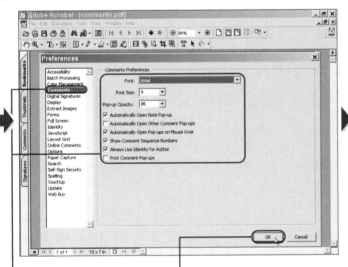

SET THE COMMENT PREFERENCES

6 Click **Comments**.

7 Make choices in the Comments Preferences area according to your liking.

Note: Always Use Identity for Author makes Acrobat use the Identity information for your comments. Also, when choosing fonts, use common fonts installed with Acrobat, such as Arial.

8 Click **OK**.

■ When you create comments, the comment title bar and properties use the Identity information for author name in the title bar. Other attributes you selected in the comment preferences are reflected in each comment.

CREATE A NOTE COMMENT

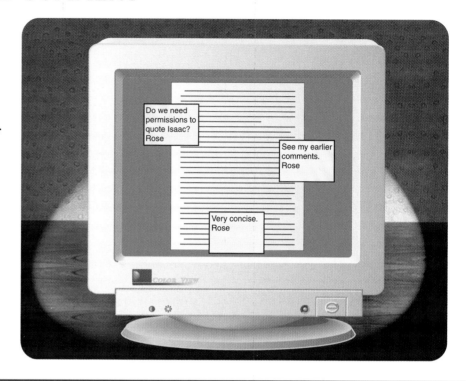

Note comments are the most common among the Acrobat comment tools. Note comments are similar to sticky notes you might attach to a piece of paper in your office. You can create note comments in Acrobat and type messages in the note window.

CREATE A NOTE COMMENT

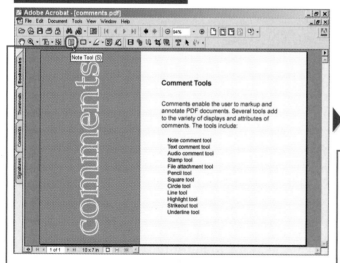

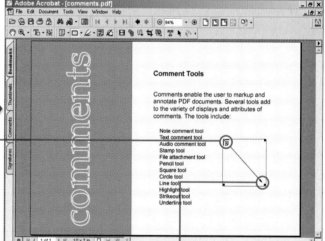

1 Click 📄.

■ You can also use a keyboard modifier by pressing **S** on your keyboard. Press **Shift** + **S** to change the comment tools.

■ The cursor changes to 📄.

2 Move the cursor to the Document Pane where you want to create your note.

3 Click the mouse button and drag a rectangle in a diagonal direction.

4 Release the mouse button.

Why do my note comment windows appear gray and the text is hard to read?

You can change the comment preferences to various degrees of transparency. Open the Comment Preferences by clicking **Edit**, then **Preferences**, then **General**, and click **Comments** in the left panel. The item denoted as Pop-up Opacity determines the amount of transparency applied to a comment note. The lower the number, the more transparent the note window appears. Raise the number by editing the value in the Pop-up Opacity field box to make the note less transparent and the text more clearly visible.

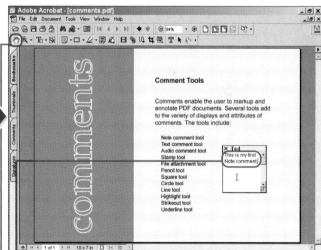

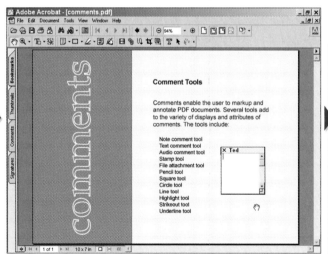

■ The note is created and the title bar reflects the Identity information you supplied in the Comments Preferences.

■ Additionally, a blinking cursor appears informing you that you can type text in the note window.

5 Type your text in the note window.

6 When you are finished typing, click 🖑.

■ Clicking the Hand tool tells Acrobat that you are finished creating notes.

SET COMMENT PROPERTIES

The Comments Preferences only partially control attributes for all comments created in Acrobat. Additionally, you can make other comment property choices for individual notes, such as editing the author name or changing the color of the note, from an on-screen context window. You can also move a note window very simply.

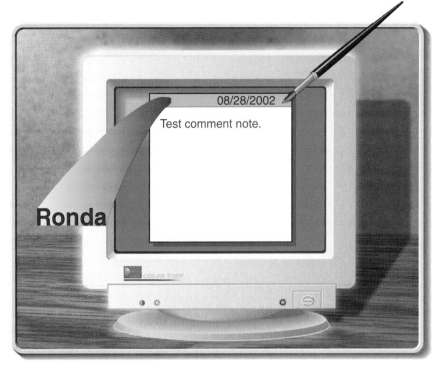

SET COMMENT PROPERTIES

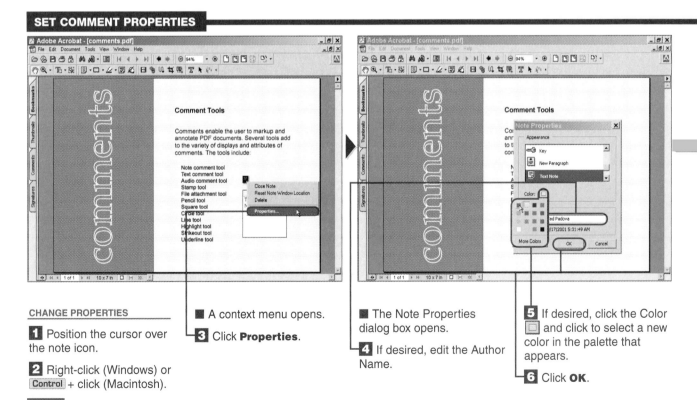

CHANGE PROPERTIES

1 Position the cursor over the note icon.

2 Right-click (Windows) or Control + click (Macintosh).

■ A context menu opens.

3 Click **Properties**.

■ The Note Properties dialog box opens.

4 If desired, edit the Author Name.

5 If desired, click the Color and click to select a new color in the palette that appears.

6 Click **OK**.

How do I delete a note?

To delete note comments, right-click (Windows) or **Shift** + click (Macintosh) and click **Delete** in the pop-up menu. You can also click the note icon and press **Delete**.

How do I move a note window?

Note icons and note windows can be moved independently of each other. To move an icon, drag it to a new location. To move a note window, click the title bar and drag it to a new location.

How do I hide a note?

Click ☒ (Windows) or ☐ (Macintosh) in the note window.

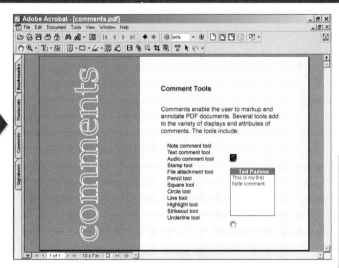

■ Acrobat closes the Note Properties dialog box.

■ The new property changes are applied to the note you selected.

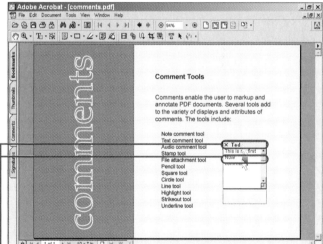

MOVE THE NOTE WINDOW

1 Click the note title bar.

2 Click and hold while dragging in a downward motion.

■ The note window is moved and the Note icon is visible.

CREATE A FREE TEXT NOTE

Note comments are limited in view to about 72 characters wide and 20 characters vertical for 12-point text. If you need to create larger text blocks, use a Free Text note. Among other differences, Free Text notes can be displayed without a window border. Therefore, the text you create can appear similar to the text on a document page.

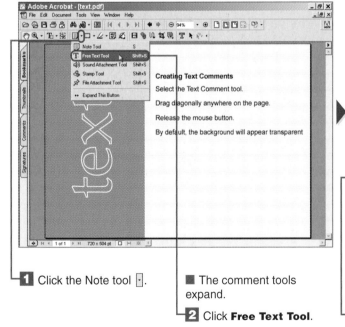

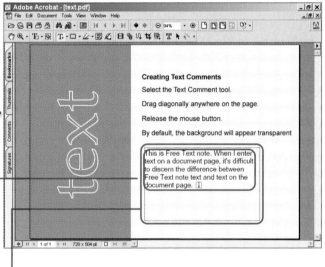

1 Click the Note tool.

■ The comment tools expand.

2 Click **Free Text Tool**.

3 Click and drag open a free text note rectangle.

4 Type text in the Free Text note window.

5 Click outside the note window to stop editing.

Note: There is no note icon available for Free Text notes. To make changes in the Free Text note properties, right-click (Windows) or **Control** *+ click (Macintosh) over the note rectangle to open the Free Text Properties.*

Acrobat can serve as something like a suitcase in which you can store a collection of different files. You can attach native document files and embed them in your PDFs. To open the files, you need to have the original authoring application. For example, if you attach a Word document, when you open the file you must have Word installed on your computer.

CREATE A FILE ATTACHMENT

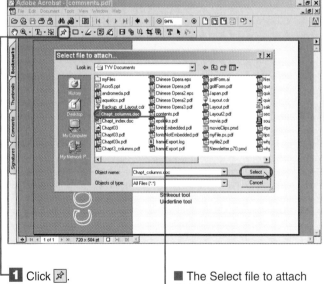

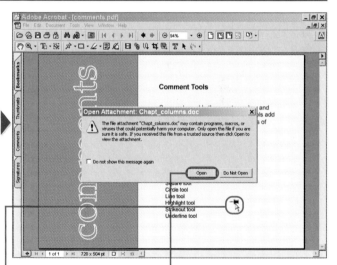

1 Click 📎.

2 Click a PDF page.

■ The Select file to attach dialog box opens.

3 Click a file to attach.

4 Click **Select**.

■ The file attachment appears as an icon in the document.

5 Double-click the icon.

■ The Open Attachment dialog box appears.

6 Click **Open**.

■ The file opens in the native authoring application.

CREATE AN AUDIO COMMENT

Audio comments enable you to import sound into PDFs. To create an audio comment, you need to have a sound file saved as WAV (Windows) or AIFF (Macintosh). When the audio comment is added to the PDF, it can be heard across platforms.

Good intro . . . can we see about punching up the second paragraph? Maybe making it shorter and more to the point. What do you think, Lindsay?

CREATE AN AUDIO COMMENT

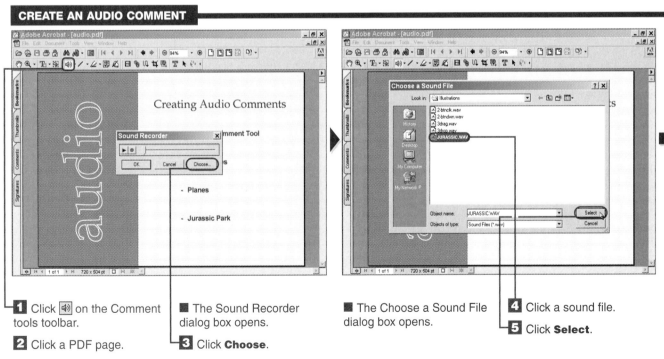

1 Click 🔊 on the Comment tools toolbar.

2 Click a PDF page.

■ The Sound Recorder dialog box opens.

3 Click **Choose**.

■ The Choose a Sound File dialog box opens.

4 Click a sound file.

5 Click **Select**.

How do I get sounds to import into my PDFs?

For recording sounds, you need to have a sound-editing program installed on your computer. You can find many public domain applications on Web sites. For Windows, search www.freewarefiles.com. For Macintosh users, search www.macupdate.com.

You can also search the Interent for other public domain software sites. Additionally, you need to have your computer properly configured with a microphone.

Record a sound with a sound editor and save the file as WAV (Windows) or AIFF (Macintosh). You can then import sound with the Sound Attachment tool.

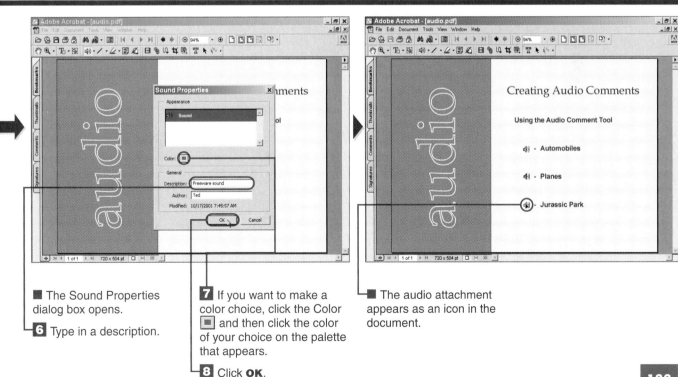

■ The Sound Properties dialog box opens.

6 Type in a description.

7 If you want to make a color choice, click the Color ▣ and then click the color of your choice on the palette that appears.

8 Click **OK**.

■ The audio attachment appears as an icon in the document.

USING THE STAMP TOOL

Stamp comments in Acrobat are like rubber stamps you might use in an office environment. You can use a stamp to mark a file as a draft, confidential, approved, or create any number of other messages.

USING THE STAMP TOOL

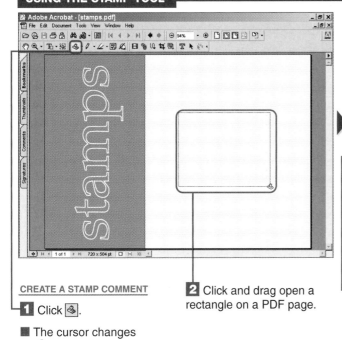

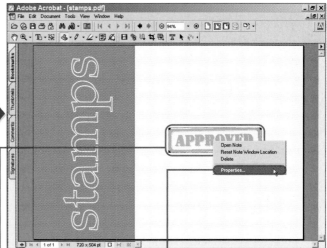

CREATE A STAMP COMMENT

1 Click 🖐.

■ The cursor changes to 🖐.

2 Click and drag open a rectangle on a PDF page.

■ The stamp appears on the document page. By default, Acrobat places the last stamp you used, but you can change the stamp properties.

CHANGE STAMP COMMENT PROPERTIES

3 Right-click (Windows) or `Control` + click (Macintosh) to open a context menu.

4 Click **Properties**.

Can I change the size of my stamp icon?

After you create a stamp comment, you can size it up or down on the PDF page. Just click the stamp icon and drag a handle in to resize it smaller or out to resize it larger.

How do I keep the note window and stamp icon together when I move the stamp?

If you click and drag the stamp or the note window, the windows will move independently of each other. To realign the two items, follow these steps:

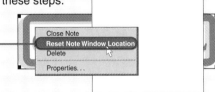

1 Click the note window or stamp icon and open a context menu.

2 Click **Reset Note Window Location**.

■ The note window is aligned with the stamp on the top-left corner.

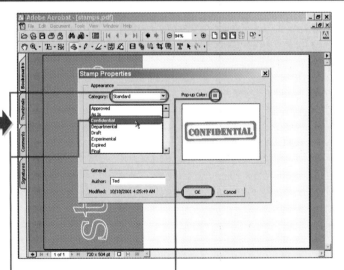

■ The Stamp Properties dialog box opens.

5 Click the Category ▼ and click a category.

6 Click a stamp in the list below the category.

■ Acrobat previews the stamp to the right.

7 If desired, click the Pop-up Color ■ and pick a new color.

8 Click **OK**, and the stamp appearance changes as indicated.

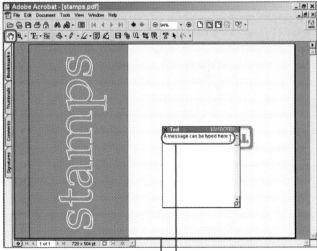

ADD A NOTE COMMENT

1 Double-click the stamp comment.

■ A note window opens.

2 Type text in the note window.

3 When you are finished typing, click 🖐.

CREATE CUSTOM STAMPS

Acrobat offers you several stamp categories from which to choose for your stamp appearances. However, you can create custom stamp icons for things like a company logo, a special office stamp, or any visual you may want to use to communicate a message. Custom stamps require that you create a page template; the name of the template is the stamp name. You also may need to create a category name under which the new stamp can be listed for later retrieval.

CREATE CUSTOM STAMPS

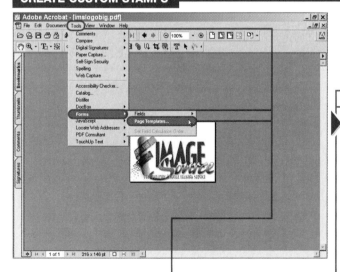

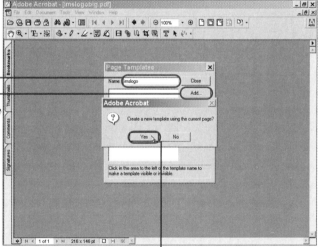

CREATE A PAGE TEMPLATE

1 Open a PDF or convert a file as described in Chapter 3.

2 Click **Tools**.

3 Click **Forms**.

4 Click **Page Templates**.

■ The Page Templates dialog box opens.

5 Type in a name.

6 Click **Add**.

■ The Adobe Acrobat dialog box opens.

7 Click **Yes**.

Why can I not change the name of the template I created?

When you add a template in the Page Templates dialog box and wish to change the name of the template, you must select the template name and click **Delete**. Type a new template name in the field box and click **Add**. The template remains the same, but the name changes.

Add...

Final=Final

Final=X

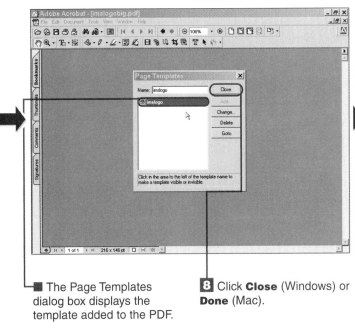

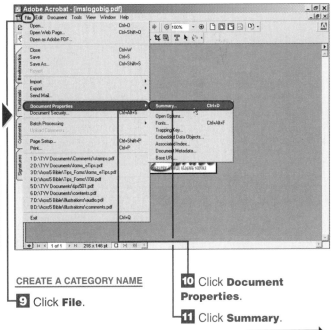

■ The Page Templates dialog box displays the template added to the PDF.

8 Click **Close** (Windows) or **Done** (Mac).

<u>CREATE A CATEGORY NAME</u>

9 Click **File**.

10 Click **Document Properties**.

11 Click **Summary**.

CONTINUED

CREATE CUSTOM STAMPS

After creating the page template to identify the individual stamps, you can create a category name for your new stamp library. You must also save the file to the proper location in order for the stamp file to be recognized by Acrobat.

APPROVED

APPROVAL PENDING

REJECTED

CATEGORY: Office Use

CREATE CUSTOM STAMPS (CONTINUED)

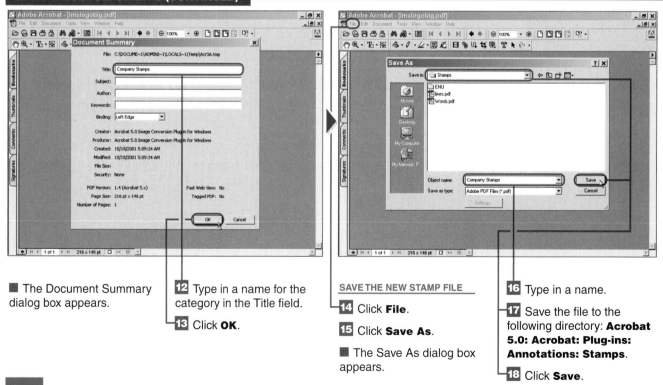

■ The Document Summary dialog box appears.

12 Type in a name for the category in the Title field.

13 Click **OK**.

SAVE THE NEW STAMP FILE

14 Click **File**.

15 Click **Save As**.

■ The Save As dialog box appears.

16 Type in a name.

17 Save the file to the following directory: **Acrobat 5.0: Acrobat: Plug-ins: Annotations: Stamps**.

18 Click **Save**.

Can I create multiple stamp icons for my new category?

The stamp category is determined in the Document Summary where you supply a name in the Title field. The individual icons are determined from page templates. If you want to create additional icons for a given category, use a multiple-page PDF with all the images you want to use. See Chapter 3 for appending pages in a PDF.

1 Open a multiple-page PDF.

2 Create a page template on the first page.

3 Create page templates for all pages.

4 Provide a name in the Title field of the Document Summary for the Category name.

5 Save the file to the Stamp Settings folder.

■ All the Page Template names appear listed in your new category.

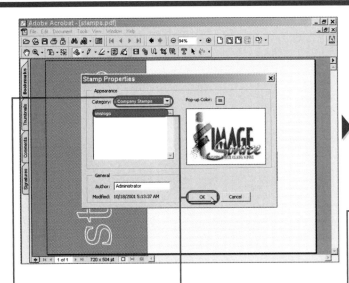

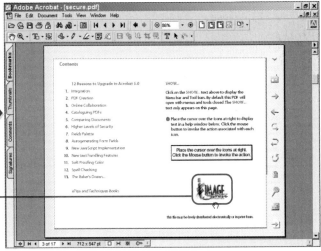

**CREATE A STAMP
WITH THE NEW ICON**

1 Create a stamp and open the Properties dialog box.

2 Click the Category ▼ and click the new category you created.

■ Note the category name is the same as the Title field in the Document Summary.

3 If not already highlighted, click the stamp name.

4 Click **OK**.

■ The new stamp icon appears on your document page.

CREATE COMMENTS WITH GRAPHIC MARKUP TOOLS

You can also create comments with the Graphic Markup tools. These tools are used for drawing circles, squares, straight, and irregularly shaped lines. All comments created with these tools can have attached notes. The line tools can have shapes such as arrowheads on either end of the line.

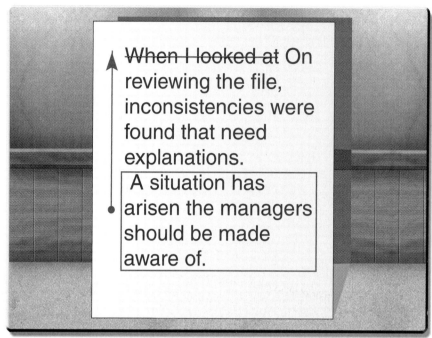

This example demonstrates how to create a note for a line; however, note windows for all the Graphic Markup tools are opened in the same manner.

CREATE COMMENTS WITH GRAPHIC MARKUP TOOLS

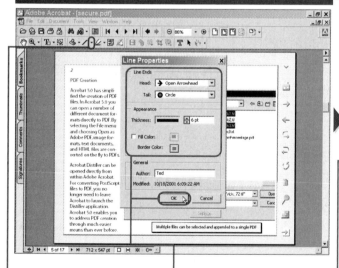

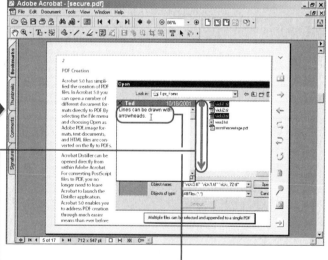

1 Click the Graphic Markup tools ⋅ and click a tool in the menu that appears.

2 Click and drag the shape on a PDF page.

3 Right-click (Windows) or `Control` + click (Macintosh) to open a context menu and click **Properties**.

4 Make any desired choices in the Properties dialog box.

5 Click **OK**.

6 Double-click the shape drawn.

■ A note window opens.

7 Type text in the note.

8 Click outside the note window to stop editing.

The Text Markup tools enable you to correct, approve, and review documents for PDF editing. You can use the Highlight tool, the Strikeout tool, or the Underline tool for markups on a document. All these tools can also have associated note windows.

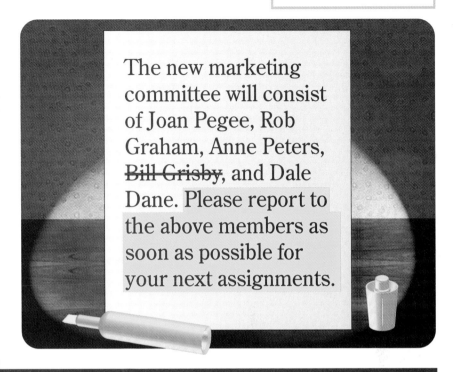

The new marketing committee will consist of Joan Pegee, Rob Graham, Anne Peters, ~~Bill Grisby~~, and Dale Dane. Please report to the above members as soon as possible for your next assignments.

USING THE TEXT MARKUP TOOLS

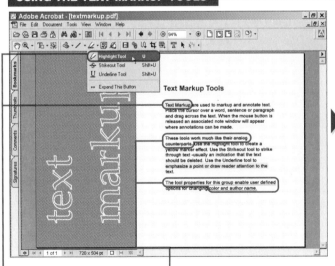

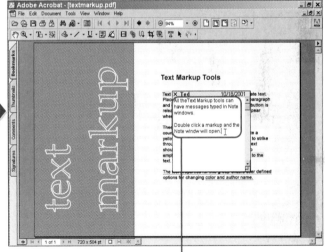

1 Click the Text Markup tools ⊡ and click the Highlight tool in the menu that appears.

2 Drag across a line of text.

3 Click 🛠 and drag through a line of text.

4 Click 🛛 and drag through a line of text.

5 Double-click one of the markups.

■ A note window opens.

6 Type a message in the note window.

7 Click outside the note window to stop editing.

FILTER COMMENTS

Several people sharing PDF documents can add comments. If you want to view only comments contributed by a given author, of a certain type, or after a certain date, you can filter the comments. Filtering enables you to sort out information of personal interest at any given moment.

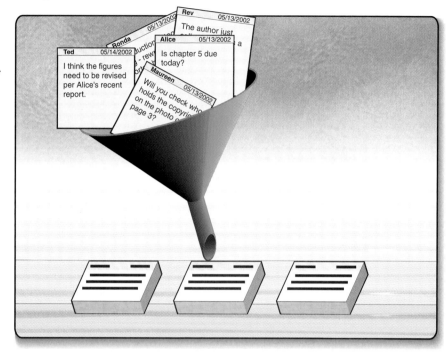

FILTER COMMENTS

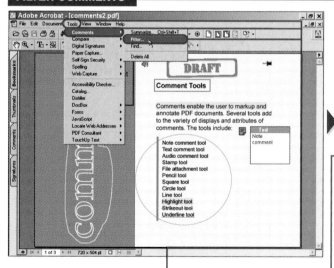

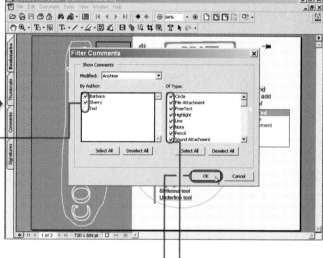

OPEN THE FILTER COMMENTS DIALOG BOX

1 Create several comments and adjust properties to change author names.

Note: See "Set Comment Properties," earlier in this chapter.

2 Click **Tools**.

3 Click **Comments**.

4 Click **Filter**.

■ The Filter Comments dialog box opens.

5 Check any author whose comments you do not want to see (☐ changes to ☑).

6 Check any types of comments you do not want to see (☐ changes to ☑).

7 Click **OK**.

How can I get back all my comments after I have filtered them to view only a single author?

If you filtered out any authors, comment types, or dates, you can retrieve the unfiltered list from the Filter Comments dialog box.

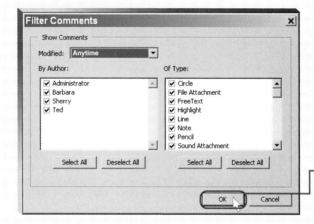

1 Click **Tools**.

2 Click **Comments**.

3 Click **Filter**.

■ When the dialog box opens, all comments are listed by default.

4 Click **OK** and all the comments appear in the Comments palette.

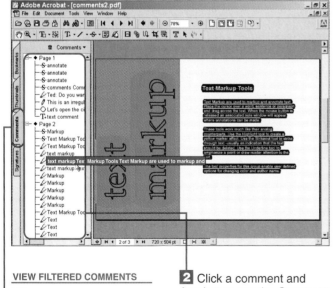

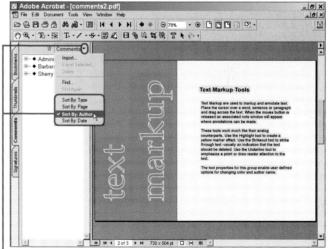

VIEW FILTERED COMMENTS

1 Click **Comments**.

■ The Comments palette opens, listing all the filtered comments in the palette.

2 Click a comment and Acrobat opens the Comment Note window.

SORT COMMENTS

1 Click the Comments palette ▼.

2 Click the sorting method you want to use.

■ Comments are sorted in the palette according to your choice – in this example, by author name.

CREATE COMMENT SUMMARIES

If you have a large document with many pages and several contributions from different authors, you may want to create a summary of the comment information. The summary makes viewing comment notes easier than navigating to pages where comments appear.

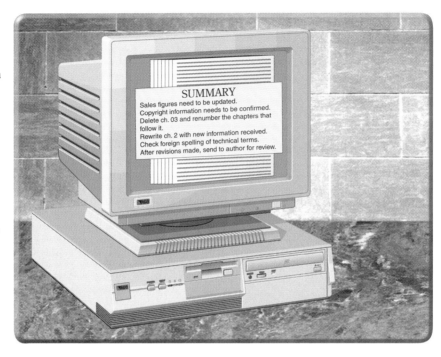

Before compiling your summary, you should filter your comments, so that your summary does not contain unwanted notes.

CREATE COMMENT SUMMARIES

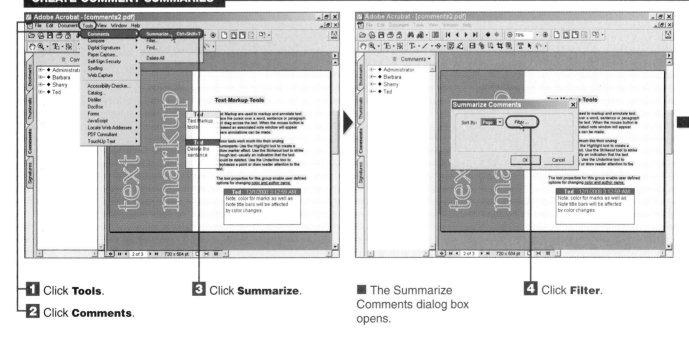

1 Click **Tools**.

2 Click **Comments**.

3 Click **Summarize**.

■ The Summarize Comments dialog box opens.

4 Click **Filter**.

**I share my PDFs with some Acrobat Reader users.
Can Reader users summarize my comments?**

Users of the Acrobat Reader software can neither
create, filter, nor summarize comments. They can,
however, view a comment summary that you
create and append to a PDF file. For appending
pages to PDFs, see Chapter 7.

How do other users make comments on my PDFs?

You can send a copy of a PDF file to another
Acrobat user who can then make comments. You
can also use Online Commenting on a network
server or Web server for workgroup collaboration.
See "Select a Network Folder for Online
Comments," later in this chapter.

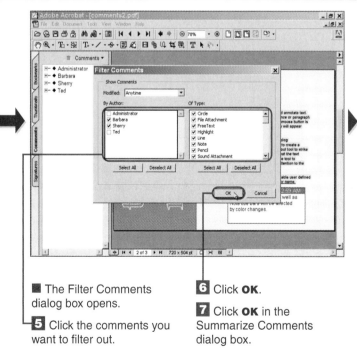

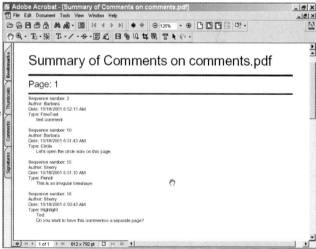

■ The Filter Comments
dialog box opens.

5 Click the comments you
want to filter out.

6 Click **OK**.

7 Click **OK** in the
Summarize Comments
dialog box.

■ The summary opens as a
new PDF file.

SELECT A NETWORK FOLDER FOR ONLINE COMMENTS

Online comments enable you to host a PDF document on a network server or Web server and allow several people to comment on the same PDF file. To create online comments, you need to have your network or Web server properly configured. Web server online commenting requires help from your system administrator.

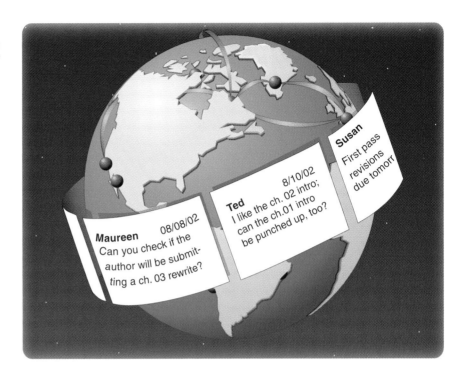

SELECT A NETWORK FOLDER FOR ONLINE COMMENTS

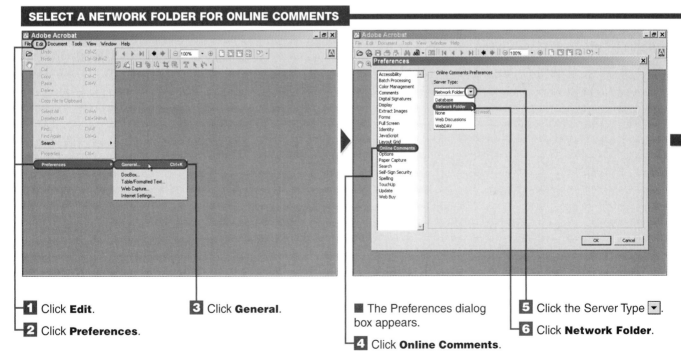

1 Click **Edit**.

2 Click **Preferences**.

3 Click **General**.

■ The Preferences dialog box appears.

4 Click **Online Comments**.

5 Click the Server Type ▼.

6 Click **Network Folder**.

How can I use online comments on a Web server?

Commenting online on a Web server requires help from your system administrator. For information to help your Web administrator, see the documentation on the Acrobat CD-ROM or visit Adobe's Web site at www.adobe.com.

Can I secure my online collaboration for a restricted group of users?

Normal network administration for user access will prevail. If you have users with permissions to access network locations, then you can provide password security on the PDFs you host for online collaboration. For more information on PDF security, see Chapter 13.

7 Click **Choose**.

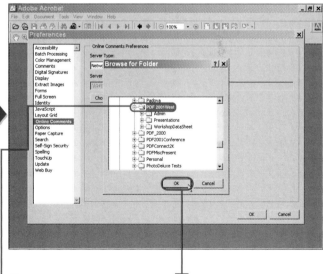

■ The Browse for Folder dialog box opens.

8 Navigate your network to locate a folder where online collaboration is performed.

9 Click **OK**.

■ The network location where your online comments are addressed is now identified.

147

WORK WITH ONLINE COMMENTS

After you select the network folder for online commenting, you can make comments online either on a network or a Web server. To use the online comment tools, you must view your PDF file inside a Web browser.

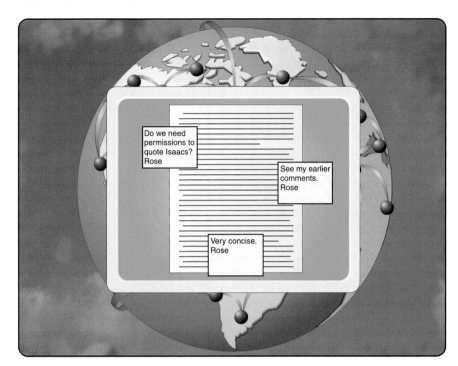

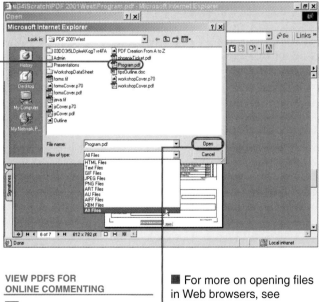

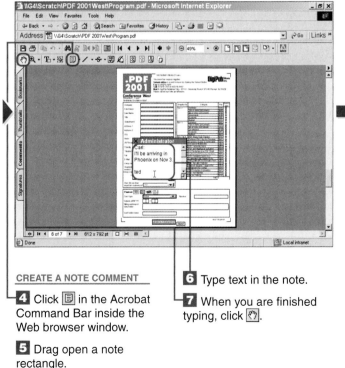

VIEW PDFS FOR ONLINE COMMENTING

1 Launch your Web browser.

2 Open the PDF to be used from a network server.

■ For more on opening files in Web browsers, see Chapter 1.

3 Click **Open**.

Note: You can also drag a PDF to your Web browser location bar to open a PDF inside the Web browser.

CREATE A NOTE COMMENT

4 Click in the Acrobat Command Bar inside the Web browser window.

5 Drag open a note rectangle.

6 Type text in the note.

7 When you are finished typing, click .

**Can I create comments in Acrobat and
upload them later to a server?**

You can create offline comments
at any time and save the PDF
on your local hard drive. When
you return to your office or
network connection, you can
upload the comments to the
server by clicking **File** and
then **Upload Comments.**

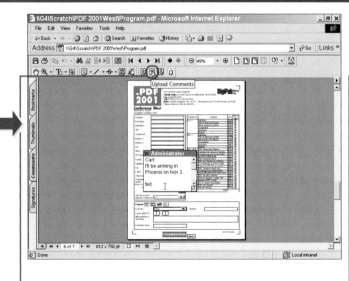

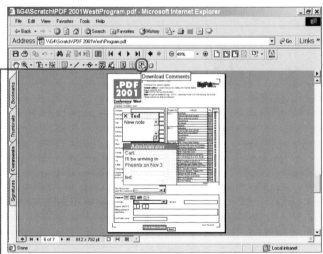

UPLOAD COMMENTS

8 Click 🖼.

■ The tool becomes active
only after you create a
comment.

■ The comment is uploaded
to the network server. Any
authorized user can access
the PDF and comment.

DOWNLOAD COMMENTS

1 Click 🖼.

■ Any user comments
added to the server are
displayed in the PDF you
view through the Web
browser.

SPELL CHECK COMMENTS AND FORM FIELDS

Acrobat has a powerful spell-checking feature that checks spelling for comments and form fields. You cannot check spelling on the PDF pages, but you can check spelling on the words you enter in comment notes and form fields.

Acrobat gives you a choice of dictionaries to use for the check, and the option to add words to dictionaries.

SPELL CHECK COMMENTS AND FORM FIELDS

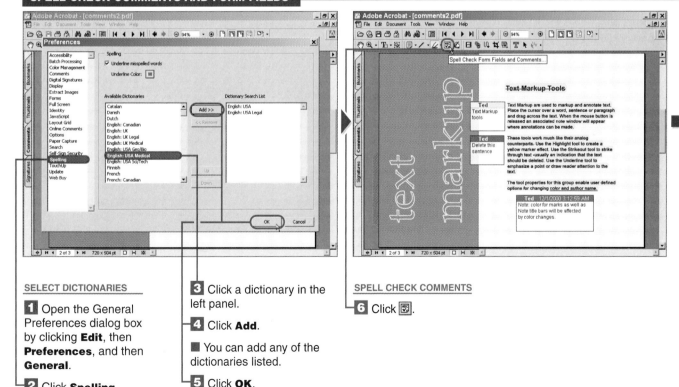

SELECT DICTIONARIES

1 Open the General Preferences dialog box by clicking **Edit**, then **Preferences**, and then **General**.

2 Click **Spelling**.

3 Click a dictionary in the left panel.

4 Click **Add**.

■ You can add any of the dictionaries listed.

5 Click **OK**.

SPELL CHECK COMMENTS

6 Click 📖.

If I add a word incorrectly to a dictionary, can I later delete it?

If you inadvertently add a misspelled word to a dictionary, you can delete it at any time.

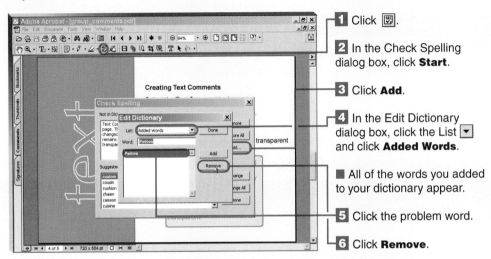

1 Click .

2 In the Check Spelling dialog box, click **Start**.

3 Click **Add**.

4 In the Edit Dictionary dialog box, click the List ▾ and click **Added Words**.

■ All of the words you added to your dictionary appear.

5 Click the problem word.

6 Click **Remove**.

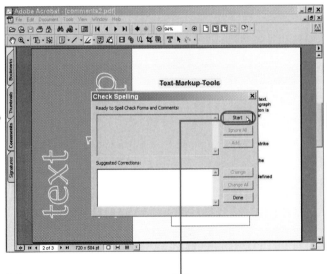

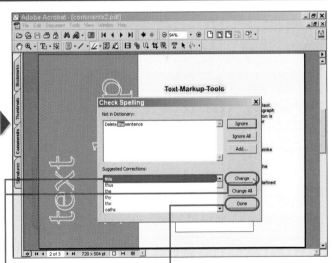

7 The Check Spelling dialog box opens.

8 Click **Start**.

■ Acrobat stops at the first suspect word.

9 Click a word in the Suggested Corrections list if the correct spelling is listed.

10 Click **Change**.

■ The misspelled word is corrected.

■ If the word is not in the dictionary, you can add a word by clicking **Add**. Be certain the spelling is correct.

11 To end the check, click **Done**.

Huge Bike Sale!!

For 3 days only, incredible savings on the bikes you've only dreamed about. Mountain bikes, touring bikes, and bikes for kids and adults at below factory price!! Helmets and other  drastically reduced in price. Don't miss this sale!!

Mountain Man Bikes
322 West Billington
Wild Hope, Utah

CHAPTER 7

Edit Pages in Acrobat

Are you ready to start mixing and merging PDF pages to complete finished documents? This chapter shows you how to edit pages and text.

Understanding PDF Page Editing 154

Copy and Paste Pages 156

Extract Pages 158

Replace Pages 159

Insert Pages 160

Edit an Image 162

Edit an Object 164

Using the TouchUp Text Tool 166

Copy Text 168

Using RTF-Formatted Files 170

Export Table-Formatted Text 171

Crop Pages 172

Add a Text Block 174

Create URL Links from Text 175

Save the World, Inc.

NEWSLETTER - JUNE 2001

Seventy-five percent of the World's people live in the Third World. These nations supply developed nations with a multitude of raw materials and natural resources, and also buy many of our exports (40% of U.S. exports are bought by the Third World). Clearly the lives of the people in the developed and underdeveloped worlds are unavoidably interrelated. It is for this reason that it is important for the rich nations to study the problems in other countries and help them to overcome them. One major problem in most underdeveloped countries (UDC), is that since the Colonial period, exploitation of their arable land has rapidly increased. Companies from the developed countries (DC) are blamed for abusing the land, but the farmers and locals are often guilty as well. Seventy-five percent of the energy supplied by UDCs is produced by wood burning. this wood they must tear rare and exotic trees until

eventually whole forests disappear. The land then no longer has anything holding it together. This results in soil erosion and loss of water retaining abilities.

Development in the Western sense is to industrialize your economy. It is essential for the Third World to develop their production techniques, especially in agriculture, in order to compete effectively on the World Markets. This kind of development, however, requires not only costly machinery, but expensive fossil fuels for operation.

Delete Page 2

Don't fade photo

UNDERSTANDING PDF PAGE EDITING

To finalize your PDF documents, you can refine them by adding, deleting, mixing, merging, and editing individual pages.

Add and Delete Pages

Acrobat provides several means for adding, inserting, and replacing pages in a PDF. If links exist on a given page that you delete, you lose the links. Managing pages for insertions and deletions is an important consideration.

Crop Pages

Just as you can crop photographic images, you can crop PDF pages to eliminate excess page margins.

Edit Text

Acrobat has limited text-editing capabilities. For minor changes, you can edit a few words. For paragraph editing and large passages, you need to use external editors.

Export Text

If you have a PDF and need to edit text paragraphs, you may need to export the text to an editing program. Make your changes and convert the edited document back to PDF.

Edit Images

You embed images in PDFs. If you need to edit an image, you must use an external editor and import the image back into the PDF.

COPY AND PASTE PAGES

Acrobat does not permit you to copy data from other programs and paste the data into a PDF. You can, however, copy and paste a page from one PDF to another PDF.

COPY AND PASTE PAGES

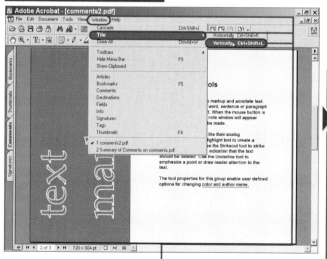

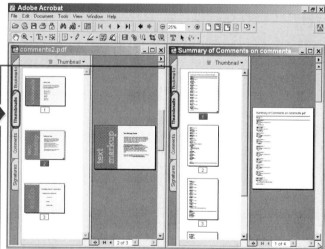

1 Create a comment summary from a PDF with comments.

Note: For instructions on creating comment summaries, see Chapter 6.

2 Click **Window**.

3 Click **Tile**.

4 Click **Vertically**.

5 Click the **Thumbnails** tab in the Navigation Pane for both documents.

Can I copy and paste a page in the same document?

You can copy and paste pages in the same document by using thumbnails.

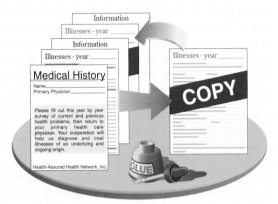

How can I cut a page from one document and paste it into another PDF?

When dragging thumbnails between documents, press **Ctrl** (Windows) or **option** (Macintosh) and drag to the destination thumbnails palette. Acrobat cuts the pages from the first file and pastes them into the second document.

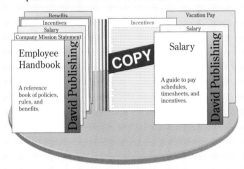

COPY AND PASTE PAGES

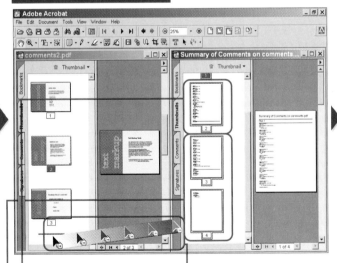

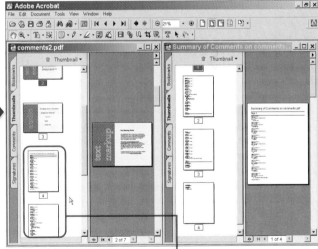

6 Click the first thumbnail in the Comment Summary panel.

7 Press **Shift** and click the remaining thumbnails.

8 Click and drag from the Comment Summary panel to the Thumbnails palette in the original file.

■ The cursor changes to ▶▣ when dragging to the second thumbnail palette.

9 Release the mouse button.

■ The pages paste in the original document.

EXTRACT PAGES

If you want to create a PDF file from one page of a multipage file, you can extract a page. Acrobat offers you the choice of deleting a page upon extraction or preserving the original file while creating a second PDF document from the extracted page(s).

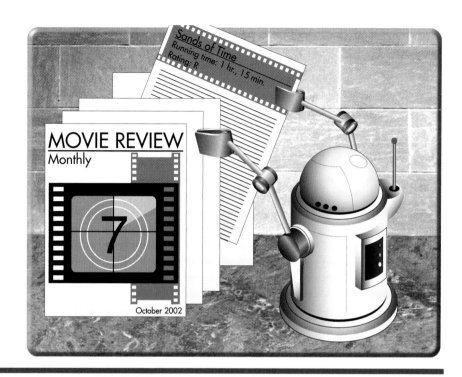

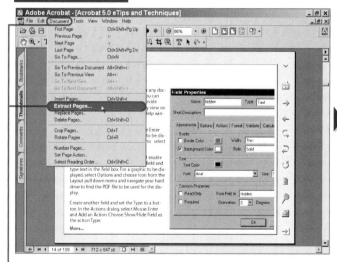

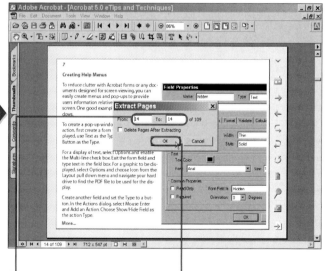

1 Click **Document**.

2 Click **Extract Pages**.

■ The Extract Pages dialog box opens.

3 Type in the page range to extract.

■ To delete the page from the original file, you can check **Delete Pages After Extracting** (☐ changes to ☑).

4 Click **OK**.

5 Save the pages as PDF.

Note: To save pages, see Chapter 1.

■ The new file contains only those pages extracted from the original file.

REPLACE PAGES

If you have a link to a page and delete the page, the link is lost. Sometimes you may need to edit a page in the original authoring program to fix the link. You can then replace the original page with the newly edited page to preserve any links.

REPLACE PAGES

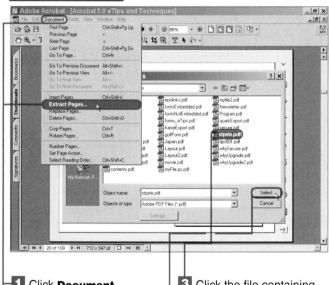

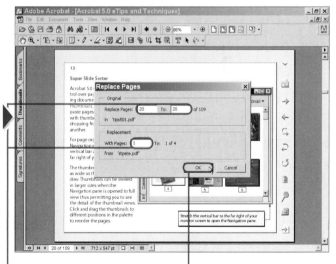

1 Click **Document**.

2 Click **Replace Pages**.

■ The Select File With New Pages dialog box opens.

3 Click the file containing the new page.

4 Click **Select**.

■ The Replace Pages dialog box opens.

5 Type the page range of the pages you want to replace.

6 Type the page number of the new page to replace the old.

7 Click **OK**.

■ Acrobat replaces the pages and preserves any links, comments, or form fields.

INSERT PAGES

You may have a PDF file in which you need to add pages. You can insert pages from a single file or from multiple files. All the pages from the files you select append to the PDF. When you insert pages, Acrobat does not disturb the links, comments, or form fields already existing in the host document.

You can also insert all file types supported with Open As Adobe PDF. For information on Open As Adobe PDF, see Chapter 3.

INSERT PAGES

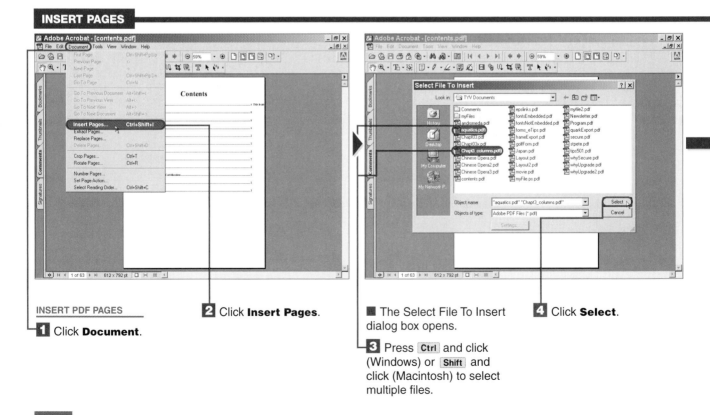

INSERT PDF PAGES

1 Click **Document**.

2 Click **Insert Pages**.

■ The Select File To Insert dialog box opens.

3 Press **Ctrl** and click (Windows) or **Shift** and click (Macintosh) to select multiple files.

4 Click **Select**.

Can I delete pages from my PDF documents?

When you need to delete pages, first check to see if any links, form fields, bookmarks, or comments appear on those pages. If any of these elements exist, then you want to use the Replace Pages command. If none of these elements exist, you can delete a single page or range of pages. You must, however, keep at least one page in the PDF document.

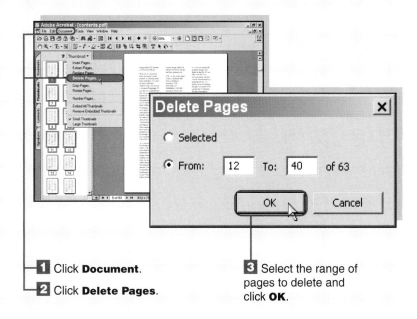

Delete Pages

○ Selected

● From: 12 To: 40 of 63

OK   Cancel

▣ Click **Document**.

▣ Click **Delete Pages**.

▣ Select the range of pages to delete and click **OK**.

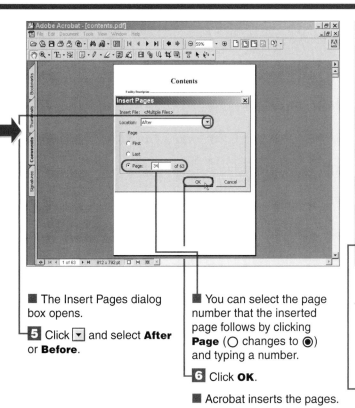

■ The Insert Pages dialog box opens.

▣ Click ▾ and select **After** or **Before**.

■ You can select the page number that the inserted page follows by clicking **Page** (○ changes to ●) and typing a number.

▣ Click **OK**.

■ Acrobat inserts the pages.

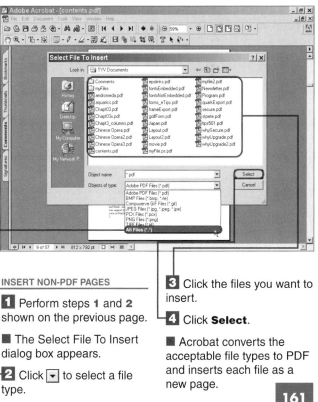

INSERT NON-PDF PAGES

▣ Perform steps **1** and **2** shown on the previous page.

■ The Select File To Insert dialog box appears.

▣ Click ▾ to select a file type.

▣ Click the files you want to insert.

▣ Click **Select**.

■ Acrobat converts the acceptable file types to PDF and inserts each file as a new page.

EDIT AN IMAGE

You may need to edit an image in an image editor and replace the image on a PDF page. Acrobat enables you to dynamically edit images in an image editor.

This example uses Adobe Photoshop, but you can use Corel Paint or similar editors. The process in other programs will be similar, although the specific steps may be different. Check your software documentation for specific steps.

LAUNCH AN EXTERNAL EDITOR

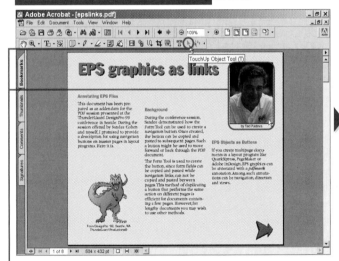

1 Open a PDF document containing an image.

2 Click ⬉.

3 Click the image.

4 Press **Ctrl** (Windows) or **option** (Macintosh) and double-click the mouse button.

■ Photoshop launches and the image opens in a Photoshop window.

5 Edit the image as desired.

My PDF did not update when I saved my image from Photoshop. Why not?

If a file is saved with the Save As command, it may not be updated. Acrobat keeps track of your file by creating a temporary file. If you disturb the temporary filename, the image will not update.

Also, if you create elements that fall on layers in Photoshop, you need to flatten all layers before saving the file. If you have layers or image modes requiring files to be saved in other than Photoshop PDF, the original image won't be updated.

SAVE THE EDITED IMAGE

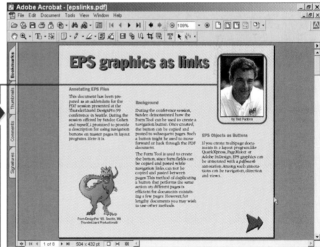

6 Click **File**.

7 Click **Save**.

*Note: Do not click **Save As**.*

8 Click ☒ to close Adobe Photoshop.

■ The image dynamically updates in the PDF.

EDIT AN OBJECT

Objects are vector art images and text. Anything other than an image edited in Photoshop qualifies as an object. You can use Adobe Illustrator, MacroMedia FreeHand, or CorelDraw to edit objects that can be dynamically updated in PDF documents.

This example uses Adobe Illustrator to edit an object. The process will be similar to other programs, although the specific steps may be different. Check your software documentation for specific steps.

OPEN THE OBJECT EDITOR

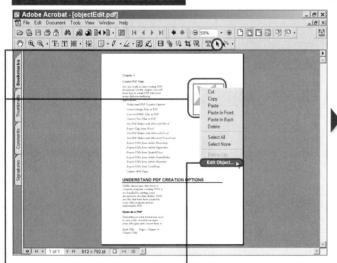

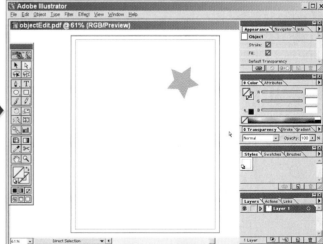

1 Click ▶.

2 Click an Object.

3 Right-click (Windows) or [Control] + click (Macintosh) the object to open a context menu.

4 Click **Edit Object**.

■ You can also double-click the object to open the object in Illustrator.

■ The object opens in Illustrator.

5 Edit the object for color and style changes.

Why is my text all broken up when I edit text as an object?

Paragraph text does not retain integrity when opening PDFs in other applications. To reform paragraphs into single text blocks, you can select all the text and cut it from the page. Use the Type tool (T) and draw a rectangle. Click **Edit** and **Paste** to paste the text into the rectangle. The text reforms into paragraphs, and you can edit it.

When the object is running away, our s h oes will help you. Noise? Work? Everyday stress? You left it behind a half-mile ago. You'll return when *you* want to. When you're running t o ward fitne ss, let us help you get there. Every step forward is a step towards fitness. Every heart beat is stronger, heal th ier. Take t hat first step now.

Whatever your goals, *Winged Feet* gets you there.

SAVE THE EDITED OBJECT

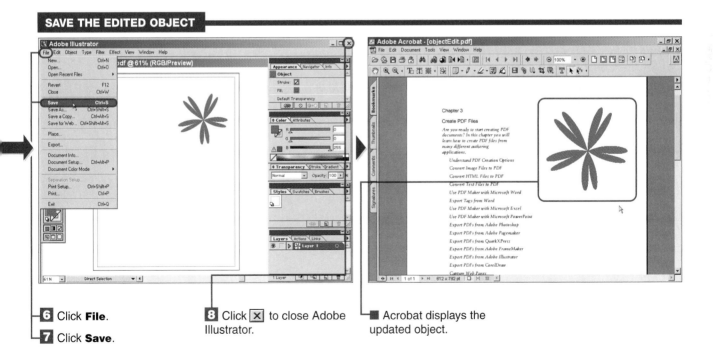

— **6** Click **File**.

— **7** Click **Save**.

8 Click X to close Adobe Illustrator.

■ Acrobat displays the updated object.

USING THE TOUCHUP TEXT TOOL

For paragraph editing, you use the Edit Object command. You use the TouchUp Text tool for minor edits on single lines of text. When using the TouchUp Text tool, keep in mind that you can edit only single individual lines of text.

USING THE TOUCHUP TEXT TOOL

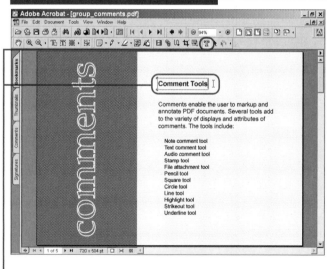

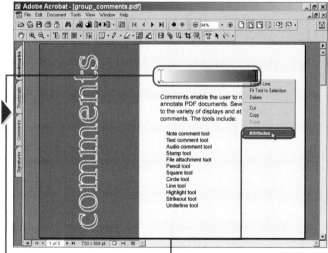

EDIT A LINE OF TEXT

1 Click ⊤.

2 Click a line of text.

■ The text appears inside a rectangle surrounding the line of text.

3 Click inside the rectangle.

4 Type in any desired changes.

CHANGE TEXT ATTRIBUTES

5 Drag the mouse ⊺ across a line of text.

6 Right-click (Windows) or **Control** + click (Macintosh) the text to open up a context menu.

7 Click **Attributes**.

Can I move a line of text?

If using the TouchUp Text tool (□), you can drag a line of text left or right horizontally on the page. To do so, click the diamond shape on the left side of the line marker and drag horizontally. To drag to any position on a page, click the TouchUp Object tool (□) and drag the text to the desired location.

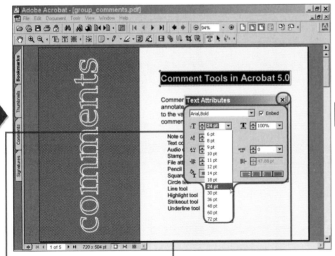

■ The Text Attributes dialog box opens.

8 Make any desired changes.

■ You can change text size, color, leading, kerning, indent, outdent, and justification.

■ Acrobat makes the changes dynamically as you go.

9 Click ☒ to close the Text Attributes dialog box.

■ The PDF now reflects the designated changes.

COPY TEXT

Major text editing
often requires re-
editing a file in an
authoring program
and converting it
back to a PDF. At
times, you need to
transfer text from a
PDF back to a text
editor or layout
application. Acrobat
provides several
means of copying
text that you can
later paste into
other programs.

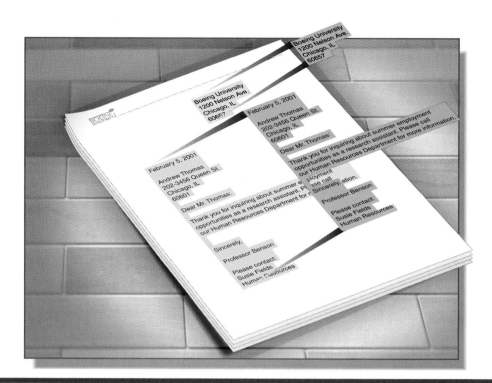

COPY TEXT

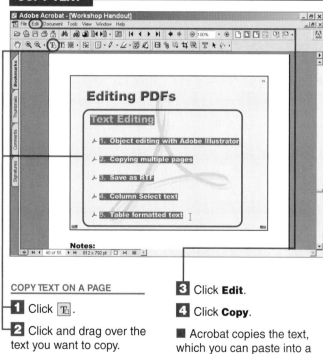

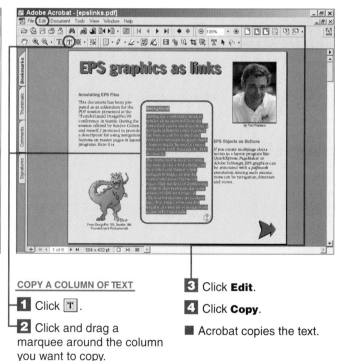

COPY TEXT ON A PAGE

1 Click 🔤.

2 Click and drag over the
text you want to copy.

3 Click **Edit**.

4 Click **Copy**.

■ Acrobat copies the text,
which you can paste into a
word processor.

COPY A COLUMN OF TEXT

1 Click 🔤.

2 Click and drag a
marquee around the column
you want to copy.

3 Click **Edit**.

4 Click **Copy**.

■ Acrobat copies the text.

168

**Can I copy text from my word processor
and paste it back into a PDF?**

You cannot paste text or graphics from
other programs into a PDF document.
After you edit text in
a word processor,
convert the newly
edited document to
PDF and use the
Replace Pages
command to
preserve links. See
Chapter 3 to
convert to PDF
and see the
section "Replace
Pages" earlier in this
chapter to preserve the links.

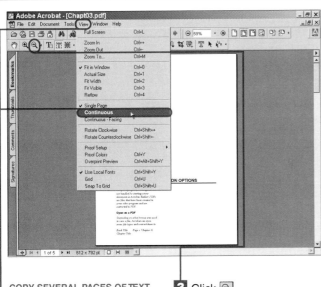

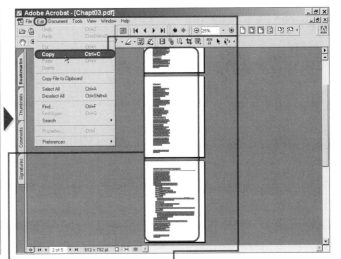

COPY SEVERAL PAGES OF TEXT

1 Click **View**.

2 Click **Continuous**.

3 Click 🔍.

4 Click several times in the
Document Pane until several
pages are visible.

5 Click 🔃.

6 Click and drag from the
top page down across all the
pages you want to copy.

■ Pages automatically scroll
until you release the mouse
button.

7 Click **Edit**.

8 Click **Copy**.

■ Acrobat copies the text,
which you can paste into a
word processor.

USING RTF-FORMATTED FILES

If you need to export the entire body of text in a PDF to a word processor for editing, you can save the file in a format recognized by word processors. The Rich Text Format (RTF) preserves most formatting from your PDFs. After saving the PDF as an RTF file, you can then open the file in a word processor.

USING RTF-FORMATTED FILES

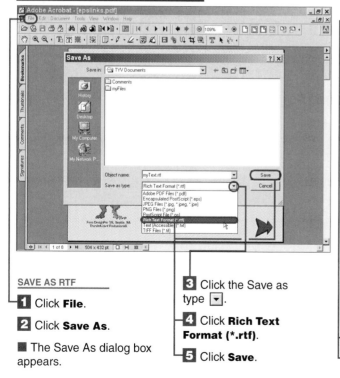

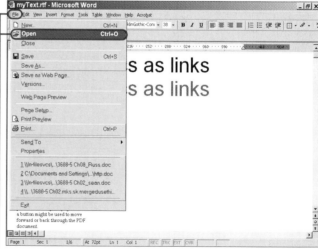

SAVE AS RTF

1 Click **File**.

2 Click **Save As**.

■ The Save As dialog box appears.

3 Click the Save as type ▾.

4 Click **Rich Text Format (*.rtf)**.

5 Click **Save**.

OPEN AN RTF FILE IN MICROSOFT WORD

1 Open Microsoft Word.

2 Click **File**.

3 Click **Open**.

4 Open the RTF file saved from Acrobat.

■ The document opens in the Word processor with formatting preserved.

You can import tables into a word processor or a spreadsheet like Microsoft Excel. RTF files do not hold the formatting for tables; therefore, you must use another tool. You can use the Table/Formatted Text Select tool to copy table data. Subsequently, you can paste copied data into word processors and spreadsheets. This feature is available only in Windows.

EXPORT TABLE-FORMATTED TEXT (WINDOWS ONLY)

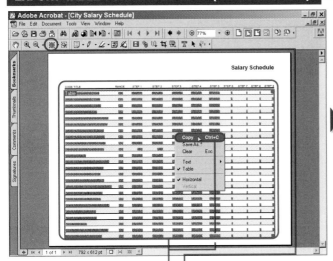

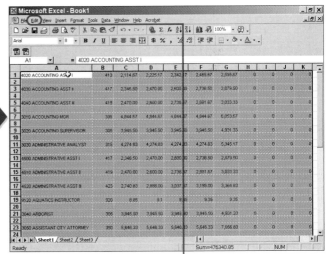

EXPORT THE TEXT

1 Launch the destination application and have a new document open before copying data.

Note: See the application's instructions for further information.

2 Click the Table button (▦).

3 Click and drag around the data to copy.

4 Right-click the table.

5 In the context menu that appears, click **Copy**.

PASTE TABLE TEXT INTO A SPREADSHEET

6 Press **Alt** + **Tab** to open the spreadsheet application.

■ If you have both Acrobat and MS Excel open, the programs switch.

7 In Excel, click **Edit**.

8 Click **Paste**.

■ The data pastes into individual cells.

CROP PAGES

You can have PDF pages of different sizes in the same file. If you want all your pages to appear at the same size, you can crop off excess page area. Acrobat enables you to crop individual pages or a range of pages.

CROP PAGES

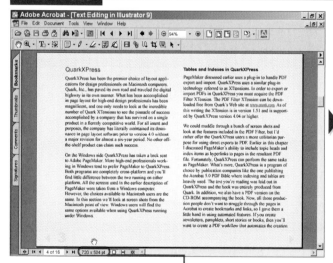

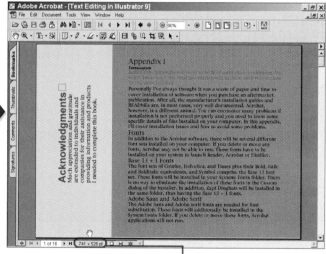

1 Navigate to a page that is the size of all of the pages you want to crop.

Note: See Chapter 2 to navigate to the appropriate page.

2 Note the page's size in the status bar.

Note: In this example, the page size is 720 by 504 points.

3 Navigate to a page that you want to crop to the page size assessed in step **2**.

4 Record the page's size on a piece of paper.

Note: In this example, the page size to crop measures 741 by 526.

5 On a piece of paper, subtract the smaller size from the larger page size.

Note: In this example, the difference in the horizontal width is 21 points (741 – 720) and the difference in the vertical height is 22 points (526 – 504)

I have a single page PDF file of a scanned photo. My file size does not get smaller when I crop an image. Why not?

Cropping pages does not eliminate data when you save files with cropped pages. The PDF retains all data and you can re-crop the page to regain the data originally cropped. To eliminate data after cropping, click **File**, click **Save As**, and then save the PDF as a TIFF file. Acrobat eliminates the excess data and reduces the size.

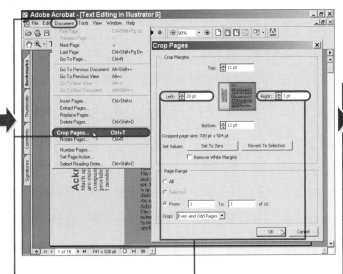

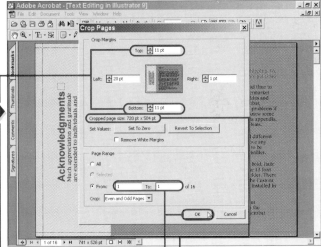

---

6 Click **Document**.

7 Click **Crop Pages**.

■ The Crop Pages dialog box opens.

8 Enter the subtracted values for the horizontal measurement in the Left and Right boxes.

Note: In this example, the 21 points horizontal is subtracted from the horizontal measurement. The Left and Right values combined should be equal to 21 points.

9 Enter the appropriate values in the Top and Bottom field boxes to equal the vertical measurement.

Note: In this example, the 22 total points are subtracted from the vertical measurement.

10 Keep adjusting the values until the Cropped Page Size equals the desired cropped size.

11 Type the range of pages you want to crop.

12 Click **OK**.

■ The respective pages crop to their new sizes.

ADD A TEXT BLOCK

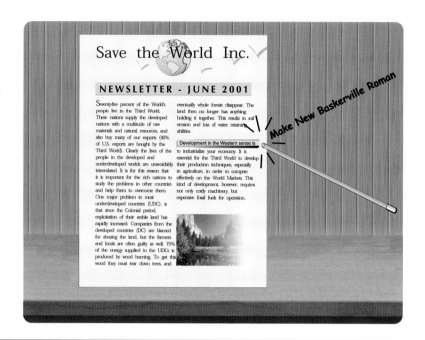

You can create raw text in Acrobat by using the TouchUp Text tool and a modifier key.

ADD A TEXT BLOCK

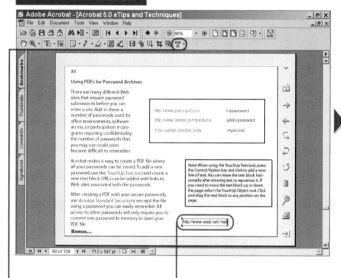

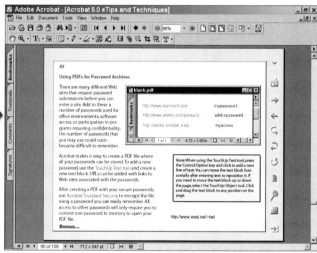

ADD A TEXT BLOCK

1 Click 🅣.

2 Position the I where you want to add a new text block.

3 Press **Ctrl** (Windows) or **option** (Macintosh) and click.

■ Acrobat opens a text block.

4 Type in the text you want to add.

5 Click outside the text block to stop editing.

■ Acrobat adds the text block.

Note: You can change the attributes of the text box to meet your specifications. See "Using the TouchUp Text Tool," earlier in this chapter, for more information.

If you create a text line as a URL, you may want to have the link active in the PDF document. When a user clicks the URL, a Web browser opens and displays the Web page. After you define text as a URL, Acrobat can automatically create the link button.

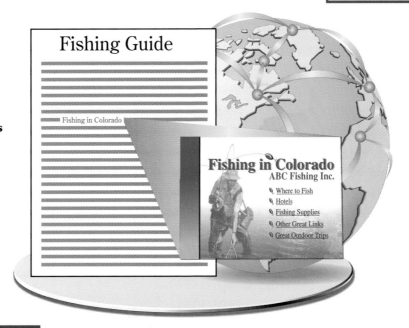

CREATE URL LINKS FROM TEXT

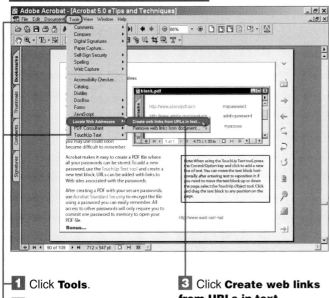

1 Click **Tools**.

2 Click **Locate Web Address**.

3 Click **Create web links from URLs in text**.

■ The Create Web Links dialog box opens.

4 Type in the page range for the links that you want to create.

5 Click **OK**.

■ Acrobat creates links from URLs specified as text in the PDF.

CHAPTER 8

Print PDFs

Are you ready to start printing your PDF files? This chapter shows you how to print files on many different printing devices. While some of the techniques described here are fairly advanced, they will come in handy as you grow in your understanding and mastery of Acrobat.

Understanding Printing Devices and Terms 178

Using the Page Setup Dialog Box 180

Set Printing Controls 182

Control Print Security 184

Print a Soft-Proof Color Separation 186

View a Soft-Proof Separation On-Screen 188

Print Proofs for Commercial Printers....190

Commercial print shops have adopted PDF as a standard in the printing industry. Take a moment to review and understand the various types of printing devices that commercial printers use to print PDF files and some of the terms used in printing.

Desktop Laser Printers

Many desktop laser printers use Adobe PostScript as a printing language. Advantages in favor of these devices include much easier imaging of PDF files. Non-PostScript printers may at times have more difficulty printing PDF files.

Desktop Color Printers

Desktop color printers are usually of the non-PostScript type. Fortunately, there are some printing alternatives available with PDF that can help ease the burden of printing difficult files.

Large Format Ink Jet Printers

Large format ink jet printers are used by professional graphic artists and advertising agencies for creating large prints for tradeshow booths and displays.

Image Setters/Plate Setters

Image setters and plate setters are used in commercial print environments as the first step in printing on offset presses.

On-Demand Printing

As a new alternative to offset printing, on-demand systems take the digital file and print to the press directly. This process bypasses the prepress work and eliminates the need for image setters and plate setters.

Film Recorders

Film recorders print to film for 4 x 5 and 35mm negatives and transparencies. You can use Acrobat PDF files to create a slide show and then print the PDFs to a film recorder to create the slides.

Photo Printers

Photo print processing machines can accept digital files directly. Rather than use a negative or transparency, you print the digital file on photo paper and process the paper with traditional photo lab chemicals.

Printing Terms

CMYK colors are called process color. Any image you see on your computer can be converted to CMYK values which represent percentages of Cyan, Magenta, Yellow, and Black. Photo images need to be converted to CMYK values to be printed at print shops.

Spot Colors are individual color values. A color like Red, for example, is a spot color. Each spot color is printed as a separate ink. If you have a CMYK photo and a spot color on the same page, the spot color needs to be converted to a process color. In the case of Red, the CMYK equivalent would be 100% Magenta and 100% Yellow.

Line Screen, also called halftone frequency, is the number of lines per inch in the printed document. This value determines the size of dots on a printed piece. If you look at a laser print, you can see dots on the page. Laser prints are commonly printed at 85 lines per inch (lpi). If you look at a good quality magazine cover, you do not see dots on the page. These prints are usually between 133 and 150 lpi. Therefore, the higher the line screen, the smaller the dot, resulting in a better-quality image.

USING THE PAGE SETUP DIALOG BOX

Regardless of the printing device you use, printing usually starts with setting attributes in the Page Setup dialog box. In this dialog box, you can make choices for paper sizes, paper types, orientation, and other similar attributes.

USING THE PAGE SETUP DIALOG BOX

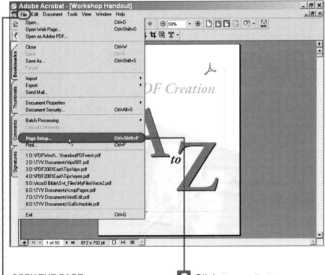

**OPEN THE PAGE
SETUP DIALOG BOX**

1 In Acrobat, click **File**.

2 Click **Page Setup**.

■ The Print Setup dialog box opens.

SELECT A PRINTER

3 In Windows, click the Name ▼, or on a Macintosh, open the Chooser.

4 Click the destination printer.

Note: On a Macintosh, open the Page Setup dialog box after making the choice in the Chooser dialog box.

5 Click **Properties**.

Why do my documents print rotated on the paper?

You may have the orientation set to Landscape when the files are in a portrait view. Revisit the Page Setup dialog box and click on the proper orientation.

Why do my documents show only a partial page when printed?

Double-check the Page Setup dialog box to make certain you have selected the page size for your paper. Be careful to avoid using Letter Small, A6, A4, or other sizes if printing on standard US Letter paper.

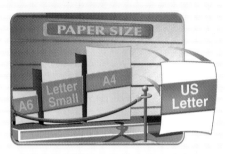

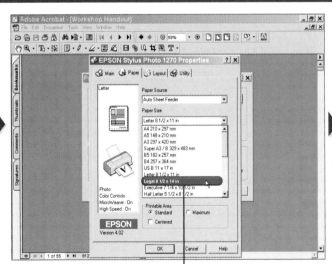

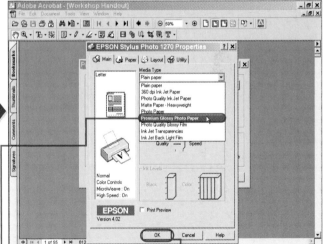

SELECT PAPER ATTRIBUTES

■ A properties dialog box specific for your printer opens.

6 Click a paper size for your printer.

Note: Not all printers are the same, and the dialog boxes vary according to the device. Consult the user documentation for your printer for attribute choices.

■ For desktop color printers, an option is usually available to choose a paper type.

7 Click the paper type for the paper you want to use.

8 Click **OK** in the printer's properties dialog box.

9 Click **OK** in the Print Setup dialog box.

■ Acrobat applies your settings.

SET PRINTING CONTROLS

Print controls in the Acrobat Print dialog box provide a huge array of attribute options to help define how a document prints. If you need help in understanding these options, the Print dialog box also offers help information.

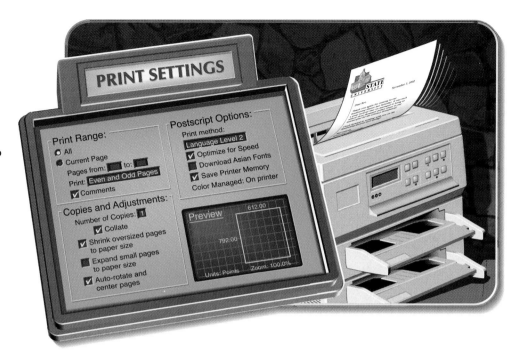

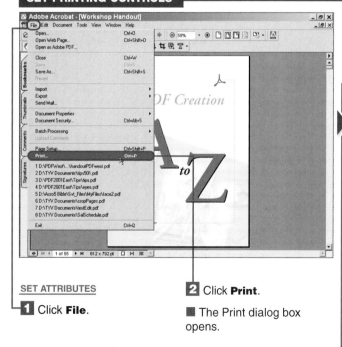

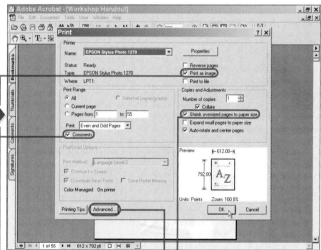

SET ATTRIBUTES

1 Click **File**.

2 Click **Print**.

■ The Print dialog box opens.

3 Select your attributes (☐ changes to ☑).

■ For printing problems with non-PostScript printers, check Print as image.

■ To print comments, check Comments.

■ To fit oversized pages onto standard page sizes, check Shrink oversized pages to paper size.

4 Click **Advanced**.

Why do I receive PostScript errors when I try to print a document?

Your printer may run low on memory and may not handle all the fonts downloaded to the printer. First try printing fewer pages in the PDF to limit the number of fonts downloading to the printer.

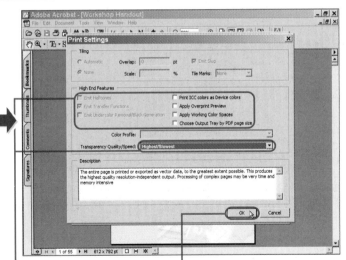

Why do my documents appear with bit-mapped fonts?

You chose to print the document as Print as image. Printing as an image converts your fonts to a bit mapped image with tiny pixels before sending them to the printer. If you do not have problems printing the file, deselect **Print as image** (☑ changes to ☐) in the Print dialog box.

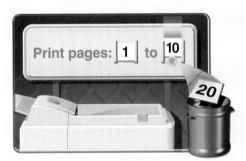

─ **5** In the Print Settings dialog box, check any features you want (☐ changes to ☑).

─ **6** Click the Transparency Quality/Speed ▾ and click a menu selection.

■ Acrobat supplies a description in the dialog box for each item you select. Follow the guidelines to make the desired attribute choices.

─ **7** Click **OK** when done.

GET HELP

1 Click **Printing Tips** in the Print dialog box.

■ Your default Web browser launches, and the Adobe Web page for printing help is loaded in your Web browser.

2 Review the Adobe Web pages for assistance with printing.

CONTROL PRINT SECURITY

You can protect your file against high-resolution printing by using Acrobat's security features. Graphic artists sometimes prefer to restrict a document to print only in low resolution. After your client approves your file, you can supply the password to unlock the document and print at high resolution.

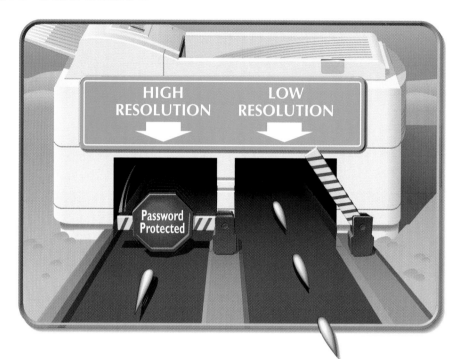

CONTROL PRINT SECURITY

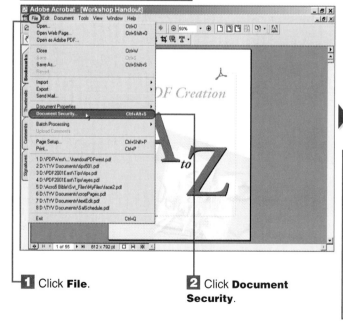

1 Click **File**.

2 Click **Document Security**.

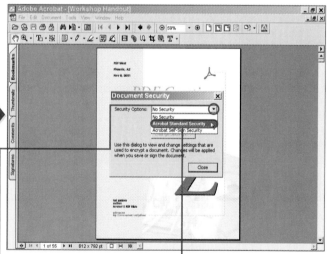

■ The Document Security dialog box opens.

3 Click the Security Options ▼.

4 Click **Acrobat Standard Security**.

■ The Standard Security dialog box appears.

How do I remove the security from my PDF?

To remove security, follow these steps:

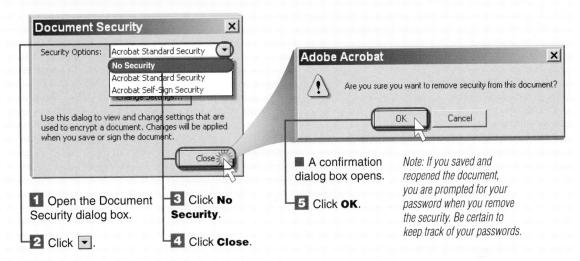

■ A confirmation dialog box opens.

1 Open the Document Security dialog box.

2 Click ▼.

3 Click **No Security**.

4 Click **Close**.

5 Click **OK**.

Note: If you saved and reopened the document, you are prompted for your password when you remove the security. Be certain to keep track of your passwords.

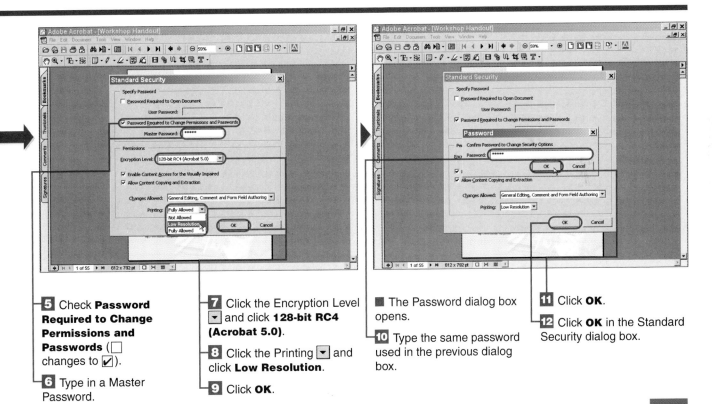

5 Check **Password Required to Change Permissions and Passwords** (☐ changes to ☑).

6 Type in a Master Password.

7 Click the Encryption Level ▼ and click **128-bit RC4 (Acrobat 5.0)**.

8 Click the Printing ▼ and click **Low Resolution**.

9 Click **OK**.

■ The Password dialog box opens.

10 Type the same password used in the previous dialog box.

11 Click **OK**.

12 Click **OK** in the Standard Security dialog box.

PRINT A SOFT-PROOF COLOR SEPARATION

Process color separations involve printing individual plates in cyan, magenta, yellow, and black. You can use Adobe Acrobat as a soft-proofing device. *Soft proofing involves producing a temporary file to verify all colors are properly produced on the right plates before sending files to imaging centers and print shops. To proof your files, print a separation as PostScript and distill the file with Acrobat Distiller. See Chapter 4 for more on PostScript and Distiller.*

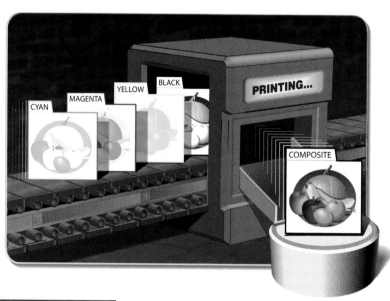

To process color separations, you must open the original file in an authoring program capable of printing separations. This example uses Adobe PageMaker; the steps with other programs will differ slightly. See the authoring program's documentation for more information.

PRINT A SOFT-PROOF COLOR SEPARATION

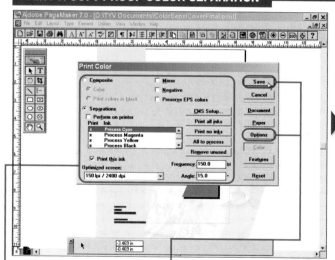

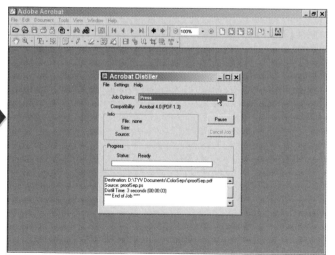

PRINT A POSTSCRIPT FILE AS SEPARATIONS

1 Open the authoring program's Print dialog box.

2 Click **Separations** (○ changes to ◉) and set other print attributes according to the program capabilities.

Note: Use the Acrobat Distiller PPD when PPD selection is available. See the "Teach Yourself" section for more on PPDs.

3 Click **Options** and select File as your destination.

4 Click **Save** and the file is printed to disk as a PostScript file.

5 Open Acrobat Distiller.

6 Distill the PostScript file in Acrobat Distiller.

Note: For more on Distiller and printing PostScript, see Chapter 4.

■ Because you only use the file for screen viewing, any choice of Job Options works.

If my file separates properly, can I send the PDF separation to my commercial printer?

Commercial printers and imaging centers usually cannot use the file you used to soft proof your job. If sending PDFs to commercial vendors, always send a composite, unseparated PDF. Check with your service provider on what Job Options are recommended.

What is a PPD?

All commercial and many desktop-printing devices use *PPDs*, or *PostScript Printer Description files*, specific to their respective devices. If you use imaging software, such as layout and illustration programs, you can make choices for PPD selection before printing a file as PostScript. In almost all circumstances, using the Acrobat Distiller PPD satisfies all your printing needs.

VIEW THE SEPARATIONS

1 Open the PDF in Acrobat.

Note: See Chapter 1 for more on opening a PDF file.

2 Click ⊞.

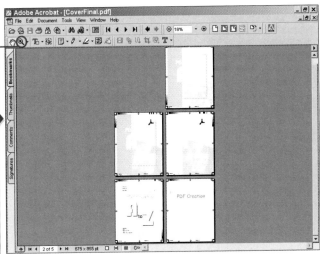

■ The PDF opens with each color separation on a separate page.

■ Click 🔍 to zoom out and see the entire PDF; click 🔍 to zoom in to the pages up close.

■ More than four pages in the PDF means that you cannot separate the file in process color correctly. Any colors other than the four CMYK colors need to be converted to CMYK values back in the authoring program.

VIEW A SOFT-PROOF SEPARATION ON-SCREEN

In addition to printing out a soft-proof separation, you can use Acrobat to view a soft proof on your computer monitor. This is particularly handy if you want to have a CMYK preview of a PDF file or view any colors overprinting in a design. Two menu options assist you in soft-proofing color.

An overprint prints one color on top of another resulting in a display of the two colors mixed together. When colors are *knocked out,* only one color prints, hiding the other color. Acrobat provides you an opportunity to check for proper overprints and knockouts.

PROOF COLOR

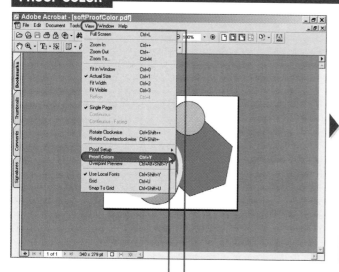

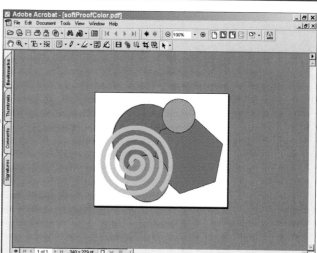

1 Open the file you want to proof in Acrobat.

Note: See Chapter 1 for more on opening files.

2 Click **View**.

3 Click **Proof Colors**.

■ Any RGB colors specified in a design display on-screen with a close approximation to a CMYK print.

Would you provide real-life examples of overprints and knockouts?

If you have a design with a yellow background and type on top of the yellow assigned magenta, when the file separates, magenta on top of the yellow knocks out the background. In essence, only the magenta color prints. However, if you assign an overprint to the magenta type, the background does not knock out, which means both magenta and yellow print. When inks mix together, the resultant color loses the magenta value and appears as red.

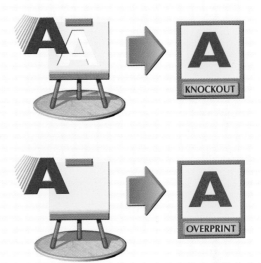

PROOF OVERPRINTS

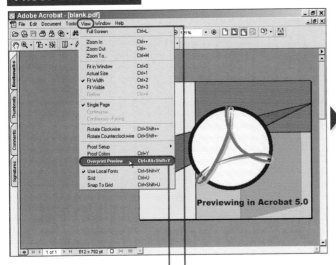

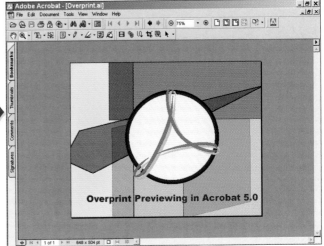

1 Open the file you want to proof in Acrobat.

Note: See Chapter 1 for more on opening files.

2 Click **View**.

3 Click **Overprint Preview**.

■ All colors assigned an overprint display as the file would print at the commercial print shop.

PRINT PROOFS FOR COMMERCIAL PRINTERS

When sending files to commercial printers, you send a composite color print and a laser printer separation to the vendor. When your printer knows how your file should appear as a final product, the job of producing the final prints becomes much easier for the vendor. When printing PDFs, you can display all crop marks and bleeds in the final proof.

To make a proof, you must open the PDF in an authoring program capable of printing separations. This example uses Adobe PageMaker; the steps with other programs will differ slightly. See the authoring program's documentation for more information.

PRINT PROOFS FOR COMMERCIAL PRINTERS

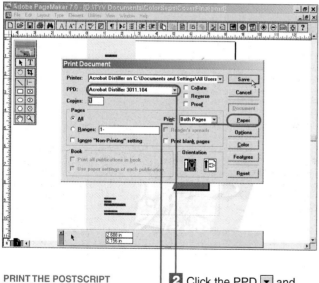

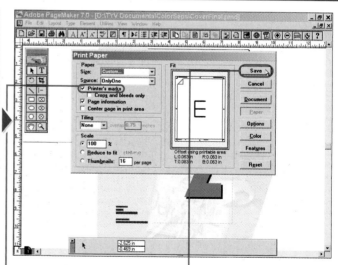

PRINT THE POSTSCRIPT

1 Open the Print dialog box in your authoring program.

2 Click the PPD ▼ and select **Acrobat Distiller**.

3 Click **Paper** to open the Print Paper dialog box.

4 Check **Printer's marks** (☐ changes to ☑).

Note: Different programs may show crop marks, registration marks, bleed sizes, and so on. Click these items respective to the program used.

5 Save the file as PostScript.

6 Distill the file in Acrobat Distiller using the Print Job Options.

Note: For more on Distiller and Job Options, see Chapter 4.

Will the color on my prints match the final offset prints from the commercial printer?

Unless you have calibrated your monitor and desktop printer to the devices at the commercial print shop, you can expect some color shifting. If color proofing is critical for your work, ask for a composite color proof from your vendor before requesting separations.

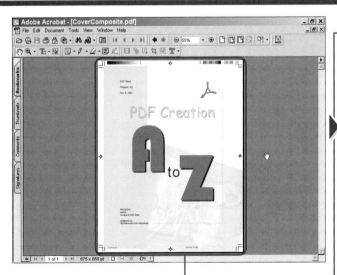

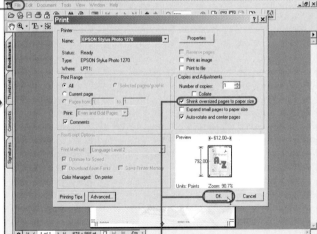

PRINT THE PDF TO
A COLOR PRINTER

1 Open the PDF in Acrobat.

2 Verify that all crop marks and bleeds display properly.

3 Click **File**.

4 Click **Print**.

■ The Print dialog box appears.

5 Check **Shrink oversized pages to paper size** (☐ changes to ☑).

■ Although smaller than actual size, the print shows the bleeds and crop marks.

6 Click **OK**.

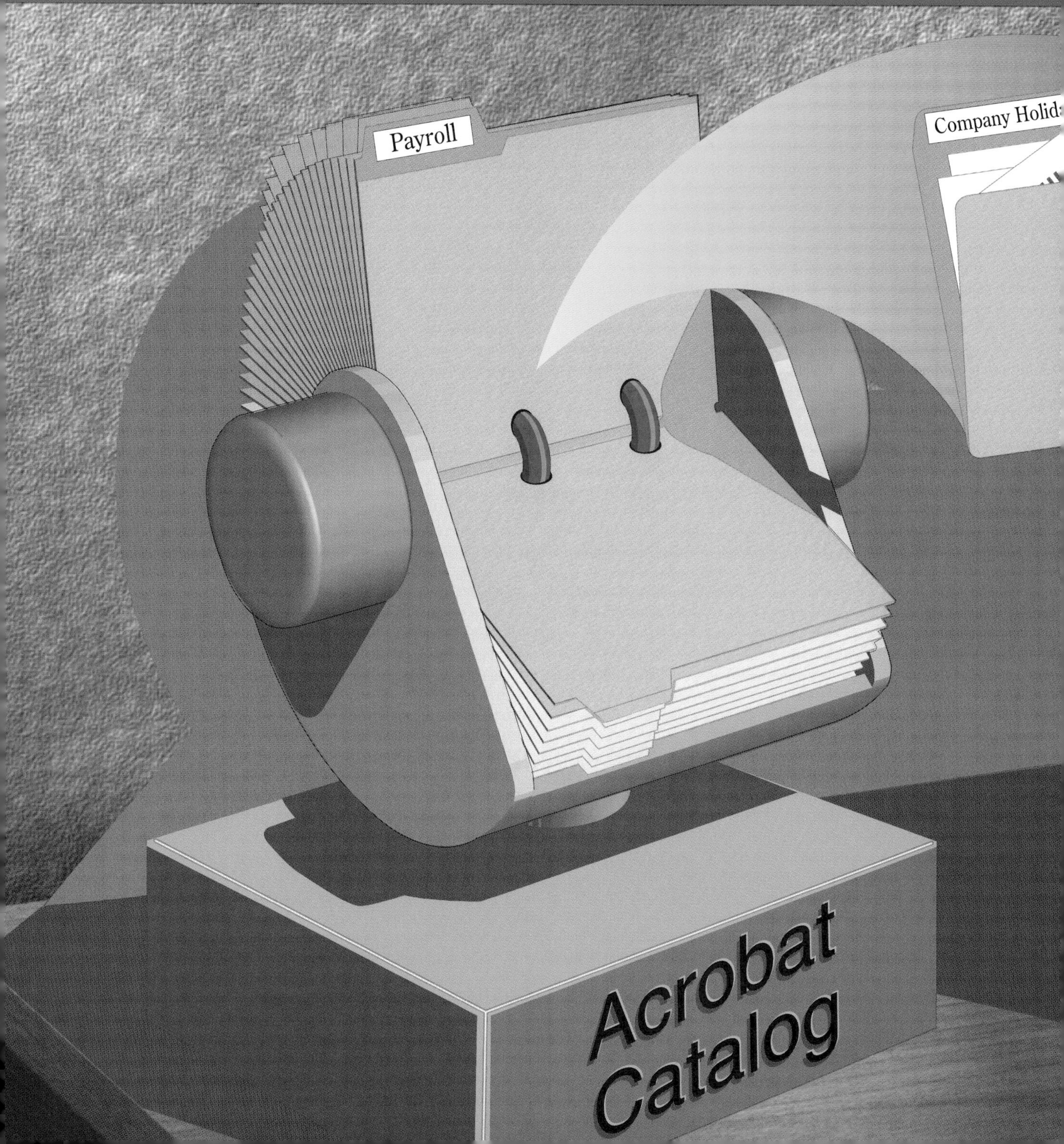

Payroll
Company Holid:
Acrobat
Catalog

CHAPTER 9

Create Search Indexes

Search indexes can help individuals and companies sort through PDF documents and find information quickly. You can create a search index with an Acrobat plug-in called Acrobat Catalog. This chapter shows you how.

Launch Acrobat Catalog and
   Set Preferences 194

Create a Search Index 196

Restrict Word Options.......................198

Rebuild or Purge an Index 199

Examine Document Summaries..........200

Create a Search Key Using the
   Document Summary 202

Document

Summary

Title

Recent Issues with
Copyrights

Subject

ubmissions without
Permissions

Author

Raymond Connors

Keyword

Copyright

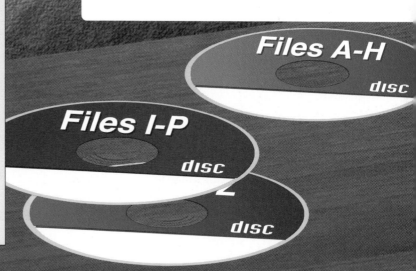

You can use the
Acrobat Catalog
plug-in to create
a search index.
To use the plug-in
in Acrobat 5.0,
you must first
launch Acrobat
and then launch
Catalog. Once
you have
launched Catalog,
you can choose
from several
preferences
settings to
customize the
functionality of
your search
index.

For example, you
can optimize a
search index for use
on CD-ROM or allow
an index to be
created on a network
server. For a
description of all the
preference settings,
use the Acrobat Help
guide. See Chapter 4
for information on
using Help.

LAUNCH ACROBAT CATALOG AND SET PREFERENCES

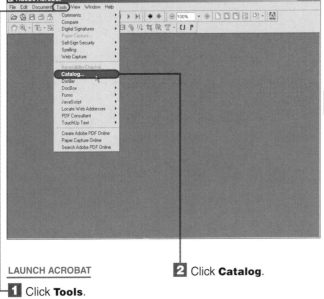

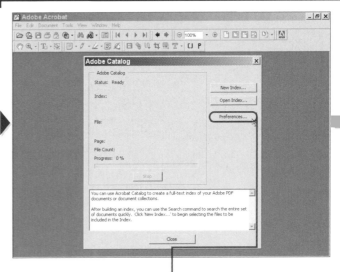

LAUNCH ACROBAT

1 Click **Tools**.

2 Click **Catalog**.

■ The Acrobat Catalog
dialog box opens.

SET CATALOG PREFERENCES

3 Click **Preferences** in the
Catalog dialog box.

■ The Catalog Preferences
dialog box opens.

Who can use my search index?

Anyone with an Acrobat viewer, including Adobe Acrobat, Acrobat Reader, and Acrobat Approval programs, can use your search index. Using indexes is covered in greater detail in Chapter 10.

Can I copy an index file and take it to another computer?

Yes. A search index is a file, like any other document, that can be stored in a folder, on a hard drive, or on a network server. You can copy the index to external media or to other computers and across platforms. Make sure that you copy the index file and all supporting folders.

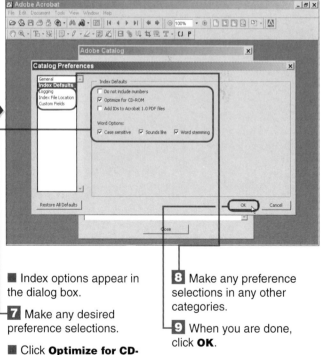

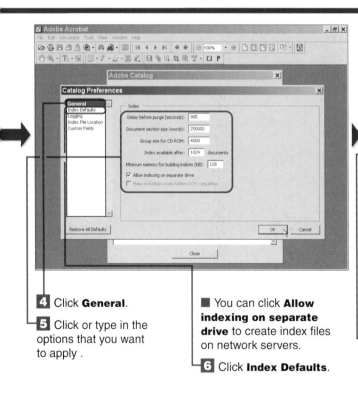

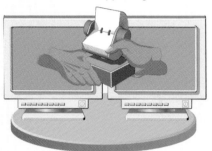

4 Click **General**.

5 Click or type in the options that you want to apply .

■ You can click **Allow indexing on separate drive** to create index files on network servers.

6 Click **Index Defaults**.

■ Index options appear in the dialog box.

7 Make any desired preference selections.

■ Click **Optimize for CD-ROM** if you want to copy your files to a CD.

8 Make any preference selections in any other categories.

9 When you are done, click **OK**.

■ The preferences are set. Catalog remains open and ready for use.

CREATE A SEARCH INDEX

Search indexes are very handy because they allow users to find a certain PDF by searching for keywords that are in that PDF. Without a search index file, a user would have to open and search each PDF individually. Fortunately, creating a search index in Acrobat Catalog is a fairly easy procedure.

Before creating a search index, make sure that you have the desired preferences set. See "Launch Acrobat Catalog and Set Preferences," earlier in this chapter. After you create an index file, you can purge and rebuild it for maintenance. See the "Rebuild or Purge an Index" section later in this chapter for more on maintaining your files.

CREATE A SEARCH INDEX

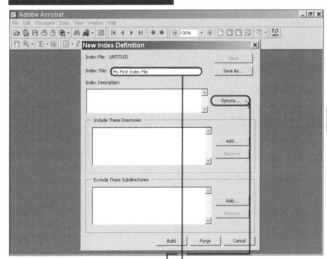

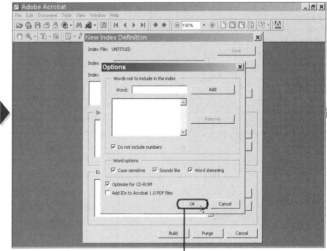

1 In the Adobe Catalog dialog box, click **New Index**.

Note: To open the Catalog dialog box, see the section "Launch Acrobat Catalog and Set Preferences."

■ The New Index Definition dialog box opens.

2 Type in an index title.

■ Acrobat does not use the name of the index file as the name, so type a descriptive name.

3 Click **Options**.

■ The Options dialog box opens.

■ If you do not have a reason to include numbers, you can check **Do not include numbers** (□ changes to ☑) to decrease the file size.

4 Click **OK**.

How can I re-index the file to include numbers?

After you create an index, you can open your index file at any time in Acrobat Catalog to retrieve your settings. In the Catalog dialog box, click **Open Index.** When the Select Index File dialog box opens, navigate through your hard drive to the index file you want to retrieve. Click the file and click **Open.** You can click **Options** in the Catalog dialog box to readjust your settings. Click **Build** after making adjustments to allow Acrobat to reflect the updated index and your new options choices.

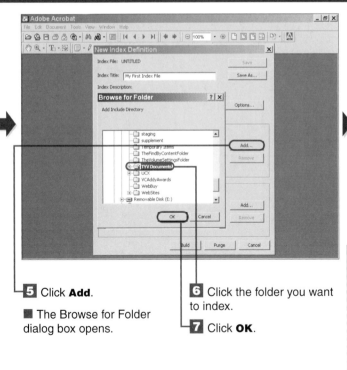

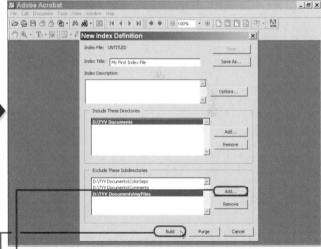

5 Click **Add**.

■ The Browse for Folder dialog box opens.

6 Click the folder you want to index.

7 Click **OK**.

8 Click **Add** to open the Browse for Folder dialog box.

9 Repeat steps **6** and **7**, but click the files you want to exclude.

10 Click **Build**.

■ The Save Index File dialog box opens.

11 Type in an index name.

12 Click **OK**.

■ Acrobat creates the index file.

RESTRICT WORD OPTIONS

Word Options offer settings for case sensitivity, synonyms, and word stems. Including these items in the search index can increase the file size. In addition, many words, like prepositions, are not usually necessary for searching. You can elect to eliminate such items when you build the search index.

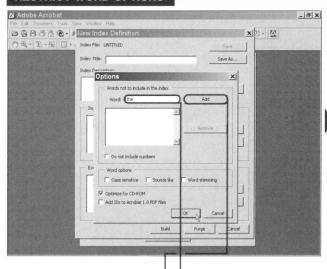

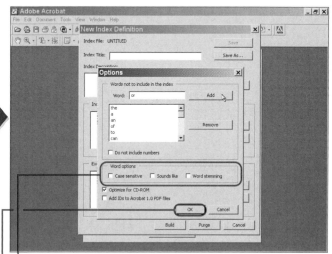

1 In the Adobe Catalog dialog box, click New Index.

2 Click **Options** in the New Index Definition dialog box.

■ The Options dialog box opens.

3 Type the words you want to exclude in the Word field box.

4 Click **Add** to place the word in the list.

5 Deselect the Word options as desired (☑ changes to ☐).

6 Click **OK**.

7 Resume building the index.

Note: For more on building an index, see "Create a Search Index."

■ Acrobat builds the index without the listed words and Word options.

At times, you may want to delete previously indexed PDFs. To eliminate the excess data, you need to purge the index file. You may also want to add files to previously indexed PDFs; you can do this by rebuilding the index file. These two tasks are performed in a very similar manner, differing only by the click of a button.

Neither task requires that you identify specific files to be purged or added. Acrobat Catalog updates the index depending on what files have been added to or deleted from the index's folder, so before you begin either task, make sure that the contents of the index's folders are current.

REBUILD OR PURGE AN INDEX

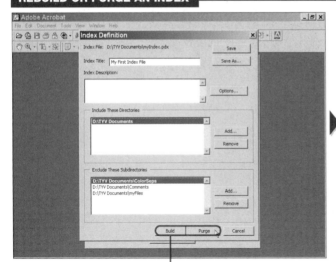

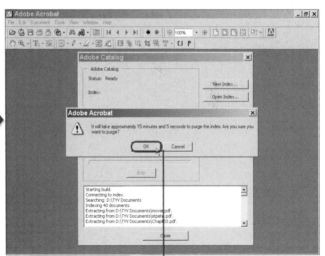

1 Click **Open Index** in the Acrobat Catalog dialog box.

2 In the Select Index File dialog box, navigate to the index file you want to purge or rebuild.

3 Click **Open**.

■ The Index Definition dialog box opens.

4 Click **Build** or **Purge**.

■ If you are rebuilding, Catalog rebuilds the index and includes words in the folders targeted for indexing and includes the new PDF documents. The index file is updated.

■ If you are purging, Catalog displays a warning indicating how much time is needed to purge the data.

5 Click **OK**.

■ Acrobat purges the index file without any further options selections.

EXAMINE DOCUMENT SUMMARIES

Perhaps one of the most overlooked information items in PDFs is the Document Summary. When the summary information is complete, users can perform searches on the Title, Subject, Author, and Keyword fields. You should provide as many details as possible in these fields to take full advantage of Acrobat's search feature.

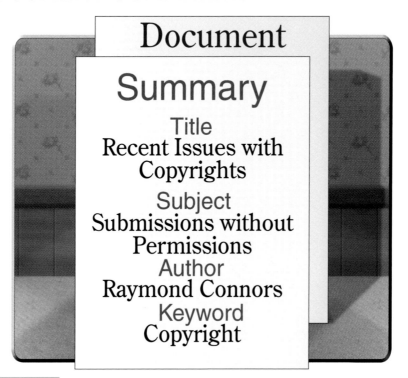

EXAMINE DOCUMENT SUMMARIES

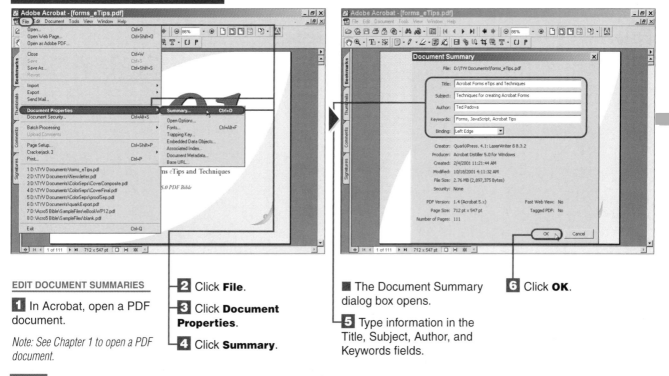

EDIT DOCUMENT SUMMARIES

1 In Acrobat, open a PDF document.

Note: See Chapter 1 to open a PDF document.

2 Click **File**.

3 Click **Document Properties**.

4 Click **Summary**.

■ The Document Summary dialog box opens.

5 Type information in the Title, Subject, Author, and Keywords fields.

6 Click **OK**.

Can I add Document Summary information at the time I create a PDF file, or do I need to add it after all my PDFs have been created?

Some authoring programs that export to PDF provide a means of adding Document Summaries to the PDFs that are produced. To export to PDF, see the programs covered in Chapter 3. When you see Document Information or Document Summary as an export option in your authoring program, edit the fields and the document summaries are included in the resulting PDF documents.

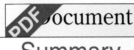

PDF Document
Summary
Title
Recent Issues with Copyrights

Document Summary. . .

Author
Raymond Connors
Keyword
Copyright

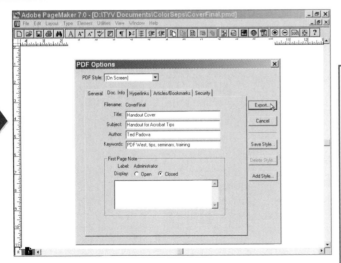

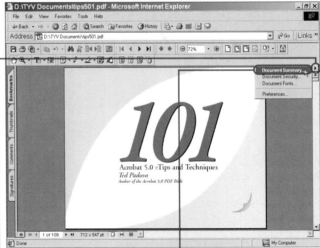

EXPORT DOCUMENT SUMMARIES

■ If you export to a PDF, you can often export Document Summary information from programs supporting PDF exports.

EXAMINE DOCUMENT SUMMARIES IN WEB BROWSERS

■ When viewing PDFs in Web browsers, you can open the Document Summary dialog box.

1 Click ▶.

2 Click **Document Summary**.

■ The Document Summary dialog box opens in the Web browser window.

CREATE A SEARCH KEY USING THE DOCUMENT SUMMARY

Perhaps one of the most overlooked search tools that you can provide your users involves the Document Summary, which can include information about titles, subjects, authors, and keywords. You can create a table that will enable users to easily search the summary information. These tables can provide users with a visual guide on where to begin searching PDFs.

For information on searching the summary information, see Chapter 10.

CREATE A SEARCH KEY USING THE DOCUMENT SUMMARY

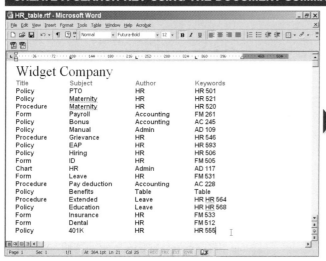

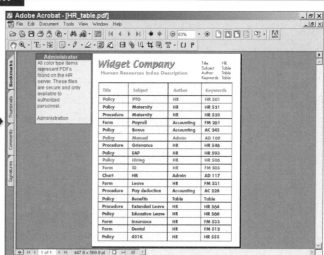

CREATE A TABLE

1 Use a word-processing program, such as Microsoft Word, to create a table identifying Title, Subject, Author, and Keyword fields.

■ For Author fields, you may want to use departments instead of worker names.

Note: Refer to your word processing program's documentation to create a table.

2 Convert the file to PDF.

Note: See Chapter 3 to convert files to PDFs.

■ You can create a layout design with color to add additional information, such as where a user can find the searched PDFs.

Why should I include my tables when I create a search index with Acrobat Catalog?

Because the tables are searchable with Acrobat Search, you should include all tables in your search index.

Why should I use a department name instead of my name?

In companies and organizations, personnel change much more frequently than department names. New employees may find it much easier to find information related to department names than to the names of former employees.

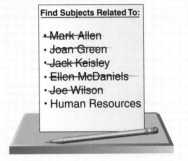

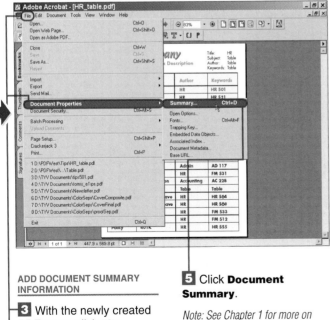

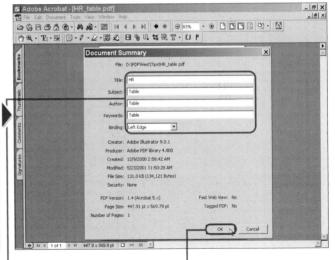

ADD DOCUMENT SUMMARY INFORMATION

3 With the newly created PDF open, click **File**.

4 Click **Document Properties**.

5 Click **Document Summary**.

Note: See Chapter 1 for more on opening a PDF.

6 Type the appropriate information in the fields.

■ Reserve words for fields like Title, Subject, and Author. When a user searches these fields for the reserved word, only PDFs created as tables are found.

7 Click **OK**.

8 Save the file.

Note: See Chapter 1 to save a file.

CHAPTER 10

Using Acrobat Search

Are you ready to start using search indexes? Acrobat offers you many powerful search features to find information in PDF files fast. This chapter shows you how to search an index file.

Load a Search Index.......................206

Using the Adobe Acrobat Search
   Dialog Box 208

Set Search Preferences 210

Search Document Summary
   Information 212

Understanding Keywords, Expressions,
   and Boolean Operators 214

Using Keywords, Expressions,
   and Boolean Operators 216

View Document Information 218

Understand Relative Referencing 219

Search Table Keys 220

Relocate a Search Index File 221

LOAD A SEARCH INDEX

You must load any search index file created in Acrobat Catalog in order to use it. After you load an index file, the Acrobat viewer can search through all the words that you indexed when you created the file.

LOAD A SEARCH INDEX

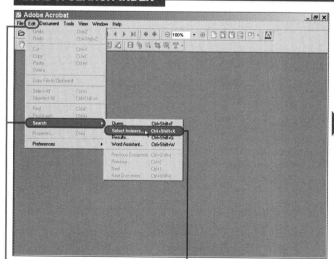

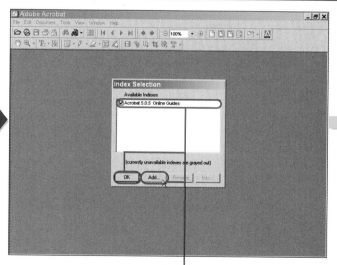

1 Click **Edit**.

2 Click **Search**.

3 Click **Select Indexes**.

Note: You do not have to open a file in Acrobat to use search features.

■ The Index Selection dialog box opens. The dialog box lists all loaded indexes currently available for use.

4 If you see the index you want to load, click the index and click **OK**; otherwise, click **Add** and continue through the steps.

Although I loaded my index file, it does not seem to work. Why?

If you relocate the index file on your hard drive or server, Acrobat loses the connection to the index file. When you revisit the Index Selection dialog box, the index file name appears grayed out. To reconnect the index, see the section "Relocate a Search Index File" later in this chapter.

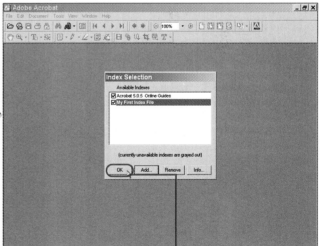

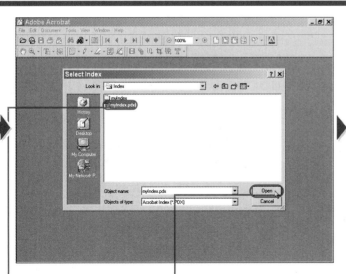

■ The Select Index dialog box opens.

5 Click the index file to open.

Note: All index files end with a .pdx extension.

6 Click **Open**.

■ The added index loads in the Index Selection dialog box.

7 Click **OK**.

■ The index is now ready for use with Acrobat Search.

USING THE ADOBE ACROBAT SEARCH DIALOG BOX

You can perform searches in the Adobe Acrobat Search dialog box. Unlike executing a Find procedure, in which you must have a PDF opened in the Document Pane, performing a search causes Acrobat to look for words in index files, so a search does not require you to open a PDF document.

SEARCH FOR A WORD

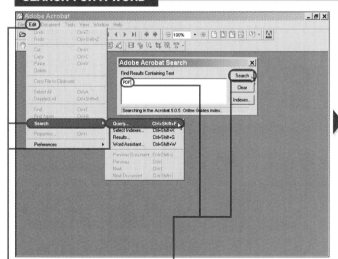

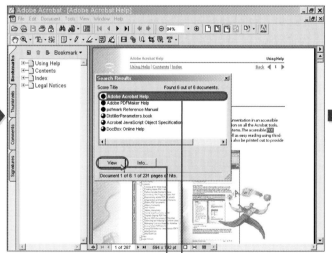

1 With Acrobat running but without a document open, click **Edit**.

2 Click **Search**.

3 Click **Query**.

■ The Adobe Acrobat Search dialog box opens.

4 Type in the words you want to search for in the Find Results Containing Text box.

5 Click **Search**.

■ The Search Results dialog box opens listing all of the documents with the search criteria.

Note: The Score column lists the strength of the result. See "Understanding Relative Referencing" later in this chapter.

6 Click the desired title.

7 Click **View**.

■ The document opens in the Document Pane behind the Search Results dialog box. Acrobat highlights the first search word example it finds.

When I try to search for a word, the Search button in the Adobe Acrobat Search dialog box grays out. Why?

You do not have an index file loaded. Open the Index Selection dialog box and load an index. By default, Acrobat loads the Acrobat 5.05 Online Guides. See the section "Load a Search Index" earlier in this chapter for more on opening the Index Selection dialog box.

FIND HIGHLIGHTS

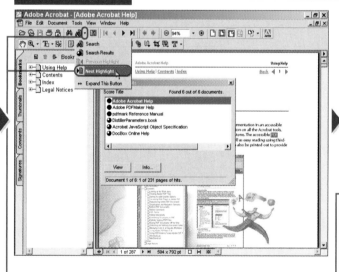

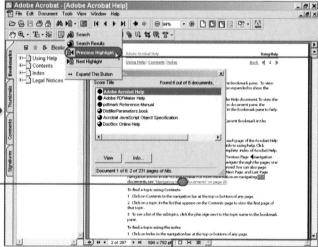

8 Click the Search tool ⬝ and click **Next Highlight**.

■ The next highlighted word from the search displays in the Document Pane.

■ To return to a prior result, click the Search tool ⬝ and click **Previous Highlight**. The last highlighted word appears.

SET SEARCH PREFERENCES

The Adobe Acrobat Search dialog box is where you begin a search. You can change the size of the Search dialog box to display more or fewer search options. At times, you may want to reduce the size of the Search dialog box in order to see more of the PDF page in the Document Pane behind the dialog box.

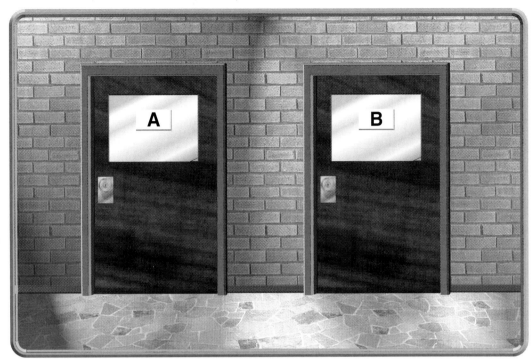

EXPAND THE SEARCH DIALOG BOX

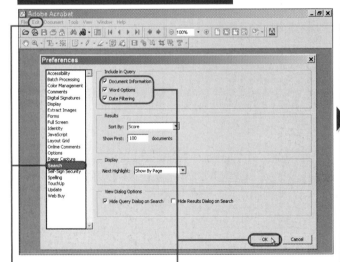

-1 Click **Edit**.

-2 Click **Preferences**.

-3 Click **General** (Windows) or **Search** (Macintosh).

-4 Click **Search** (Windows).

■ The Preferences dialog box appears on both platforms.

-5 Check all options under **Include in Query** (□ changes to ☑).

-6 Click **OK**.

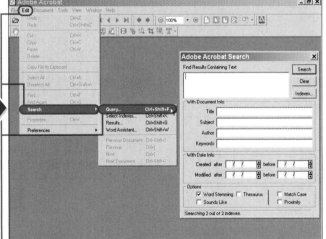

-7 Click **Edit**.

-8 Click **Search**.

-9 Click **Query**.

■ The Adobe Acrobat Search dialog box opens at full size.

What is the advantage of reducing the size of the Adobe Acrobat Search dialog box.

Most often you search for words that occur more than once in a document. When you expand the dialog box, you cannot see the search results behind the dialog box. Reducing the size helps display more search results.

When I reduce the Search dialog box in size, does it mean that I cannot use the hidden options?

You can use keywords and expressions explained later in this chapter to get the same results from a reduced search box as with an expanded search box.

REDUCE THE SEARCH DIALOG BOX

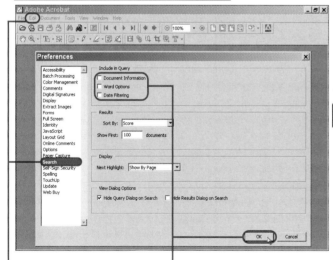

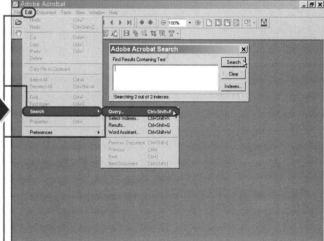

1 Perform steps **1** through **4** on the previous page to open the Preferences dialog box.

2 Deselect all the options in **Include in Query** (☑ changes to ☐).

3 Click **OK**.

4 Click **Edit**.

5 Click **Search**.

6 Click **Query**.

■ The Adobe Acrobat Search dialog box opens at reduced size.

SEARCH DOCUMENT SUMMARY INFORMATION

You can use the Document Summary information to help narrow down a search. The more Document Summary information you use for your search, the more precise Acrobat is when it returns your results. For more information on Document Summaries, see Chapter 9.

SEARCH DOCUMENT SUMMARY INFORMATION

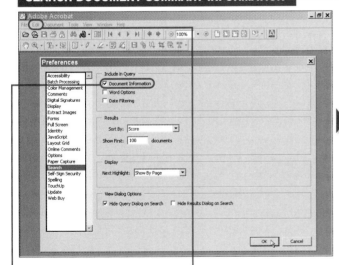

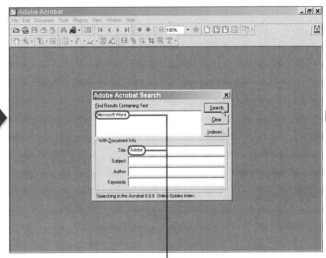

1 Follow steps 1 through 6 of "Expand the Search Dialog Box" earlier in this chapter, but only check the **Document Information** check box (☐ changes to ☑).

2 Click **Edit**.

3 Click **Search**.

4 Click **Query**.

■ The Adobe Acrobat Search dialog box opens with fields for the Document Summary information.

5 Type in an entry in the Find Results Containing Text field.

6 Type in a desired Document Summary search field.

How can I re-index a file to include numbers?

After you create an index, you can open your index file at any time in Acrobat Catalog to retrieve your settings. In the Catalog dialog box, click **Open Index.** When the Select Index File dialog box opens, navigate in your hard drive to the index file you want to retrieve. Click the file and click **Open.** You can click **Options** in the Catalog dialog box to readjust your settings. Click **Build** after making adjustments to allow Acrobat to reflect the updated index and your new options choices.

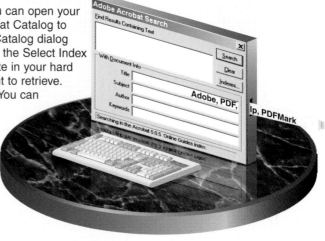

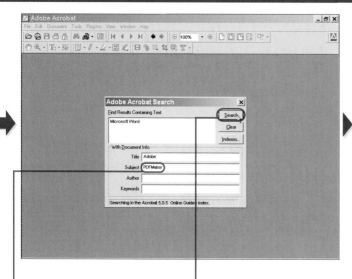

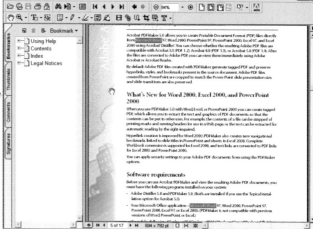

7 Type in any other desired Document Summary search fields.

8 Click **Search**.

■ Acrobat displays the result. In this case, only one document matched the criteria, so Acrobat opened the document and highlighted the matched criteria.

UNDERSTANDING KEYWORDS, EXPRESSIONS, AND BOOLEAN OPERATORS

The disadvantage to using the Document Summary fields in the Adobe Acrobat Search dialog box is that the dialog box can take up too much room and cover too much of the background document. Fortunately, Acrobat allows you to use expressions in the collapsed Search dialog box that enable you to search for the Document Summary field items. You can also use special commands known as Boolean operators to further refine your search.

Defining Search Categories

The first step in using keyword expressions is to define exactly for which category from the Document Summary fields you want Acrobat to search.

Keyword	Meaning
Title	A title may include the PDF filename or a descriptive name for the document you supply in the Document Summary. All Title field contents can be searched.
Subject	A Subject field might contain more information to elaborate on the document Title words. All Subject field data can be searched.
Author	Words supplied for the Author field might include the name of the author who created the PDF file or a department or company that was used to define the PDF author. Any of the words in this field can likewise be searched.
Keywords	Keywords might contain a miscellaneous selection of words to help describe the contents of the PDF. These keywords can also be searched.

Special Expressions

Acrobat does not limit you to exact matches in the search categories. You can pair special expressions with the search object.

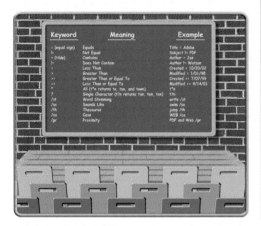

Keyword	Meaning	Example
= (equal sign)	Equals	Title = Adobe
!=	Not Equal	Subject != PDF
~ (tilde)	Contains	Author ~ Joe
!~	Does Not Contain	Author !~ Watson
<	Less Than	Created < 10/20/02
>	Greater Than	Modified > 1/01/98
>=	Greater Than or Equal To	Created >= 7/07/99
<=	Less Than or Equal To`	Modified <= 4/14/01
*	All (t*n returns to, too and town)	t*n
?	Single character (t?n returns tan, ten, ton)	t?n
/st	Word Stemming	write /st
/so	Sounds Like	swim /so
/th	Thesaurus	jump /th
/ca	Case	WEB /ca
/pr	Proximity	PDF and Web /pr

Boolean Operators

The Boolean operators AND, OR, and NOT allow you to specify conditions existing between words or fields for narrowing your search. You can also combine operators in the same search string. These expressions are shown in uppercase for clarity, but they are not case-sensitive.

Operator	Meaning	Example
AND	Find both terms/expressions	Gone AND Wind
OR	Find either term/expression	Gone OR Wind
NOT	Exclude given term/expression	Gone NOT Wind

USING KEYWORDS, EXPRESSIONS, AND BOOLEAN OPERATORS

When the Adobe Acrobat Search dialog box is collapsed, you can narrow a search for Document Summary information, as well as the PDF content, by using keywords and expressions. Boolean operators also allow you to refine your search.

USING KEYWORDS AND EXPRESSIONS

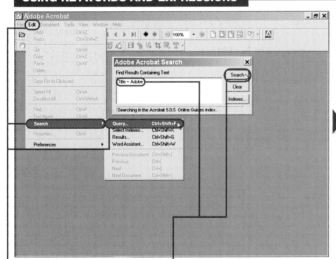

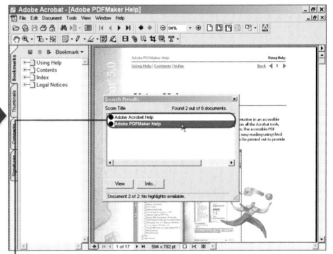

1 Set your search preferences for a collapsed Search dialog box.

2 Click **Edit**.

3 Click **Search**.

4 Click **Query**.

5 In the Search dialog box, type in the keyword, expression, and search term.

■ This example searches for all PDFs containing the word Adobe in the Title field.

6 Click **Search**.

■ The Search Results dialog box displays the fruits of the search. In this example, two PDFs were found with the matching criteria.

What is proximity?

Proximity is a powerful feature when performing searches. You can ask Acrobat Search to seek out two or more words that are found within three pages of each other in a PDF file. Use the /pr expression or display the **Word Options** in the Search Preferences and click **Proximity.**

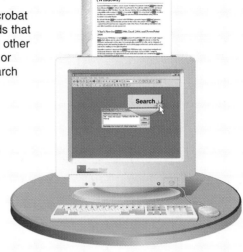

USING BOOLEAN OPERATORS

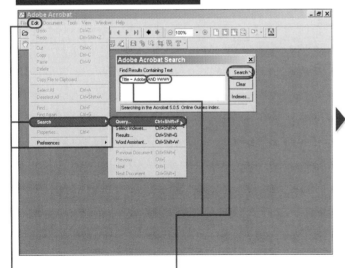

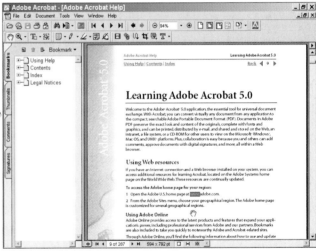

1 Set your search preferences for a collapsed Search dialog box.

2 Click **Edit**.

3 Click **Search**.

4 Click **Query**.

5 In the Search dialog box, type in the keyword, expression, and search term.

6 Type in a Boolean operator and a second search term.

7 Click **Search**.

■ Acrobat displays the results.

VIEW DOCUMENT INFORMATION

You can view the Document Summary information about a PDF, such as the date created, date modified, and so on, in the Search Results dialog box without having to open the PDF.

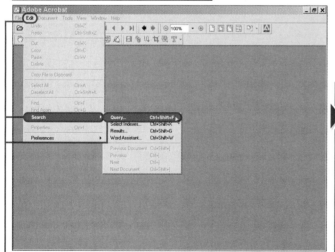

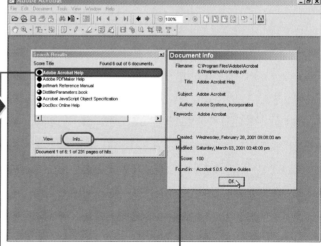

1 Click **Edit**.

2 Click **Search**.

3 Click **Query**.

4 Enter the words you want to search for in the Adobe Acrobat Search dialog box.

5 Click **Search**.

■ The Search Results dialog box opens.

6 Click a file listed in the dialog box.

7 Click **Info**.

■ The Document Summary information appears.

When the search results appear, the list displays circular relevancy icons next to the names of the PDFs. The amount of shading in an icon indicates the percentage of found words in a PDF compared to the total words in the document.

Full Circles

Full circles (●) indicate the highest order of found words.

Empty Circles

Empty circles (○) indicate the lowest percentage of found words.

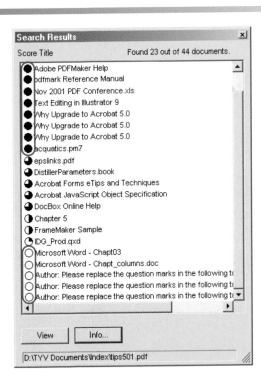

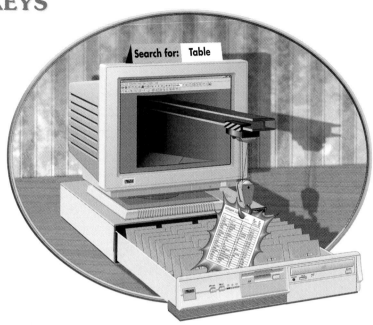

As other sections in this chapter convey, Document Summary information is important when searching PDF documents. To help organize your Document Summary information, create a PDF file with a table containing words used for the Document Summaries. The PDF file can be used as a guide to show you at a glance the words contained in the summary fields.

SEARCH TABLE KEYS

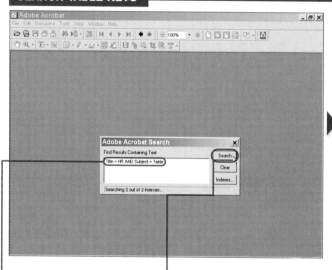

1 Create a PDF file containing words used in summary fields for your PDF files

2 Open the Search dialog box and search on a Title field and a Subject field using the words from your guide.

Note: See "Using the Adobe Acrobat Search Dialog Box," earlier in this chapter.

Note: In this example, the Title field contains HR and the Subject field contains Table, words which have been used in PDFs.

3 Click **Search**.

■ A table appears displaying the Document Summary information that you need to supply in the query to find the respective PDFs.

Note: Without a table guide, a user might not know the Document Summary terms to search. In this example, a user might search Title ~ HR AND compensation. This search returns only PDFs for the human resources department, thus narrowing the search.

Search index files behave in a similar manner to external document links. When an index file is loaded in the Index Selection dialog box, Acrobat remembers the directory path. If you move the file, Acrobat will not be able to find the index and thus considers it unavailable. If you move index files, you need to redirect Acrobat to find them.

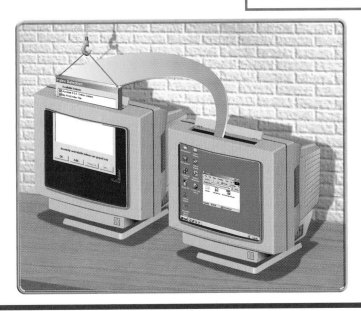

RELOCATE A SEARCH INDEX FILE

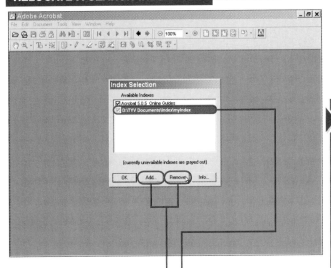

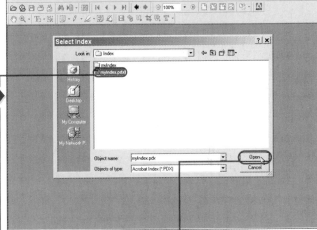

1 Open the Index Selection dialog box.

Note: See "Load a Search Index," earlier in this chapter.

■ If an index file has been moved, it appears grayed out in the Index Selection dialog box.

2 Click the grayed-out index name.

3 Click **Remove**.

4 Click **Add**.

■ The Select index dialog box opens.

5 Click the index you want to reload.

6 Click **Open**.

■ The index is now available for use.

CHAPTER 11

Create Acrobat Forms

Are you ready to start creating forms in Acrobat? Adobe Acrobat offers tools and features to create interactive and impressive forms. In this chapter you learn how to use the Form tool and menu commands to create forms for use in offices and on Web sites.

Understanding Acrobat Forms 224

Understanding Field Properties 226

Create Text Fields 228

Create Table Arrays 230

Create Radio Buttons 232

Create Check Boxes 234

Create Combo Boxes 236

Set Tab Order 238

Align Form Fields 240

Resize Form Fields 241

Export and Import Form Field Data....242

Save Populated PDF Forms 244

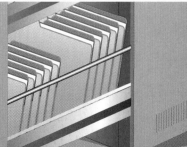

UNDERSTANDING ACROBAT FORMS

Acrobat forms are created with form fields. After you have designed a form in an authoring program and converted it to PDF, you can assign different actions to the field types to produce an almost indefinite number of results. Before creating forms, you should become familiar with the different field types.

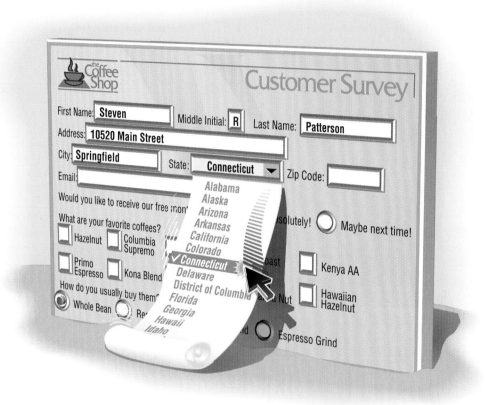

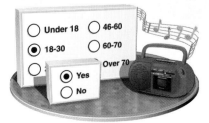

Text Fields

Any field in which text characters or numbers are input is a text field. You can use text fields for data entries and calculations.

Button Fields

You can design buttons to be links, or you can assign an almost infinite number of action types to a button.

Radio Buttons

Radio buttons are on/off buttons that offer a user a choice between several options or a yes/no response to a question.

Check Boxes

Check boxes are like radio buttons. Many forms authors distinguish radio buttons from check boxes to imply that multiple check boxes can be selected for a given question, whereas radio buttons imply the user can only make a single choice. Their behavior, however, is identical, with one exception. When a radio button is clicked, you need to click another radio button to deselect the first button. A check box can be selected and deselected by clicking the same check box.

List Boxes

List boxes offer several choices from a list. List boxes appear with scroll bars.

Combo Boxes

Combo boxes enable you to design a field with a drop-down menu. You can create your own menus and offer options for making choices from the menus.

Signature

You can use signature fields to have a user sign a form and secure it after the user completes it. After a user signs a form, the fields are locked to prevent other users from changing the responses. For more on signature fields, see Chapter 13.

UNDERSTANDING FIELD PROPERTIES

Each form field type can have many different assigned properties. Properties extend the opportunity to create fields with dynamic attributes for rendering a vast array of results.

Appearance

Depending on the field, form fields can be displayed with borders, colors, icons, and various other attributes.

Options

Options vary according to field type. Text field options include text formatting, spell checking, justification, and so on. Button fields offer choices for displays of the button contents. For examples of button fields, see Chapter 5.

Actions

All the properties available for bookmarks and links described in Chapter 5 are available for form fields. You can assign actions to execute menu commands, show or hide fields, open files, and more in the Actions dialog box.

Calculations

Validating data, formatting data, and performing calculations are various options assigned to text fields. For fields containing calculations, see Chapter 12.

JavaScript

The Acrobat implementation of JavaScript enables you to write JavaScripts to extend the capabilities of Acrobat to almost any action you wish to perform. For more on JavaScript, see Chapter 12.

CREATE TEXT FIELDS

Text fields are the most common field types used in Acrobat forms. Any text or numeric values to be supplied in completing the form are typed into text fields. You can create a text field and change its appearance easily.

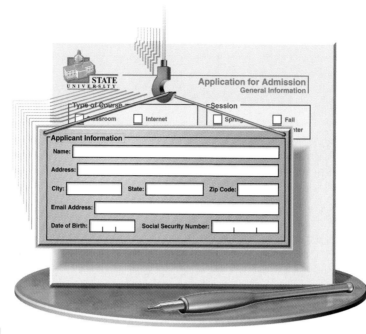

Remember that to start creating form fields, you must start with a PDF designed as a form in an authoring program and then converted to PDF.

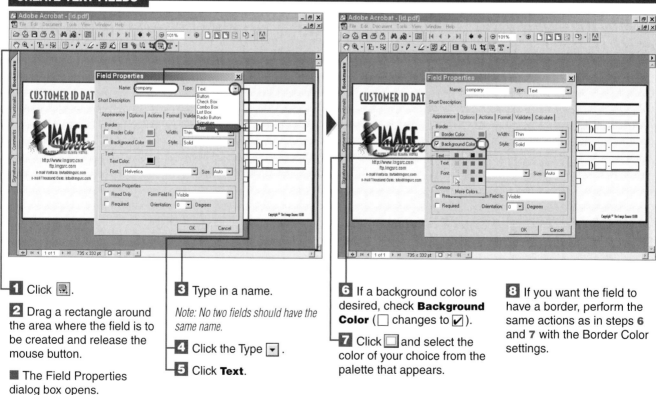

1 Click 📋.

2 Drag a rectangle around the area where the field is to be created and release the mouse button.

■ The Field Properties dialog box opens.

3 Type in a name.

Note: No two fields should have the same name.

4 Click the Type ▼.

5 Click **Text**.

6 If a background color is desired, check **Background Color** (☐ changes to ☑).

7 Click ☐ and select the color of your choice from the palette that appears.

8 If you want the field to have a border, perform the same actions as in steps **6** and **7** with the Border Color settings.

228

Why do all my fields have the same response when I fill out the form?

You probably named several fields with the same name. Acrobat thinks you want the same data in each field with the exact same name.

Field Properties

Name: address.1

Short Description:

Appearance | Options | Actio

BILL TO/COMPANY | My Company
ADDRESS | My Company
| My Company
CITY | My Company
YOUR NAME | My Company

BILL TO/COMPANY
ADDRESS | name
| name
CITY | name | ST | nan | ZIP | name
YOUR NAME | name

To correct the problem, follow these steps:

1 Click 🔲.

2 Double-click a field rectangle.

3 Change the name in the Field Properties dialog box.

4 Repeat the process for all fields with the same name.

---

9 Click the Width ▾ and click a selection.

10 Click the Style ▾ and click a selection.

11 Make any desired Text section selections.

12 Click **OK**.

13 Repeat the process for additional fields.

14 Click 🖑 to see the field appearances.

■ The form fields are displayed with the selected appearance settings.

CREATE TABLE ARRAYS

If you design forms with columns and rows, creating individual fields for each row and column could take some time. Acrobat can ease the burden of creating fields down a column or across a row by generating table arrays.

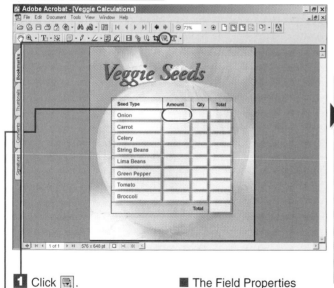

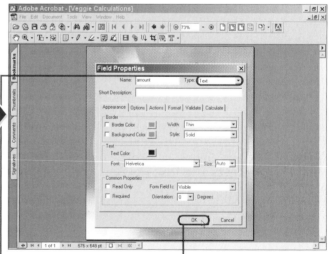

1 Click 🖳.

2 Drag a rectangle to create a text field at the top of the first column.

■ The Field Properties dialog box opens.

3 Type in a name and click **Text** for the field type.

Note: If the form design clearly illustrates where a field would appear, uncheck the Appearance items for Border Color and Background Color.

4 Click **OK**.

5 Repeat steps **2** through **4** to create all the text fields across the first row.

**My fields do not align properly when I create a
table. How can I move them into position?**

The table is undoubtedly misaligned. To
select a group of fields to be moved,
press `Ctrl` (Windows) or `Shift`
(Macintosh) and draw a marquee around
the fields to be moved. Press the arrow
keys on your
keyboard to
move in the
desired
direction.

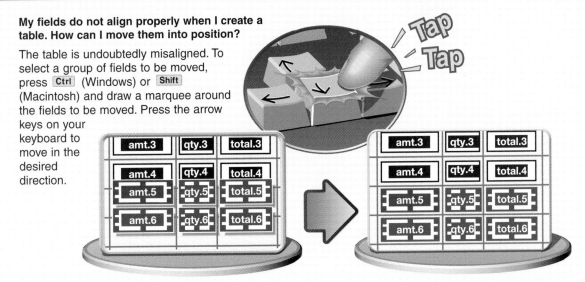

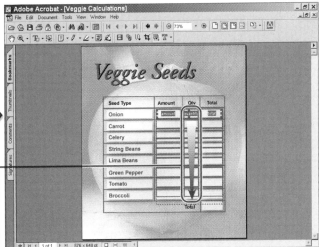

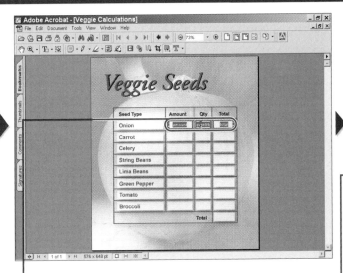

6 Press `Shift` (Windows)
or ⌘ (Macintosh) and drag a
marquee around the fields.

7 Release the mouse
button.

■ A rectangle with a dashed
line displays the selection.

8 Press `Ctrl` (Windows) or
⌘ (Macintosh) and drag the
center handle down to the
bottom row.

9 Press `Enter` on the
numeric keypad of your
computer.

■ Acrobat creates all the
fields and provides a unique
name for each field.

CREATE RADIO BUTTONS

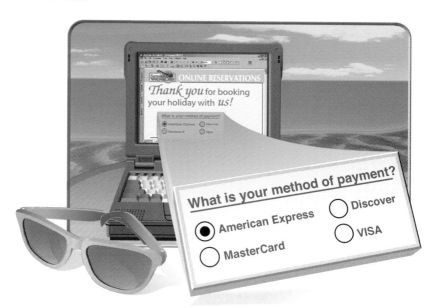

You can use radio buttons to provide an either/or choice among several options. Choices like gender, credit card types, and columns for consumer choices of products are good candidates for radio buttons. When a field name is identical for two or more button fields, clicking on one field deselects the other fields; therefore, only one field in a group can be selected. Once you have created radio buttons, you can duplicate them.

CREATE RADIO BUTTONS

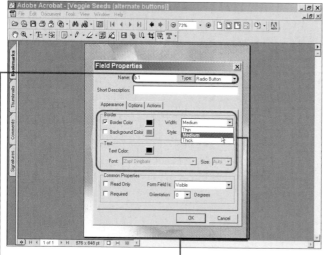

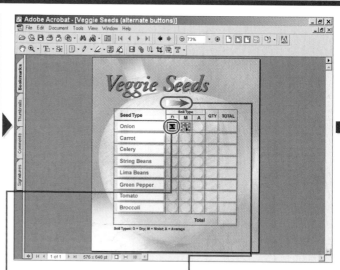

CREATE RADIO BUTTONS

1 Repeat steps **1** and **2** of "Create Text Fields," earlier in this chapter.

2 Make the field a Radio Button type and give the field a name.

Note: This field uses an extension in the name.

3 Make any desired Appearance tab changes.

■ A medium-width border with a color is advantageous.

4 Click **OK**.

DUPLICATE A FIELD

5 Press **Ctrl** (Windows) or **option** (Macintosh).

6 Click the field rectangle.

7 Press **Shift**.

8 Drag away from the field to the next field location.

9 Release the mouse button.

■ Acrobat duplicates the field.

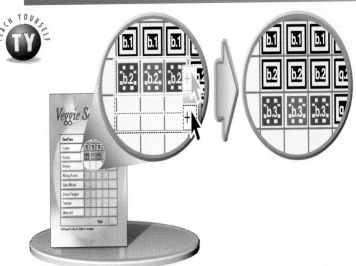

How do I create a table array for button fields?

You cannot create a button array for fields with duplicate names. To duplicate fields and change names for fields in each row, do the following:

1 Name a row of fields with parent/child names such as name.1, address.1, and so forth.

2 Press `Ctrl` (Windows) or `Shift` (Macintosh) and drag a marquee around the fields to be duplicated.

3 Click one of the fields in the selected group.

4 Press `Ctrl` (Windows) or `option` (Macintosh) and drag the group to the next row (or column).

5 Press the `+` key.

■ The child names are incremented, something like name.2, address.2, etc.

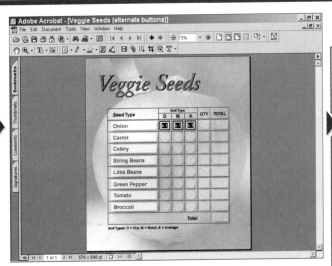

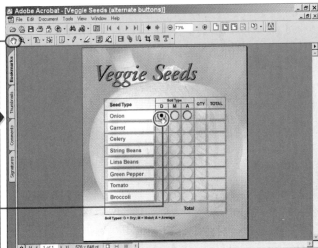

■ Repeat the duplication process until all fields are completed across a row or down a column.

Note: All field names should remain as the same name.

TEST THE FIELDS

10 Click 👋.

11 Click one of the fields.

12 Click another field.

■ The circle inside the field activates when selected. Previously selected circles are deselected.

CREATE CHECK BOXES

You can create check boxes in Acrobat that work like radio buttons. The default appearance is a square instead of a circle. To add more flair to any kind of field type, you can create different actions when the field is clicked. For actions associated with form fields, use the Actions tab in the Field Properties dialog box.

CREATE CHECK BOXES

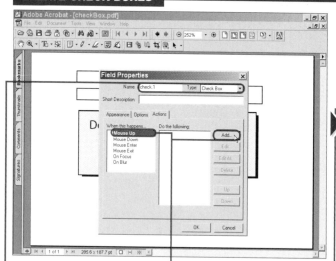

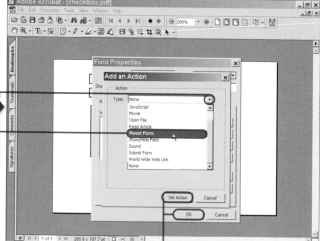

ASSIGN AN ACTION TO A CHECK BOX

1 Repeat steps **1** and **2** of "Create Text Fields," earlier in this chapter.

2 Make the field a Check Box type and give the field a name.

3 Click the **Actions** tab.

4 Select the desired action trigger in the When this happens… column.

Note: The default is Mouse Up.

5 Click **Add**.

■ The Add an Action dialog box opens.

6 Click the Type ▾.

7 Click the desired action type.

■ This example shows Reset Form, which clears all the form fields on the form when the check box is clicked.

8 Click **Set Action**.

9 Click **OK** in the Field Properties dialog box.

Can I change the appearance attributes of check marks?

All attribute assignments are handled in the Appearance properties in the Field Properties dialog box. For example, if you wish to change the size of the check mark, you can edit the text point size in the Appearance properties dialog box. To change attributes, double-click a form field. The text color and point size can be modified. For exaggerated text sizes, type a number with a higher point size in the Size field box.

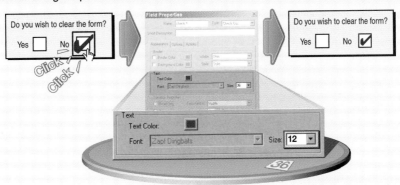

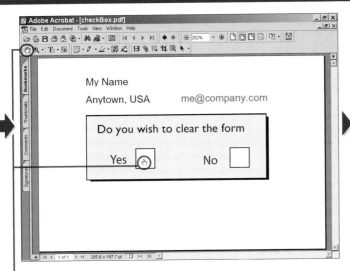

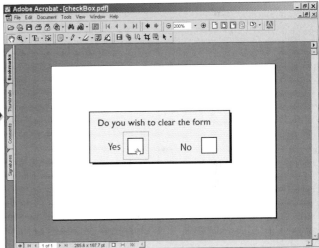

INVOKE THE ACTION

10 Click 🖐.

■ You can also press the **H** key.

11 Place the cursor over the action trigger.

■ In this example, the cursor is over the check box where the form is to be reset.

12 Click the mouse button.

■ The form is cleared of all data fields.

CREATE COMBO BOXES

You can use combo boxes to create fields with drop-down menus. This allows your users to select an option from a list of many options. Combo boxes can help conserve space on a form.

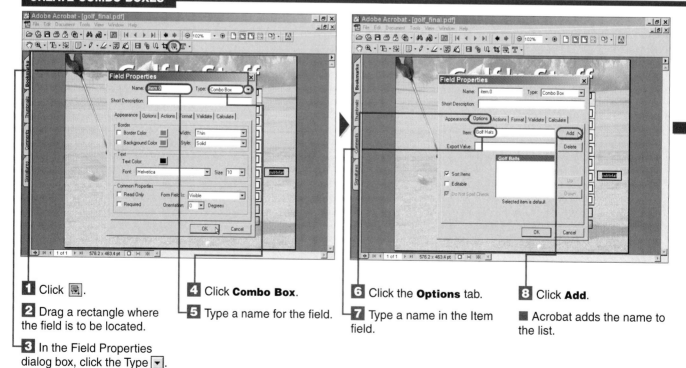

1 Click 📇.

2 Drag a rectangle where the field is to be located.

3 In the Field Properties dialog box, click the Type ▾.

4 Click **Combo Box**.

5 Type a name for the field.

6 Click the **Options** tab.

7 Type a name in the Item field.

8 Click **Add**.

■ Acrobat adds the name to the list.

236

What is the difference between a combo box and a list box?

List box

A list box displays the list contents in a window with a scroll bar and up and down arrows. With a list box, you can size the box to a small size and scroll the contents in a long list.

Combo box

With a combo box, a pull-down menu opens, and all the choices are visible without having to scroll the list.

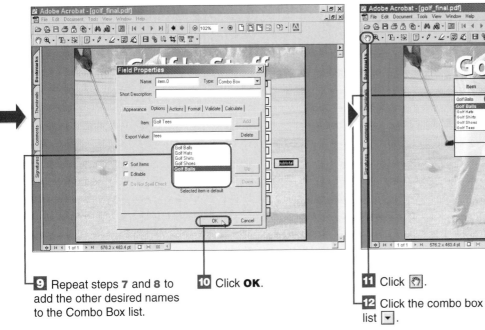

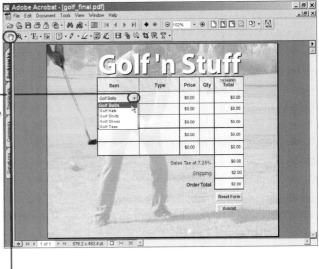

9 Repeat steps **7** and **8** to add the other desired names to the Combo Box list.

10 Click **OK**.

11 Click 🖑.

12 Click the combo box list ▾.

■ The combo box list displays the items created in the Options dialog box.

SET TAB ORDER

When a user fills in a form, pressing the `Tab` key places the cursor in the next field. Field order is determined by the order in which fields are added to a PDF. At times, you may need to reorder the tabs so the cursor does not jump around the page, thereby confusing the user.

SET TAB ORDER

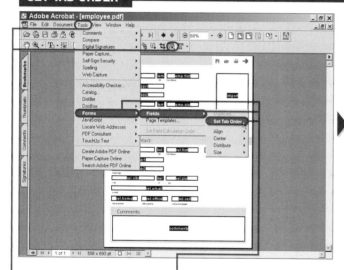

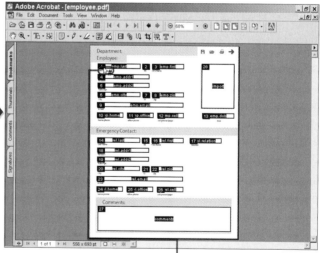

CHANGE TAB ORDER

1 Open a form where fields have been created and click 🖳.

2 Click **Tools**.

3 Click **Forms**.

4 Click **Fields**.

5 Click **Set Tab Order**.

Note: You cannot click Set Tab Order unless 🖳 is selected.

■ The fields appear numbered according to tab order and the cursor changes appearance to 🄗#.

6 Click the field you want first in the new order.

7 Click each successive field in the desired order.

If I have several pages in my form, can I set the tab order across all pages?

A user can tab to the next field from one page to another. To set tab order across multiple pages, use the navigation tools to scroll document pages and continue clicking the fields to be ordered.

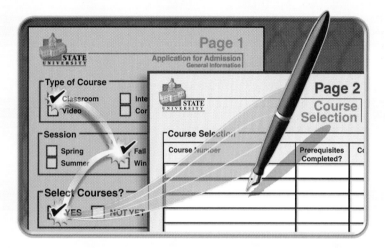

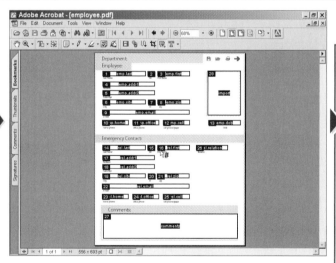

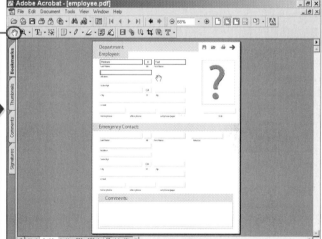

CHANGE MIDDLE ORDER

8 Press `Ctrl` (Windows) or `option` (Macintosh).

9 Click the field preceding the field to be changed.

10 Release the mouse button and modifier key.

11 Click the next field in logical order.

■ The field order changes to the next logical order following the first field selected.

TEST TAB ORDER

12 Click 🖑.

13 Type in the first field.

14 Tab through the fields to check the tab order.

ALIGN FORM FIELDS

If you create fields randomly, you may need to align them in columns or rows. Rather than clicking and dragging individual fields to an aligned position, you can use a menu command to create perfect alignment.

ALIGN FORM FIELDS

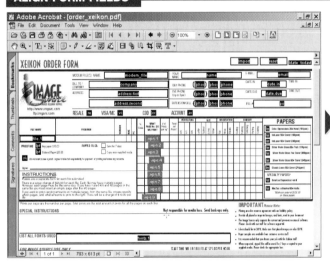

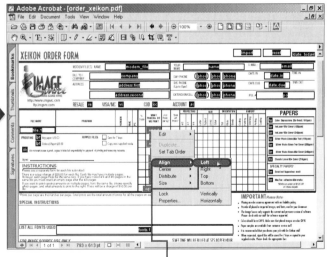

1 Drag through a group of fields to be aligned.

Note: You don't need to surround the fields with the marquee to select them all. Just drag the marquee through the fields.

2 Release the mouse button.

3 Click the field where all the other fields will be aligned.

Note: The target field changes color from blue to red.

4 Right-click (Windows) or `Control` + click (Macintosh).

■ A context menu appears.

5 Click **Align**.

6 Click **Left**.

■ The fields are aligned per the target field.

You can use a context menu to resize fields to make them all the same size. This makes your forms appear much neater and makes them easier to follow.

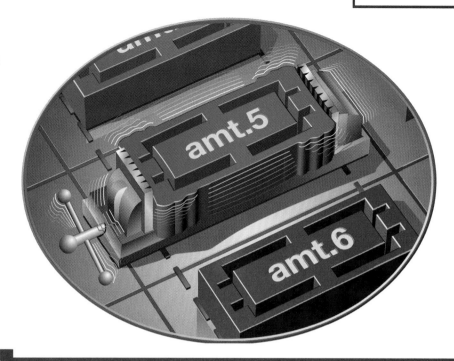

RESIZE FORM FIELDS

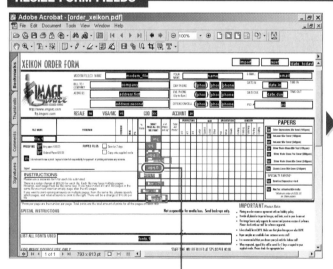

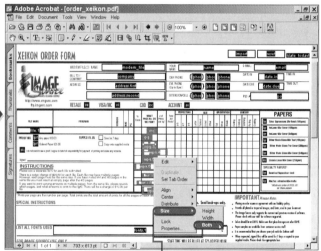

1 Click **Ctrl** (Windows) or **Shift** (Macintosh).

2 Drag through the fields to be resized.

3 Release the mouse button and modifier key.

4 Click the field to be sized to.

■ The target field appears with a red highlight.

5 Right-click (Windows) or **Control** + click (Macintosh).

■ A context menu appears.

6 Click **Size**.

7 Click **Both**.

■ The fields are sized for width and height equal to the target field.

EXPORT AND IMPORT FORM FIELD DATA

You can export common
data with exact field names
from one PDF and import
that data into another PDF.
The fields must have exact
names in both PDF files,
including case sensitivity.
Among other uses,
identifying information
used many times through
various forms saves the
user time in entering the
same data on every form.

EXPORT FORM FIELD DATA

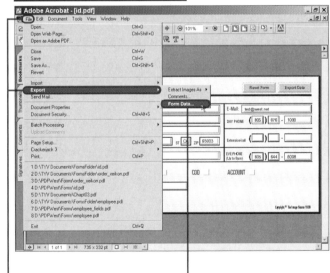

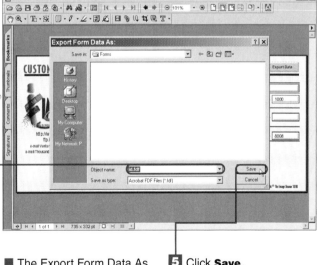

1 In a source PDF with
populated fields, click **File**.

2 Click **Export**.

3 Click **Form Data**.

■ The Export Form Data As
dialog box opens.

4 Type in a name for
the data.

*Note: All form data are saved as fdf
(Form Data File) with an .fdf
extension.*

5 Click **Save**.

■ The data are saved to
disk.

How can I easily ensure that all form fields are named identically in several PDFs?

You can copy and paste form fields between PDFs, thereby ensuring all form fields are identically named.

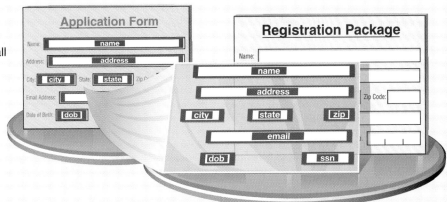

IMPORT FORM FIELD DATA

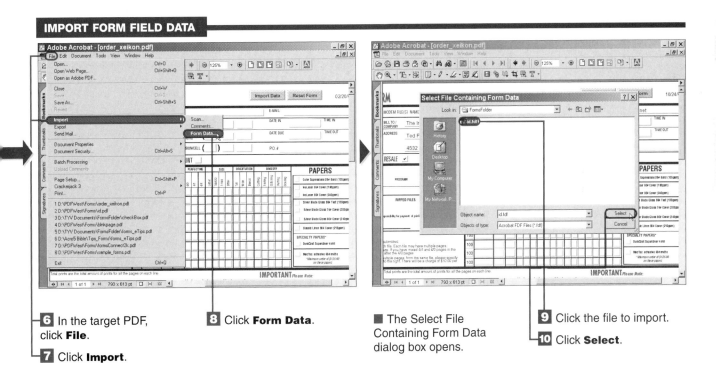

6 In the target PDF, click **File**.

7 Click **Import**.

8 Click **Form Data**.

■ The Select File Containing Form Data dialog box opens.

9 Click the file to import.

10 Click **Select**.

SAVE POPULATED PDF FORMS

After filling in a form, you can save your data entries. You can use the Save command to update the file or you can use the Save As command to rewrite the file to disk. When using Save As, the file size can be significantly reduced.

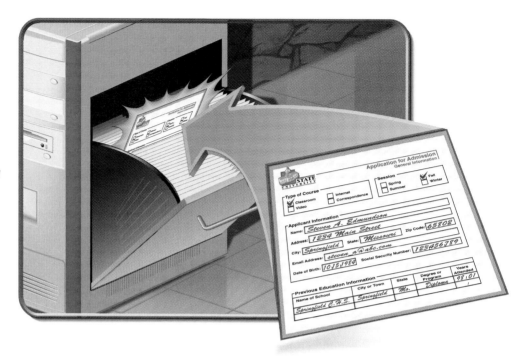

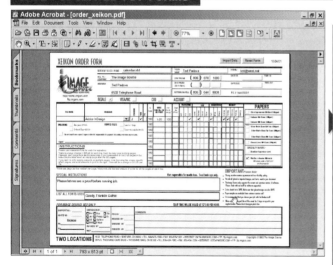

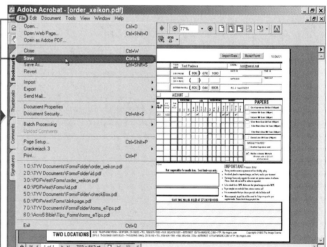

USING THE SAVE COMMAND

1 Fill in an Acrobat form.

-**2** Click **File**.

-**3** Click **Save**.

■ The form is updated with the last edits.

Why does my file size reduce in size when I use Save As instead of Save?

Acrobat clutters a document with unnecessary data when you add and delete fields and other elements. Rewriting the file eliminates the clutter. To be certain you get the best optimization out of rewriting files, open the General Preferences dialog box.

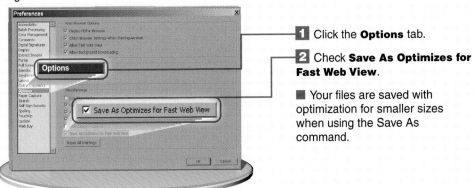

1 Click the **Options** tab.

2 Check **Save As Optimizes for Fast Web View**.

■ Your files are saved with optimization for smaller sizes when using the Save As command.

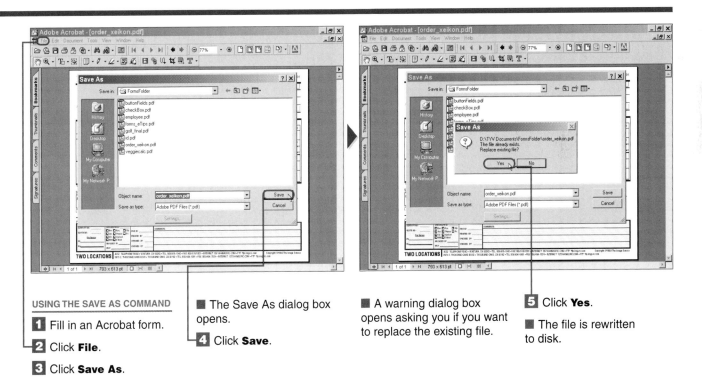

USING THE SAVE AS COMMAND

1 Fill in an Acrobat form.

2 Click **File**.

3 Click **Save As**.

■ The Save As dialog box opens.

4 Click **Save**.

■ A warning dialog box opens asking you if you want to replace the existing file.

5 Click **Yes**.

■ The file is rewritten to disk.

CHAPTER 12

Create JavaScripts

Are you ready to learn some simple JavaScripts to add flair to your forms? The Acrobat implementation of JavaScript can help you create impressive forms.

Understanding Acrobat JavaScript 248

Create an Application Beep 250

Import an Image..............................252

Navigate Pages with JavaScript 254

Calculate a Sales Tax 256

Spawn a Page from a Template 258

Add Page Numbers 260

Set Document Actions 262

Create a JavaScript Repository 263

UNDERSTANDING ACROBAT JAVASCRIPT

Before you begin using
JavaScript, you should
understand some
fundamental
points. Take a
moment to
become
familiar with
some of the
definitions on this
page.

What is JavaScript?

JavaScript is a programming language commonly
used in programming routines for Web pages.
Acrobat's implementation of JavaScript enables you to
script routines for PDF documents.

Uses for JavaScripts

You can use JavaScripts with links, form fields,
bookmarks, page actions, and document actions.
Wherever you can create a button or page action, you can
invoke a script to produce an event or action.

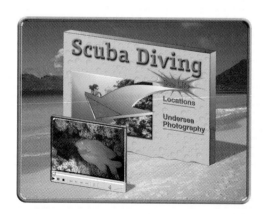

Creating JavaScripts

You write JavaScripts in a dialog box that you access from an action type. In Windows, you can assign a JavaScript editor to an external text editor, such as Windows Notepad.

Help for Writing JavaScripts

Acrobat ships with an impressive reference manual called the AcroJS.pdf. This PDF document is installed inside your Help folder. Open the reference manual to learn more about JavaScript usage with Acrobat PDFs.

Copying and Pasting JavaScripts from the Web

To become a sophisticated programmer, you need to spend much time learning the programming language. However, you can find many JavaScripts in PDF documents on the Web. You can copy and paste form fields with JavaScripts and modify them for your own use.

CREATE AN APPLICATION BEEP

An application beep is a common event in many computers. It causes the computer to emit a sound when you attempt to perform a task that the program does not allow. You can create a short JavaScript routine to add a beep on an Acrobat form to warn users before they attempt an action.

This example demonstrates how to assign an application beep to a button. While a button is probably the most common field type to assign an application beep to, you can assign an event to any field. See Chapter 11 for more about creating fields.

CREATE AN APPLICATION BEEP

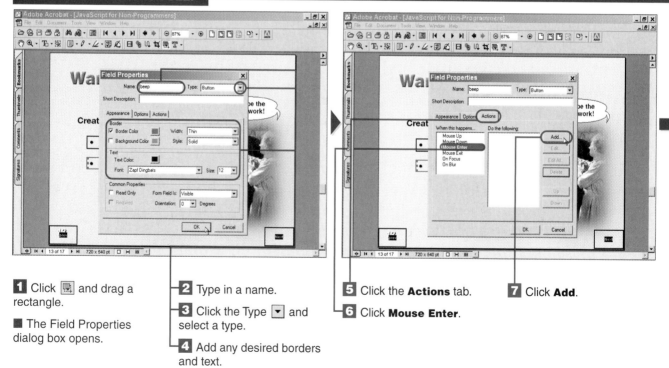

1 Click 🖳 and drag a rectangle.

■ The Field Properties dialog box opens.

2 Type in a name.

3 Click the Type ▾ and select a type.

4 Add any desired borders and text.

5 Click the **Actions** tab.

6 Click **Mouse Enter**.

7 Click **Add**.

Why does a dialog box open when I click my button?

JavaScript requires the use of precise syntax. If you type an error in the code, Acrobat prompts you with a warning dialog box informing you that an error has been found in the script. If you enter **appbeep** instead of **app.beep,** the warning will not sound and an error dialog box opens. Edit the script and use the proper syntax to correct the problem.

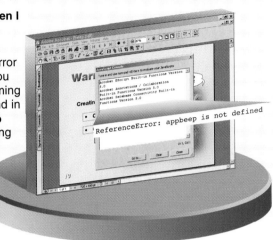

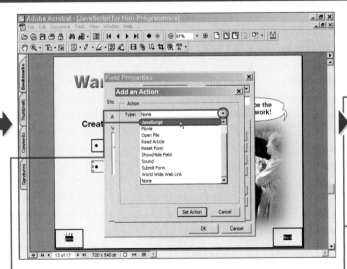

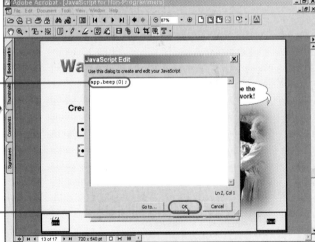

■ The Add an Action dialog box opens.

8 Click ▼.

9 Click **JavaScript**.

10 Click **Edit**.

■ The JavaScript Edit dialog box opens.

11 Type **app.beep (0);**.

12 Click **OK**.

■ The JavaScript Edit dialog box closes.

13 Click **Set Action** in the Add an Action dialog box.

14 Click **OK** in the Field Properties dialog box.

■ When the mouse enters the field, a warning beep sounds.

IMPORT AN IMAGE

You can import images into PDF documents with a simple JavaScript routine. You may need to create a template in which the fields remain the same, but different images are imported according to the design you want to produce. A Christmas card, an employee data sheet, or an insurance claim form are examples of such templates.

This example demonstrates how to import an image to a button. You can import an image to a button field by simply clicking the button and selecting a new image to import. See Chapter 11 for more about creating fields.

IMPORT AN IMAGE

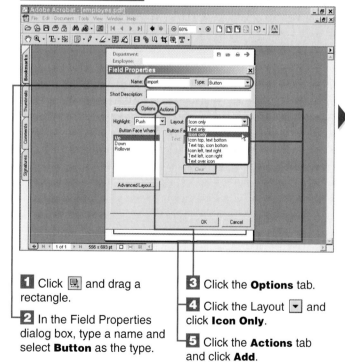

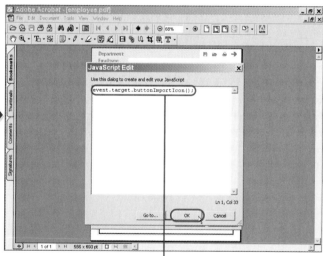

1 Click  and drag a rectangle.

2 In the Field Properties dialog box, type a name and select **Button** as the type.

3 Click the **Options** tab.

4 Click the Layout ▼ and click **Icon Only**.

5 Click the **Actions** tab and click **Add**.

■ The Add an Action dialog box appears.

6 Click **JavaScript**.

7 Click **Edit**.

■ The JavaScript Edit dialog box opens.

8 Type **event.target. buttonImportIcon();**.

9 Click **OK**.

10 Click **Set Action** and then click **OK**.

What kind of images can I import?

You can import all the file types you have access to with the Open as Adobe PDF command and any other PDF document. When you wish to import images other than PDF, click the **Objects of type** drop-down menu and select a file type. For file formats compatible with the Open as Adobe PDF command, see Chapter 3.

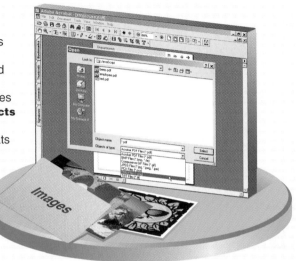

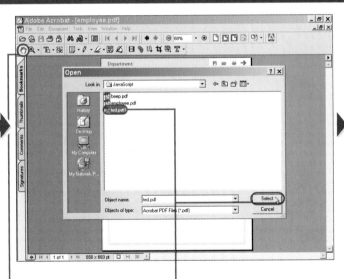

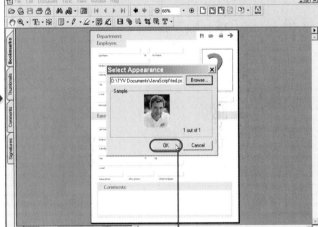

■ The field is ready to import an image.

–11 Click 🖑.

12 Click the button field.

■ The Select Appearance dialog box opens.

13 Click **Browse**.

–14 In the Open dialog box, click the file to import.

–15 Click **Select**.

■ The Select Appearance dialog box now displays a sample of the selected picture.

16 Click **OK**.

■ The JavaScript routine imports the image into the field.

NAVIGATE PAGES WITH JAVASCRIPT

You may have an index or table of contents in a PDF document and may need to create links to the document pages. If you attempt to use the Link tool, you have to manually navigate to each page and set the link. With JavaScript, you can simplify the process and work much faster. You can also duplicate navigation form fields and edit the scripts.

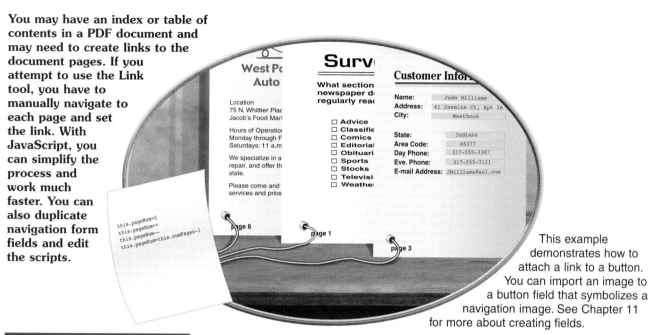

This example demonstrates how to attach a link to a button. You can import an image to a button field that symbolizes a navigation image. See Chapter 11 for more about creating fields.

SET THE NAVIGATION SCRIPT

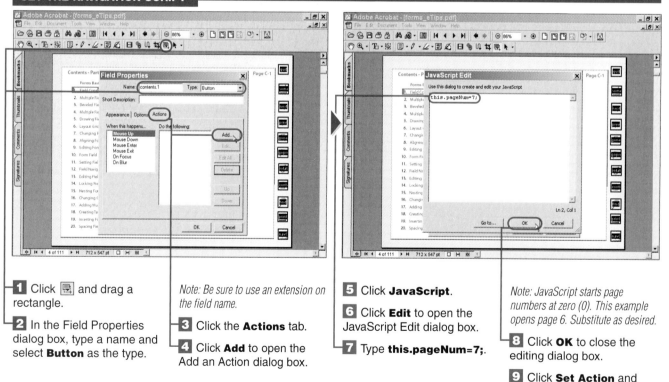

1 Click 🖺 and drag a rectangle.

2 In the Field Properties dialog box, type a name and select **Button** as the type.

Note: Be sure to use an extension on the field name.

3 Click the **Actions** tab.

4 Click **Add** to open the Add an Action dialog box.

5 Click **JavaScript**.

6 Click **Edit** to open the JavaScript Edit dialog box.

7 Type **this.pageNum=7;**.

Note: JavaScript starts page numbers at zero (0). This example opens page 6. Substitute as desired.

8 Click **OK** to close the editing dialog box.

9 Click **Set Action** and then click **OK**.

Can I use JavaScript to navigate pages forward and back in my document?

You can use JavaScript to navigate pages forward and backward through a document. Use the code in the following table for the respective actions:

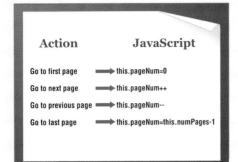

Action	JavaScript
Go to first page	this.pageNum=0
Go to next page	this.pageNum++
Go to previous page	this.pageNum--
Go to last page	this.pageNum=this.numPages-1

EDIT THE NAVIGATION SCRIPT

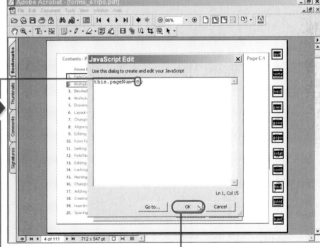

1 Click the field.

2 Press **Ctrl** (Windows) or **option** (Macintosh) and drag down.

■ The field is duplicated and given a default name indicative of a copy – here, contents.2.

3 With the Form tool selected, press +.

4 Double-click the field with 🔲.

5 In the Field Properties dialog box, click the Actions tab and click **JavaScript**.

6 Click **Edit**.

7 Change the page number as desired.

■ Here, the page is changed from 7 to 8, meaning the new navigation link opens page 7.

8 Click **OK**.

9 Click **Set Action** and then click **OK**.

10 Continue duplicating and editing fields for all contents or index items.

CALCULATE A SALES TAX

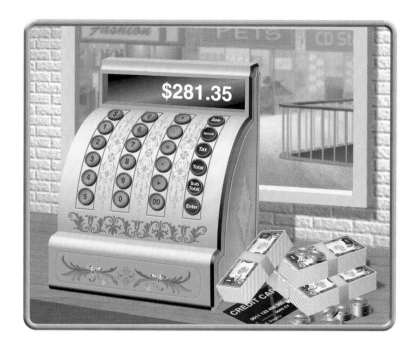

Among the many uses for JavaScript are math operations. When you create Acrobat forms, you may want to apply automatic calculations for fields of data. One of the more common math operations is calculating a sales tax, a process that you can simplify by creating a subtotal field and then writing JavaScript to do the math.

CREATE A SUBTOTAL FIELD

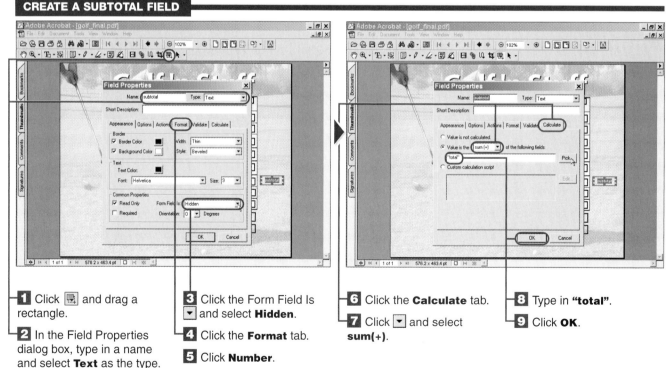

1 Click ▦ and drag a rectangle.

2 In the Field Properties dialog box, type in a name and select **Text** as the type.

■ This example uses the name subtotal.

3 Click the Form Field Is ▾ and select **Hidden**.

4 Click the **Format** tab.

5 Click **Number**.

6 Click the **Calculate** tab.

7 Click ▾ and select **sum(+)**.

8 Type in **"total"**.

9 Click **OK**.

How do I add the numbers for my subtotal field?

In the Calculate dialog box, Acrobat has several built-in calculation operations. For summing, click the **Calculate** tab and follow these steps:

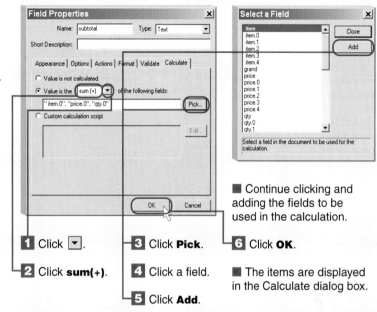

■ Continue clicking and adding the fields to be used in the calculation.

1 Click ▼.

2 Click **sum(+)**.

3 Click **Pick**.

4 Click a field.

5 Click **Add**.

6 Click **OK**.

■ The items are displayed in the Calculate dialog box.

WRITE THE TAX JAVASCRIPT

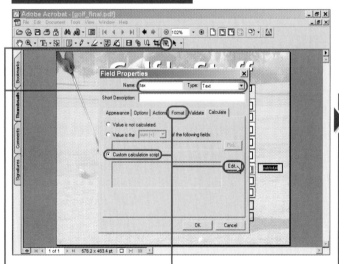

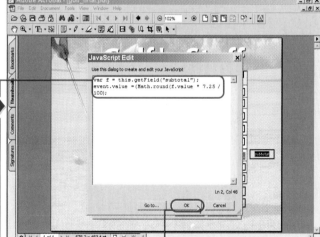

1 Click and drag a rectangle.

2 In the Field Properties dialog box, type the name **tax** and select **Text** as the type.

3 Click the **Format** tab and click **Number**.

4 Click the **Calculate** tab and click **Custom calculation script** (○ changes to ◉).

5 Click **Edit**.

6 In the JavaScript Edit dialog box, type the following: **var f = this.getField ("subtotal");**, **event.value = (Math.round (f.value * 7.25) / 100);**.

Note: Replace "subtotal" with the name of the hidden field from step 2. 7.25 is the tax rate; to change the rate to 8.5%, replace 7.25 with 8.5.

7 Click **OK**.

■ The sales tax is automatically calculated in the form.

257

SPAWN A PAGE FROM A TEMPLATE

Creating new pages from a template, a process called *spawning,* can be useful for forms on which the same fields are used on each page. Something like a Rolodex or address book would be a good candidate for such forms. To spawn a page from a template, you first need to create a template page.

CREATE A PAGE TEMPLATE

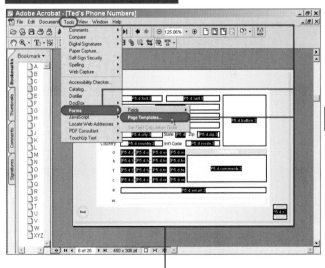

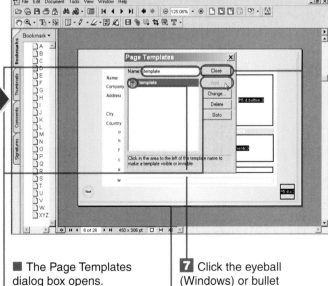

1 Create a PDF with form fields to be identical on each page spawned.

Note: Create a cover page that appears different than the template page.

2 Click **Tools**.

3 Click **Forms**.

4 Click **Page Templates**.

■ The Page Templates dialog box opens.

5 Type in a name.

6 Click **Add**.

7 Click the eyeball (Windows) or bullet (Macintosh) to hide the template.

8 Click **Close**.

Why does Acrobat not show my new page after I spawn it?

When you spawn a page from a template, you return to the page where the button exists to spawn the page. The spawned page appears at the end of your file. If you want to jump to the page immediately after spawning it, add another JavaScript.

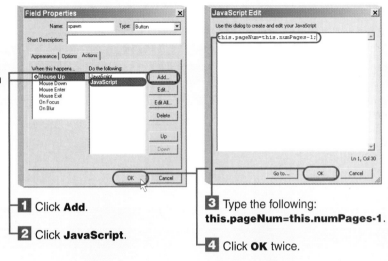

1 Click **Add**.

2 Click **JavaScript**.

3 Type the following:
this.pageNum=this.numPages-1.

4 Click **OK** twice.

■ Acrobat spawns the page then navigates to the last page in the document.

SPAWN A PAGE FROM A TEMPLATE

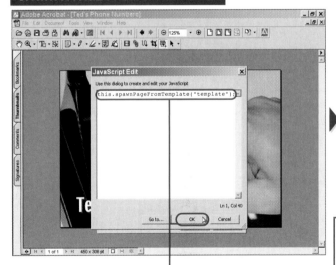

1 Create a form field button on the cover page.

2 In the Field Properties dialog box, click the Actions tab.

3 Click **JavaScript**.

4 In the JavaScript Edit dialog box, type the code shown.

Note: The code is case-sensitive. Type the code exactly as shown. The "template" item is the name you provided for your template.

5 Click **OK**.

6 Click **OK** in the Field Properties dialog box.

7 Click the field button you created.

■ A new page is spawned from the template.

Note: Acrobat creates new field extensions for all fields on the page.

ADD PAGE NUMBERS

When you create PDFs from multiple document files, you may want to add page numbers to the PDF pages. If files are converted to PDF and inserted in a document, then the authoring programs cannot effectively create page numbers. With a little JavaScript code, page numbers can be added to the final PDF document with the help of a field button.

The field button is temporary. After the button is clicked and page numbers added, you can delete it.

ADD PAGE NUMBERS

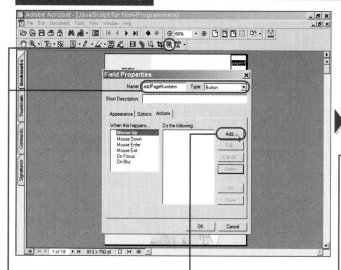

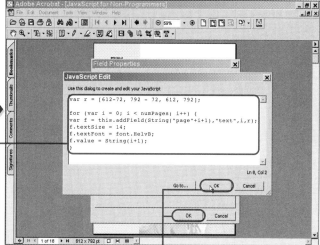

WRITE THE PAGE NUMBER ROUTINE

1 Click 🖳 and drag a rectangle.

2 In the Field Properties dialog box, type in a name and select **Button** as the type.

3 Click the **Actions** tab and click **Add**.

4 In the Add an Action dialog box, click the Type ▼ and select **JavaScript**.

5 Click **Edit**.

6 In the JavaScript Edit dialog box, type in the code shown.

■ Tweak as desired. For example, you can adjust the font – here, HelvB – and the text size – here, 14 point.

7 Click **OK** to close the JavaScript Edit dialog box.

8 Click **OK** again in the Field Properties dialog box.

Can I change the position and type attributes of my page numbers?

You can modify the code to change fonts and point sizes. For size and color changes, you can specify point sizes and different colors. The position of the page numbers is one inch from the top and right side of the page. The code reads as follows:

var r = [612-72, 792-72, 612, 792];

To set the page numbers one-half inch from top and right side, change the code to read:

var r = [612-36, 792-36, 612, 792];

30pt Times Italic

24pt Courier Italic

24pt Helvetica Bold

12pt Helvetica Bold Italic

14pt Times

8pt Courier Bold

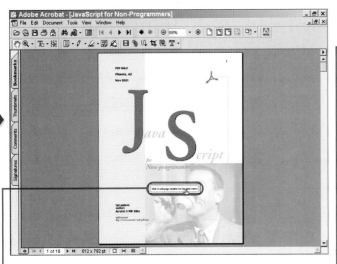

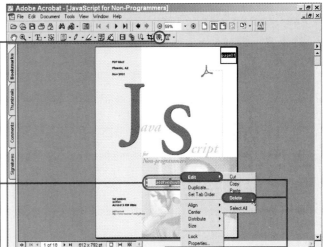

CREATE THE PAGE NUMBERS

9 Click the button you created.

■ Page numbers appear in the top-right corner.

DELETE THE FIELD BUTTON

1 Click 🔲.

2 Position the cursor over the field button.

3 Right-click (Windows) or Control + click (Macintosh).

4 In the pop-up menu that appears, click **Edit**.

5 Click **Delete**.

■ The field button is deleted.

SET DOCUMENT ACTIONS

You can instruct Acrobat to execute a JavaScript on document actions, such as opening a file, closing a file, printing, or saving. Message alert boxes are among the many different routines you can assign to a document action.

This example demonstrates how to display a dialog box with a message when someone closes a PDF. Substitute where appropriate to meet your needs.

SET DOCUMENT ACTIONS

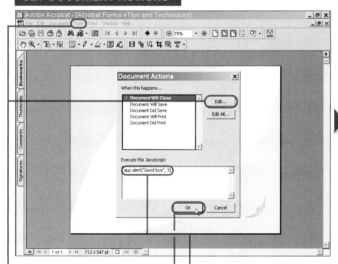

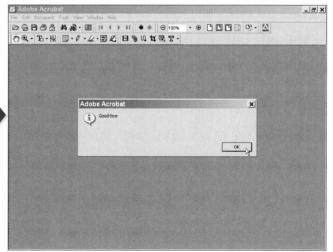

1 Click **Tools** and then click **JavaScript**.

2 Click **Set Document Actions**.

3 Click **Edit** in the Document Actions dialog box.

4 Type in **app.alert ("Good-bye");**.

5 Click **OK**.

■ The Document Actions dialog box displays the script in the window.

6 Click **OK**.

7 Save the PDF.

8 Close the PDF.

■ The Document Action displays a dialog box with the message.

Rather than retype commonly used scripts each time you create a form, you can create a formula template in which form fields contain JavaScripts. Copying and pasting the form fields into new documents saves you a great deal of time. The script used for creating Page Numbers is a good example of a routine you can use many times over. You can also find forms on the Web, copy the fields, and paste them into your formula library.

CREATE A JAVASCRIPT REPOSITORY

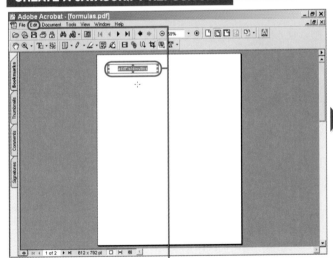 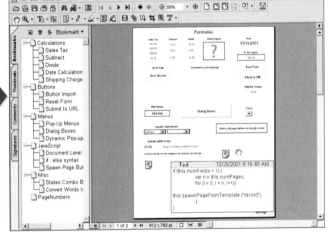

1 Create a blank page PDF document.

Note: See Chapter 3 for PDF creation methods.

2 On another form, click 📑 and click a JavaScript field.

3 Right-click the field and, in the context menu that appears, click **Edit** and then click **Copy**.

4 Open the blank PDF and click **Edit**.

5 Click **Paste**.

■ Acrobat copies the JavaScript into the document.

■ As you find more scripts, copy and paste them to your template.

■ You can create bookmarks for zooming into a field box.

■ You can also create comment notes to write messages or other routines.

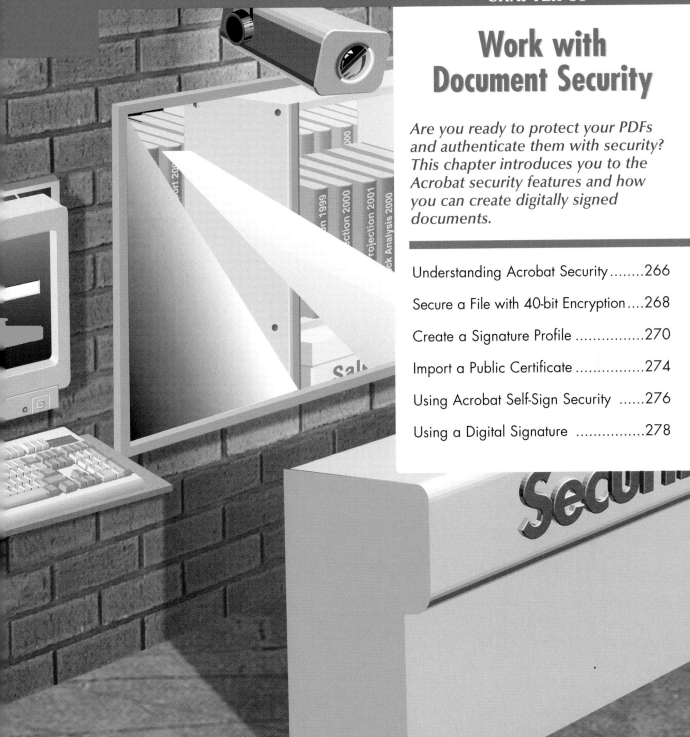

CHAPTER 13

Work with Document Security

Are you ready to protect your PDFs and authenticate them with security? This chapter introduces you to the Acrobat security features and how you can create digitally signed documents.

Understanding Acrobat Security 266

Secure a File with 40-bit Encryption 268

Create a Signature Profile 270

Import a Public Certificate 274

Using Acrobat Self-Sign Security 276

Using a Digital Signature 278

Acrobat offers two levels of security, referred to as either *40-bit* or *128-bit* encryption. Both levels of encryption provide a means for protecting PDF documents against unauthorized viewing or changes. Before securing documents, you should understand some general terms used with Acrobat security.

User Password

When a PDF is secured with a user password, the PDF can be opened and viewed only by those who know the password.

ONLY AUTHORIZED USERS BEYOND THIS POINT

Master Password

A master password enables you to secure a document against various change options to prevent users from altering your PDFs. You can secure PDFs with both a user password and a master password.

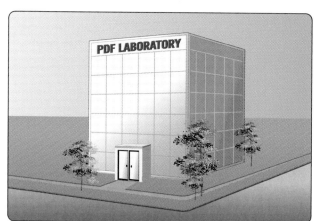

PDF LABORATORY

Digital Signature

You can create a profile for your signature. The profile you create contains your password and is not distributed to anyone else. This profile is like a master password.

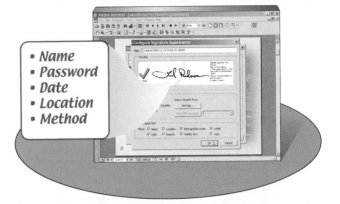

- *Name*
- *Password*
- *Date*
- *Location*
- *Method*

Public Certificates

When you create a digital signature profile, you can share a public certificate with others. This certificate is like a user password and does not compromise your personal profile. In addition, you can use public certificates to authenticate digitally signed documents.

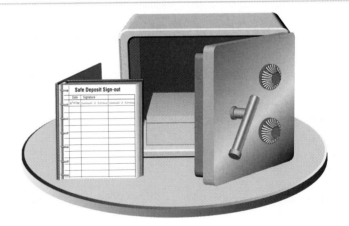

Self-Sign Security

You can secure documents to prevent access by anyone outside a workgroup. When using self-sign security, you collect the public certificates of those who can open your PDFs.

SECURE A FILE WITH 40-BIT ENCRYPTION

Acrobat's 40-bit encryption is the most common form used in securing PDF files. You can add user password security, master password security, or both to a PDF. This level of security enables you to protect against unauthorized viewing or changing of the document. For information on 128-bit encryption, see Chapter 8.

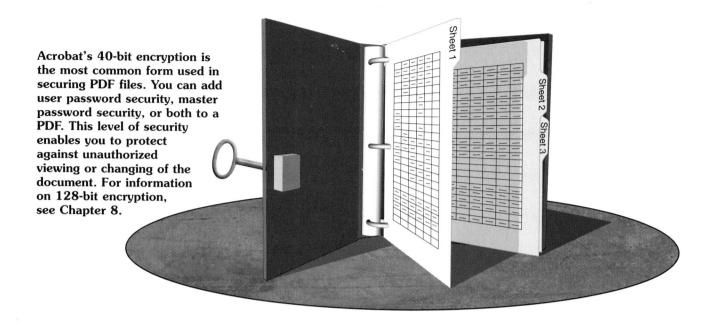

SECURE A FILE WITH 40-BIT ENCRYPTION

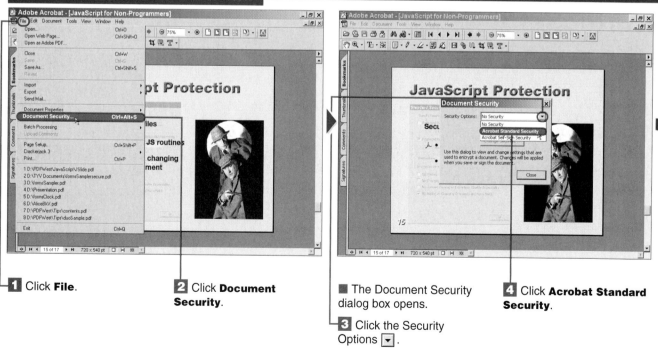

1 Click **File**.

2 Click **Document Security**.

■ The Document Security dialog box opens.

3 Click the Security Options ▾.

4 Click **Acrobat Standard Security**.

How can I open a PDF if I forget my password?

If you forget a password, you cannot access the PDF the same way it was protected. Be certain to write down all your passwords and keep them safely stored. A good way of storing passwords is to create a PDF file containing all your passwords for all your files. Secure the document with a user password and you need to remember only one password to gain access to all the passwords you use.

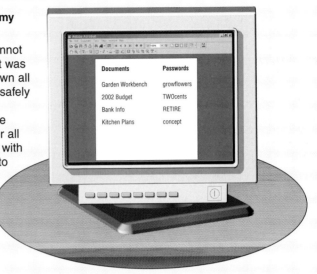

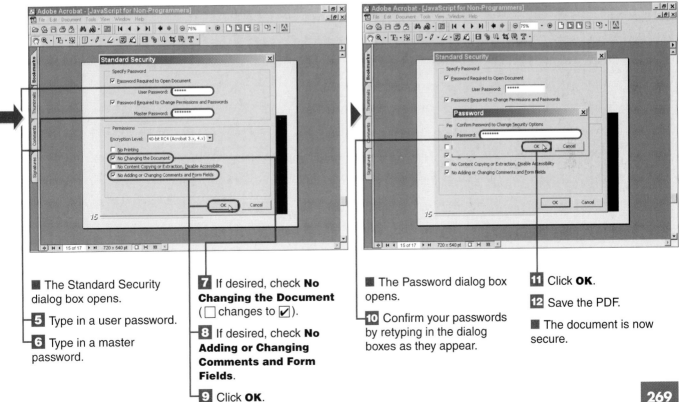

■ The Standard Security dialog box opens.

5 Type in a user password.

6 Type in a master password.

7 If desired, check **No Changing the Document** (☐ changes to ☑).

8 If desired, check **No Adding or Changing Comments and Form Fields**.

9 Click **OK**.

■ The Password dialog box opens.

10 Confirm your passwords by retyping in the dialog boxes as they appear.

11 Click **OK**.

12 Save the PDF.

■ The document is now secure.

CREATE A SIGNATURE PROFILE

Before you can create a digital signature or use the Acrobat self-sign security, you must first create an individual user profile. After you create your personal profile, you can use it when signing documents with digital signatures.

Signature appearances are imported from files saved as PDF, so you should prepare your PDF before beginning the procedure.

CREATE A SIGNATURE PROFILE

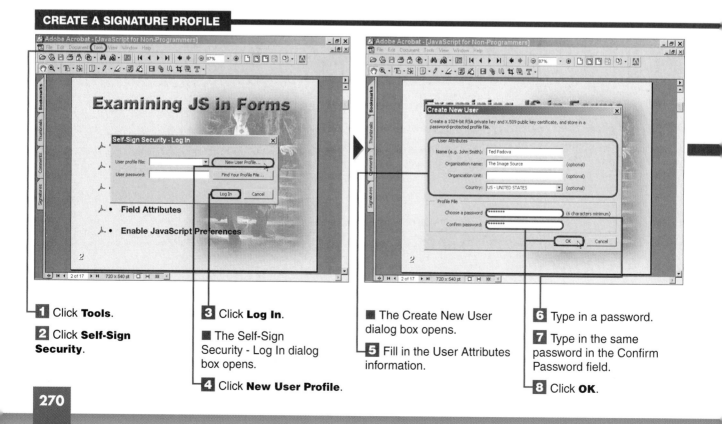

1 Click **Tools**.

2 Click **Self-Sign Security**.

3 Click **Log In**.

■ The Self-Sign Security - Log In dialog box opens.

4 Click **New User Profile**.

■ The Create New User dialog box opens.

5 Fill in the User Attributes information.

6 Type in a password.

7 Type in the same password in the Confirm Password field.

8 Click **OK**.

Can I create more than one user profile?

You can create as many user profiles as you like. To create a second profile, follow the same steps to create the profile. If you are logged in as a user, click **Tools**, click **Self-Sign Security**, and then click **Log In As Different User**. Again, follow the same steps to create a new user profile. When you use multiple signatures, you can select which user you want to log in as in the Self-Sign Security - Log In dialog box.

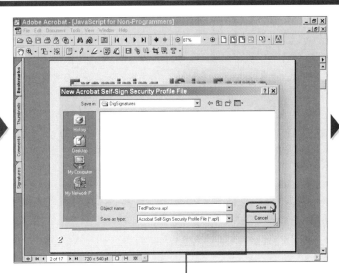

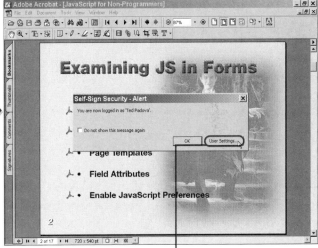

■ The New Acrobat Self-Sign Security Profile File dialog box opens.

9 Click **Save**.

Note: Leave Object name and Save as type at the default values.

■ The Self-Sign Security - Alert dialog box opens.

10 Click **User Settings**.

CONTINUED

CREATE A SIGNATURE PROFILE

You can use an analog signature that you scan, a seal, an icon, or any visual to display your signature appearance. The file can be any design saved as a PDF file.

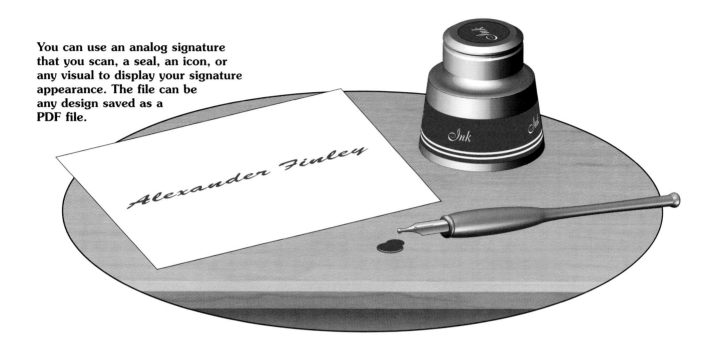

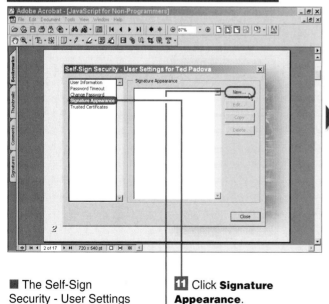

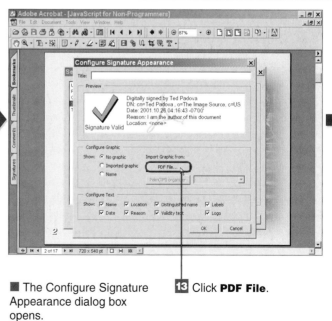

■ The Self-Sign Security - User Settings dialog box opens.

11 Click **Signature Appearance**.

12 Click **New**.

■ The Configure Signature Appearance dialog box opens.

13 Click **PDF File**.

Do I send my user profile to others so that they can authenticate my signatures or open self-signed documents?

Your workgroup users need to receive a public certificate and not your personal profile. To send a Public Certificate derived from your User Profile, follow these steps:

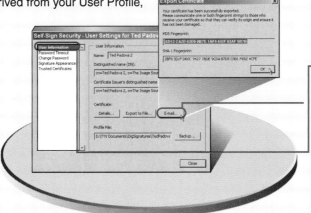

1 Click **User Settings** after logging in as a user or at the time you create your profile.

2 Click **User Information**.

3 Click **E-mail**.

■ Your default e-mail program opens. Add the recipient and send the e-mail. Your public certificate is attached to the e-mail.

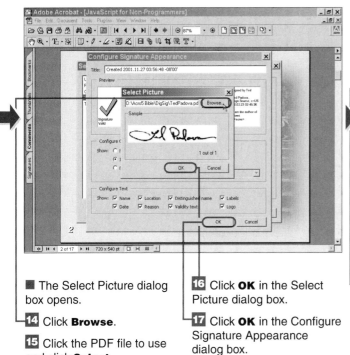

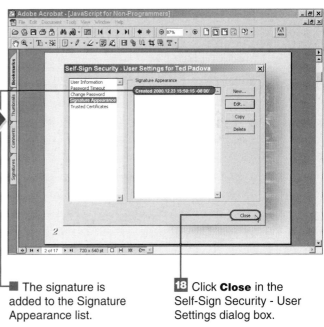

■ The Select Picture dialog box opens.

14 Click **Browse**.

15 Click the PDF file to use and click **Select**.

16 Click **OK** in the Select Picture dialog box.

17 Click **OK** in the Configure Signature Appearance dialog box.

■ The signature is added to the Signature Appearance list.

18 Click **Close** in the Self-Sign Security - User Settings dialog box.

■ Your User Profile is complete.

IMPORT A PUBLIC CERTIFICATE

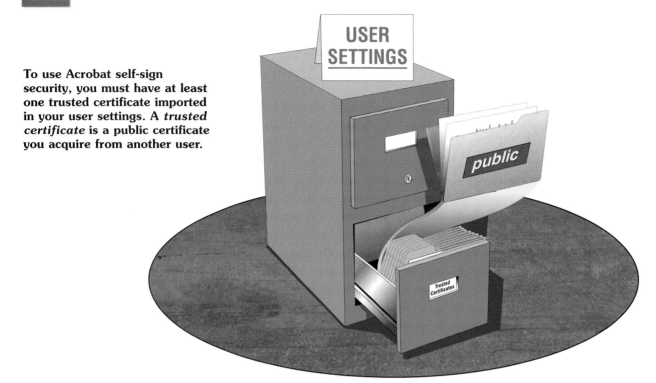

To use Acrobat self-sign security, you must have at least one trusted certificate imported in your user settings. A *trusted certificate* is a public certificate you acquire from another user.

IMPORT A PUBLIC CERTIFICATE

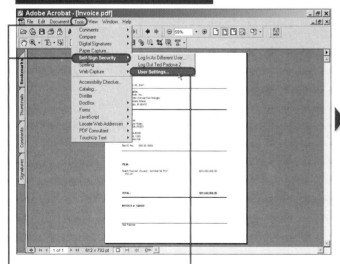

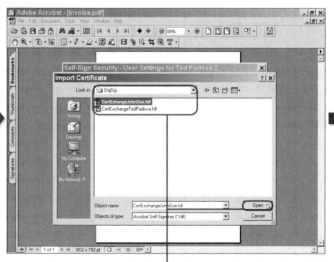

■1 Click **Tools**.

■2 Click **Self-Sign Security**.

■3 Click **User Settings**.

■ The Self-Sign Security - User Settings dialog box opens.

■4 Click **Trusted Certificates**.

■5 Click **Import from File**.

■ The Import Certificate dialog box opens.

■6 Select the certificate to open.

■7 Click **Open**.

Do I need my own trusted certificate to open a file I sign with self-sign security?

If you sign a document and later want to open it, you need to log in with your own profile. Once logged in, you can open any documents you have secured with self-sign security.

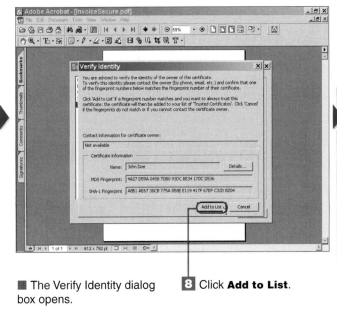

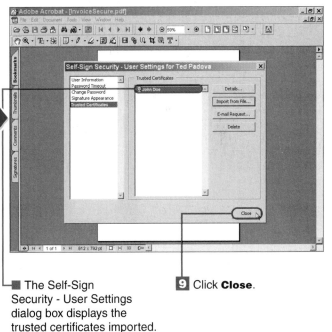

■ The Verify Identity dialog box opens.

8 Click **Add to List**.

└─■ The Self-Sign Security - User Settings dialog box displays the trusted certificates imported.

9 Click **Close**.

USING ACROBAT SELF-SIGN SECURITY

Acrobat self-sign security enables you and other members of a workgroup to exchange secure files. If all the members of the group have all the public certificates for each other, they can access the secure files. Anyone outside the group is prevented from opening the documents. Before you self-sign a document, you must be logged in.

USING ACROBAT SELF-SIGN SECURITY

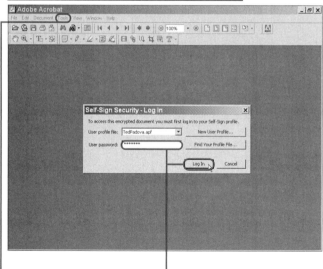

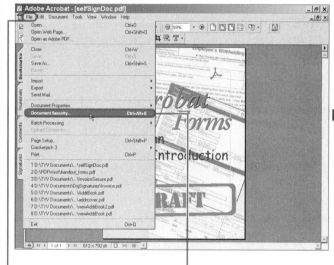

LOG IN TO SELF-SIGN SECURITY

1 Click **Tools**.

2 Click **Self-Sign Security**.

3 Click **Log In**.

■ The Self-Sign Security - Log In dialog box opens.

4 Type in your password.

5 Click **Log In**.

SECURING THE FILE WITH SELF-SIGN SECURITY

1 Click **File**.

2 Click **Document Security**.

Why am I not able to open a document I signed with self-sign security?

To open a file you have secured, you need to log in with your password. If you do not log in with the profile and password used to secure the file, Acrobat displays the Self-Sign Security Alert dialog box. Try logging in again and type in the identical password first used to secure the file.

If my hard drive crashes, will I lose all my profiles?

You must keep your personal profile and public certificates backed up on external media cartridges or CD-ROMs. The profiles are files like any other files on your computer. If you lose your hard drive, then you lose your profiles.

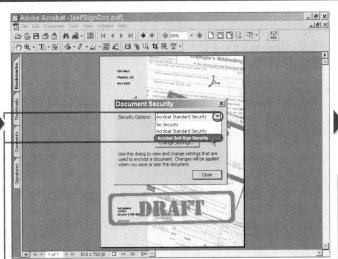

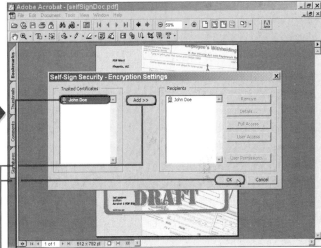

■ The Document Security dialog box opens.

3 Click the Security Options ▼.

4 Click **Acrobat Self-Sign Security**.

■ The Self-Sign Security - Encryption Settings dialog box opens.

5 Click a user in the Trusted Certificates list.

6 Click **Add**.

7 Repeat steps **5** and **6** as needed to add others you want to have access.

8 Click **OK**.

9 Click **Close** in the Document Security dialog box.

10 Save the PDF.

■ The file is now secure with self-sign security. Only certificate holders can open the file.

USING A DIGITAL SIGNATURE

You can use digital signatures to sign a document on your computer. In order for an end user to authenticate a digital signature, you must send your public certificate to the user who needs to verify your signature.

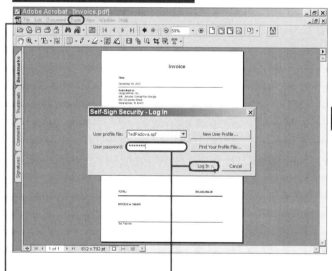

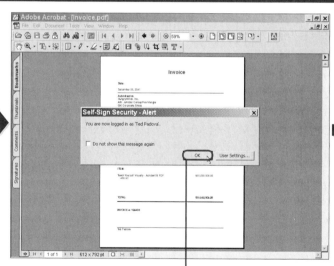

1 Click **Tools**.

2 Click **Self-Sign Security**.

3 Click **Log In**.

■ The Self-Sign Security - Log In dialog box opens.

4 Type in your password.

5 Click **Log In**.

■ The Self-Sign Security - Alert dialog box opens.

6 Click **OK**.

278

When I sign a document with a digital signature, is it a secure document?

Using a digital signature is very much like signing a paper document. No security is imposed on the file.

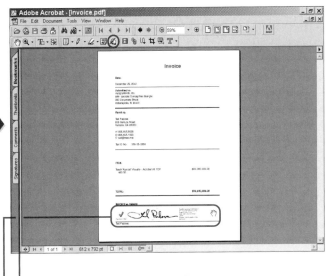

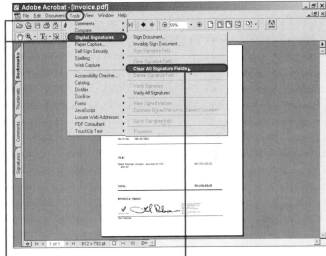

7 Click .

8 Drag a rectangle to where the signature will be applied.

9 In the Self-Sign Security - Sign Document dialog box that appears, confirm your password.

10 Click **Save**.

■ The document is saved with your signature.

<u>CLEAR A SIGNATURE</u>

1 Click **Tools**.

2 Click **Digital Signatures**.

3 Click **Clear All Signature Fields**.

■ The signature(s) is cleared from the document.

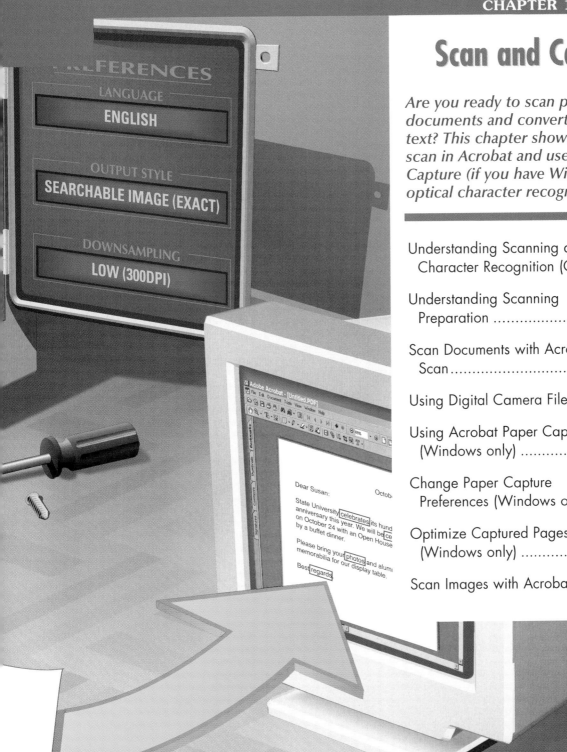

Are you ready to scan paper documents and convert the scans to text? This chapter shows you how to scan in Acrobat and use Paper Capture (if you have Windows) for optical character recognition.

Understanding Scanning and Optical Character Recognition (OCR) 282

Understanding Scanning Preparation 284

Scan Documents with Acrobat Scan..286

Using Digital Camera Files 288

Using Acrobat Paper Capture (Windows only) 290

Change Paper Capture Preferences (Windows only) 292

Optimize Captured Pages (Windows only) 294

Scan Images with Acrobat Scan........296

UNDERSTANDING SCANNING AND OPTICAL CHARACTER RECOGNITION (OCR)

Acrobat provides several tools that you can use with different hardware to convert scanned images to readable and searchable text.

Acrobat Scan

Acrobat Scan is a plug-in that is automatically installed with Acrobat. When Acrobat is open, you can scan a document and it opens as a PDF page. Additional pages can be scanned and appended to the open file.

Paper Capture (Windows only)

Paper Capture is optical character recognition (OCR) software designed to convert image scans to text. The Paper Capture plug-in was first released for Windows only. Mac users should check the Adobe Web site for a Mac version when made available.

Paper Capture Online

Adobe provides an online service for capturing pages. With a scanned document, the file is an image and no text can be searched in the image, even when it has been converted to PDF. Send Adobe a scanned document and, for a small fee, you can have your document converted to rich text and e-mailed back to you.

Acrobat Capture

Acrobat Capture is a standalone product sold separately from Acrobat. For industrial-strength document conversions, Acrobat Capture meets strong OCR conversion demands.

Scanners

To use Acrobat Scan, you need to connect a scanner to your computer. Be certain your scanner is configured correctly before using Acrobat Scan.

Digital Cameras

You can use digital cameras to photograph documents and then open the image files in Acrobat via the Open as Adobe PDF command. The PDF files can then be converted with Paper Capture. If resolution is not sufficient on the original photos, you can upsize them in Photoshop before capturing the pages.

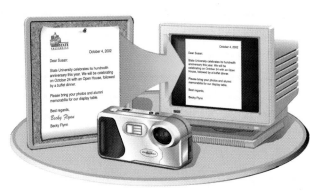

UNDERSTANDING SCANNING PREPARATION

Before scanning any document, you need to understand how to prepare your original documents for scanning. The initial preparation you make before scanning saves you editing time later.

Clean the Scanner

Be certain to use a lint-free cloth and clean the scanner glass before scanning images or text. The cleaner the scan, the fewer corrections you need to make in the final documents.

Using the Right Source Material

If you have manuals or bound documents that need OCR conversion, you may find that photocopying the originals yields better results. If material is not placed flat on the scanner glass, the scans may be unusable.

Preview

When opening your scanner software, click the Preview button to see a thumbnail preview. Adjust the scan borders and crop out any unneeded edges. Be certain to straighten the source material before scanning.

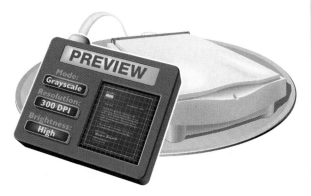

Set Image Resolution

Paper Capture requires at least 200 dpi (dots per inch) to sufficiently convert image data to text. Make certain you have enough resolution, but also be aware that too much resolution slows down your workflow.

Control Brightness

Contrast is important in scanning for OCR conversion. Most scanner software is capable of adjusting contrast before you scan. Run some tests and find the right contrast adjustment for producing good scans.

Select a Color Mode

If scanning for OCR conversion, grayscale images are sufficient. Color images require more memory and take longer to scan.

SCAN DOCUMENTS WITH ACROBAT SCAN

You can use the Acrobat Scan plug-in, which is automatically installed with Acrobat, to scan a document.

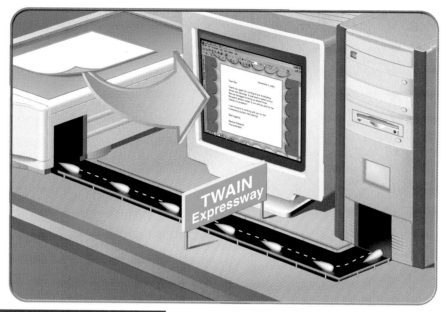

This example shows a typical scanning sequence. The specifics of using your scanner may differ. Before attempting a scan in Acrobat, be certain your scanner is properly configured. You should have a TWAIN (Technology With An Important Name) driver installed with your scanner software. For installation instructions, see your scanner's manual.

SCAN DOCUMENTS WITH ACROBAT SCAN

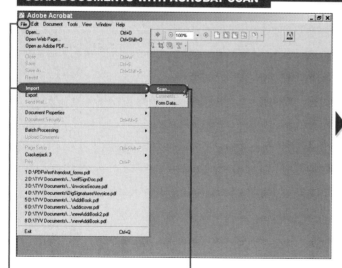

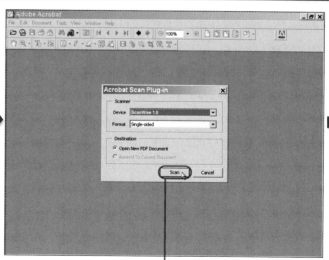

1 Click **File**.

2 Click **Import**.

3 Click **Scan**.

■ The Acrobat Scan Plug-in dialog box opens.

Note: The scanner device should appear. If no device is found, recheck your scanner's connection and configuration.

4 Click **Scan**.

Why can I not see my scanner when I open the Acrobat Scan plug-in dialog box?

Launch your scanner software or the program you usually use to scan. Check the scanner to see if it is working properly. If the scanner works, then you may not have the TWAIN driver installed for your scanner. Check your scanner installer CD or visit the manufacturer's Web site for an updated driver. Install the new driver per your manufacturer's instructions.

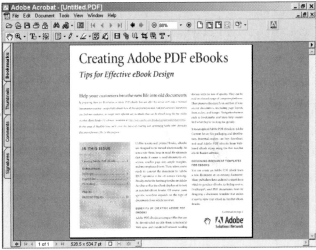

■ The dialog box for your scanner opens. Each dialog box differs according to scanner manufacturer.

5 Click **Preview**.

6 Crop the area to be scanned with a rectangle in the preview area.

7 Make adjustments for image resolution, brightness, and color mode.

8 Click **Scan**.

■ The scan opens as a PDF in the Document Pane.

USING DIGITAL CAMERA FILES

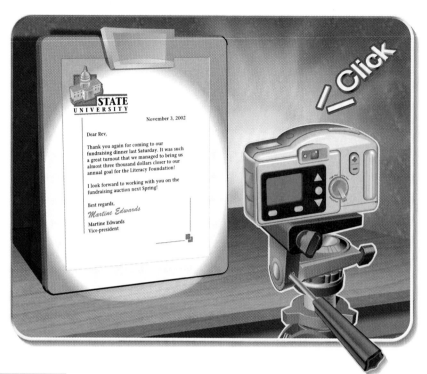

Digital cameras can often capture pages much faster than flatbed scanners. You can set up a copy stand and photograph pages that you can later convert with Acrobat Paper Capture. If the photo images are not of sufficient resolution, you can resample the images in a program like Photoshop.

You can set up a Photoshop Action to automate the process. For more on Photoshop Actions, see the Photoshop user documentation.

USING DIGITAL CAMERA FILES

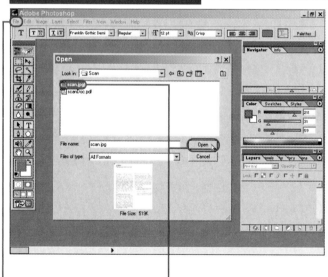

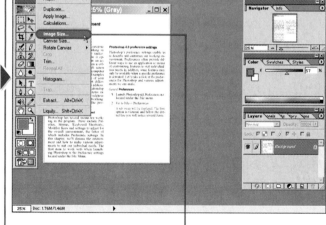

RESAMPLE AN IMAGE IN PHOTOSHOP

1 Open Photoshop.

2 Click **File**.

3 Click **Open**.

■ The Open dialog box appears.

4 Click the file to open.

5 Click **Open**.

6 Click **Image**.

7 Click **Image Size**.

Can I bypass using Photoshop if my digital camera images are sufficient resolution for OCR conversion?

If you have a digital camera capable of capturing images at sufficient resolution, use the Open as Adobe PDF command and select JPEG for the file type. Almost all digital cameras save files as JPEG images. You can append pages to an open PDF file and import multiple images. (See Chapter 3 for more on opening JPEG files in Acrobat and appending pages.)

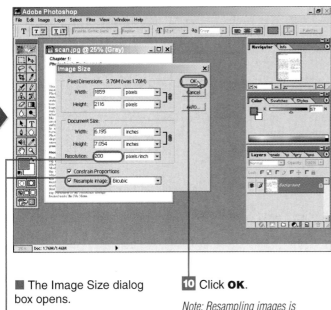

■ The Image Size dialog box opens.

8 Check **Resample Image** (□ changes to ✓).

9 Type **200** for Resolution.

10 Click **OK**.

Note: Resampling images is recommended only for OCR conversion.

■ Convert the color mode to grayscale and adjust brightness if necessary.

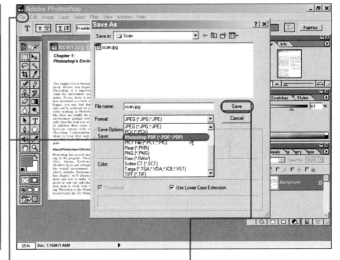

SAVE AS PDF

1 Click **File**.

2 Click **Save As**.

3 Click the Format ▾ and click **Photoshop PDF**.

4 Click **Save**.

■ The file is ready for Paper Capture.

Note: For more on Paper Capture, see "Using Acrobat Paper Capture," later in this chapter.

If you have properly converted a scan to PDF and you have the Windows operating system, you can use Acrobat Paper Capture to convert the scanned image to recognizable text. Any words not recognized by Paper Capture are listed as Capture Suspects. When you capture a page, you may need to correct these Capture Suspects.

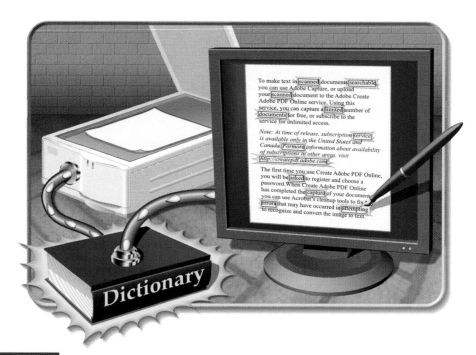

USING ACROBAT PAPER CAPTURE

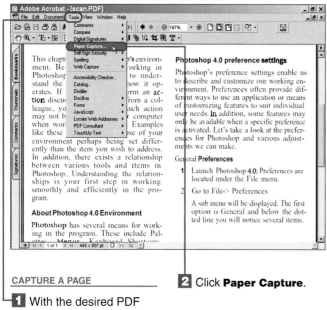

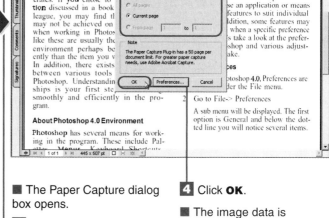

CAPTURE A PAGE

1 With the desired PDF open in Acrobat, click **Tools**.

2 Click **Paper Capture**.

■ The Paper Capture dialog box opens.

3 Make any desired capture setting changes.

4 Click **OK**.

■ The image data is converted to text.

Why are some of the words denoted as suspects when they are spelled correctly?

Paper Capture matches its interpretation of a word to its dictionary. If the interpretation is not found in the dictionary, the word is tagged as a suspect. When words are spelled correctly, click **Accept (TAB)** or press the Tab key and Paper Capture's interpretation is accepted.

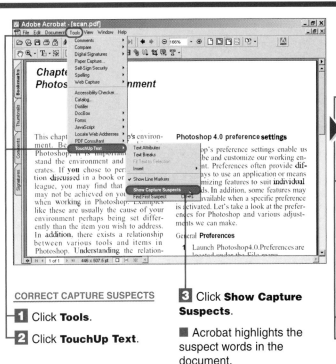

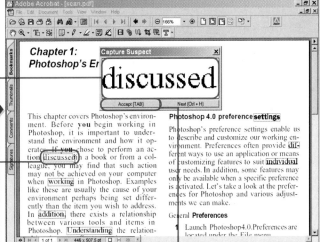

CORRECT CAPTURE SUSPECTS

1 Click **Tools**.

2 Click **TouchUp Text**.

3 Click **Show Capture Suspects**.

■ Acrobat highlights the suspect words in the document.

4 Click [T].

5 Click a suspect.

6 If the word is misspelled, type in the correct spelling in the Capture Suspect dialog box.

7 Click **Accept (TAB)** to accept any changes and move to the next suspect.

8 Continue tabbing through the suspects and make any needed changes.

CHANGE PAPER CAPTURE PREFERENCES

Paper Capture offers several choices for converting text. You can convert text from different languages and output styles. You can also adjust the image resolution during the conversion. These choices are all available in Paper Capture Preferences.

CHANGE PAPER CAPTURE PREFERENCES

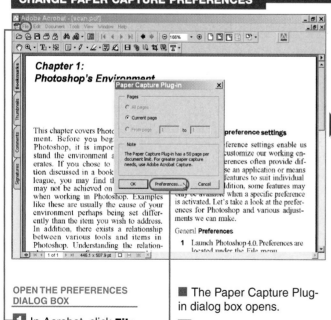

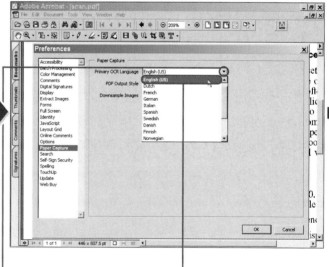

OPEN THE PREFERENCES DIALOG BOX

1 In Acrobat, click **File**.

2 Click **Import**.

3 Click **Scan**.

■ The Paper Capture Plug-in dialog box opens.

4 Click **Preferences**.

■ The Preferences dialog box opens.

SELECT A LANGUAGE

5 Click the Primary OCR Language ▼.

6 Click a language dictionary to use.

**My document does not display text changes I make when I scan with
the Searchable Image (Exact) PDF Output Style option. Why not?**

When you use Searchable Image
(Exact), Acrobat preserves the original
look of the scanned document. The
actual text appears much like a hidden
layer. This option is designed to
preserve document integrity for legal
documents, yet offer the capability to
search the file from the text not
displayed on the PDF page. You
can make text edit changes
with the TouchUp Text tool,
but the changes do not
compromise the original
document integrity.

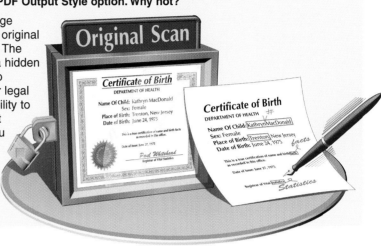

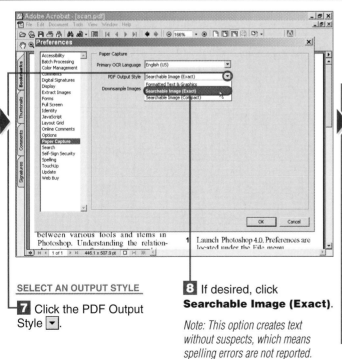

SELECT AN OUTPUT STYLE

7 Click the PDF Output
Style ▾.

8 If desired, click
Searchable Image (Exact).

*Note: This option creates text
without suspects, which means
spelling errors are not reported.*

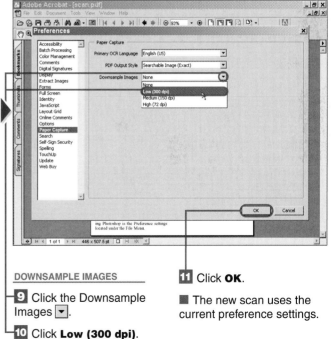

DOWNSAMPLE IMAGES

9 Click the Downsample
Images ▾.

10 Click **Low (300 dpi)**.

11 Click **OK**.

■ The new scan uses the
current preference settings.

OPTIMIZE CAPTURED PAGES

Paper Capture converts image scans to text. The original image scans are much larger in file size than text documents converted from authoring programs. If you want to economize disk space, you can eliminate the original image scans after you capture the text.

OPTIMIZE CAPTURED PAGES

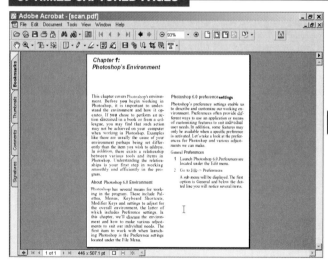

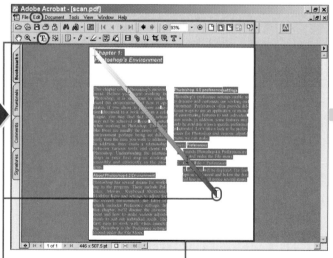

1 Scan a document with Acrobat Scan.

Note: See "Scan Documents with Acrobat Scan," earlier in this chapter.

2 Convert the text with Paper Capture.

Note: See "Using Acrobat Paper Capture," earlier in this chapter.

3 Click 🔳.

4 Click at the beginning of the text and drag through the text on the page.

5 Click **Edit**.

6 Click **Copy**.

Note: For multiple pages, save the file as RTF. See Chapter 7 for saving as RTF.

I have many pages to scan and convert to text. Can Paper Capture efficiently do the job?

You can purchase scanners with automatic document feeders and let Acrobat Scan and Paper Capture work overnight scanning big projects. Paper Capture has a 50-page limit. For more impressive solutions in large offices, you can purchase Adobe's stand-alone product Acrobat Capture. Acrobat Capture converts documents with fewer suspects.

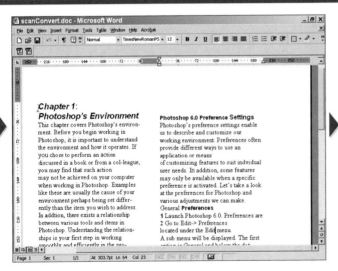

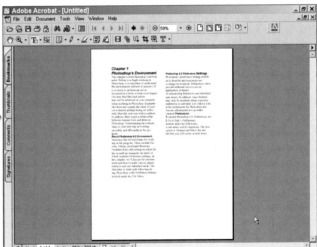

7 Open a word processor.

8 Paste the copied text into a new document.

9 Format the text and make necessary corrections.

10 Convert the document to PDF.

Note: If using Microsoft Word, you can use the PDF Maker tool. See Chapter 3 for more on converting documents, with or without PDF Maker.

■ The new PDF is a smaller file size than the scanned image.

SCAN IMAGES WITH ACROBAT SCAN

You can scan images just like the documents you scan for OCR conversion. Images can be appended to a PDF with different orientations and sizes. If you need to edit an image, you can use the Acrobat Edit Image command to perform edits in Photoshop and have them dynamically updated in the PDF. (See Chapter 7 for more on editing images.)

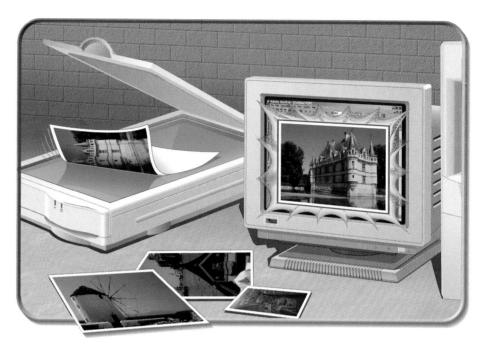

SCAN IMAGES WITH ACROBAT SCAN

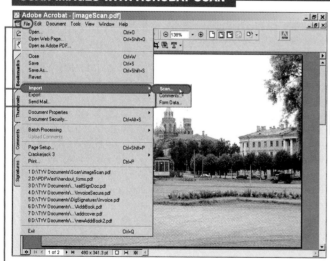

SCAN AN IMAGE

1 Click **File**.

2 Click **Import**.

3 Click **Scan**.

4 Click **Scan** in the Acrobat Scan Plug-in dialog box.

Note: To append images to a file, open the file and then click Scan.

■ The dialog box for your scanner opens. Each dialog box differs according to scanner manufacturer.

5 Marquee the scan area.

Note: If image rotation is needed, the scan area should be larger than the image scanned.

6 Click **Scan**.

■ The image is appended to the document.

If I have both images and text on a PDF page, can I capture the text?

Any PDF page originally scanned with the proper resolution can later have the text converted with Paper Capture. Acrobat ignores the images and leaves them undisturbed. However, if text has been rasterized (that is, converted from text to a bit map image) in an image file, the text cannot be converted with Paper Capture.

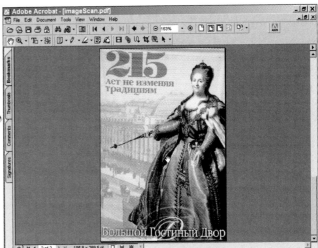

EDIT AN IMAGE

7 Click ⬆.

8 Right-click (Windows) or `Control` + click (Macintosh) the image.

9 In the pop-up menu that appears, click **Edit Image**.

■ The image opens in Photoshop.

10 Crop, rotate, and/or edit the image for brightness in Photoshop.

11 Click **File**.

12 Click **Save**.

13 Close Photoshop.

■ The image is edited accordingly. In this example, the image is cropped and rotated.

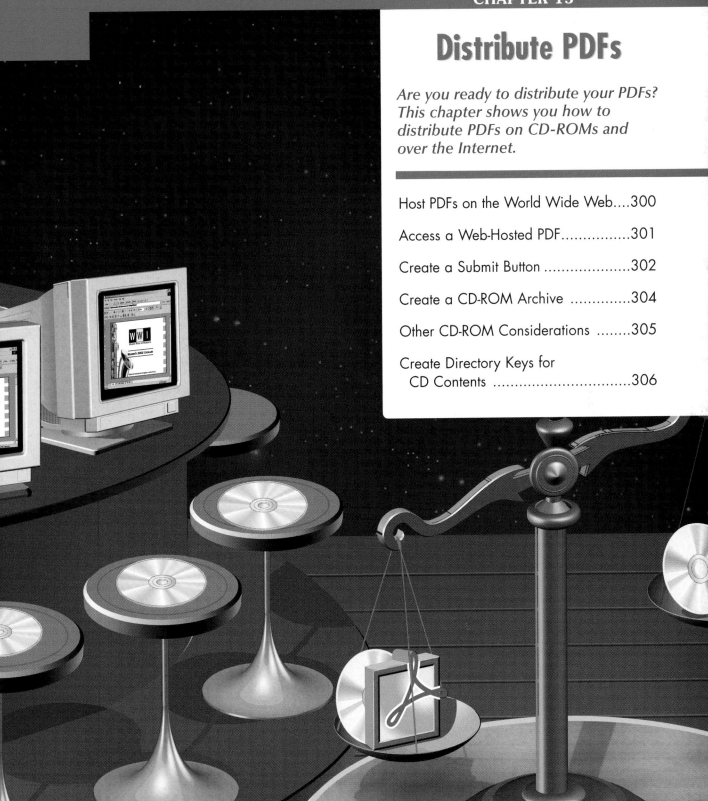

CHAPTER 15

Distribute PDFs

Are you ready to distribute your PDFs? This chapter shows you how to distribute PDFs on CD-ROMs and over the Internet.

Host PDFs on the World Wide Web....300

Access a Web-Hosted PDF................301

Create a Submit Button 302

Create a CD-ROM Archive 304

Other CD-ROM Considerations 305

Create Directory Keys for
    CD Contents 306

HOST PDFS ON THE WORLD WIDE WEB

Hosting a PDF on the World Wide Web is almost identical to hosting Web pages and image files. You need an FTP application to send your files to your Web site. After you transfer the PDF to the Web, you create a link to the PDF on your Web page just as you would to another HTML page.

HOST PDFS ON THE WORLD WIDE WEB

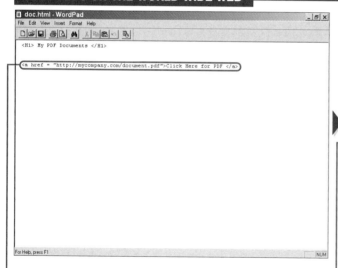

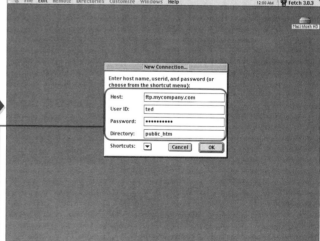

1 Open the HTML document for your Web page in your HTML editor and add code indicating the URL of the PDF.

2 Save the HTML file.

3 Open your ftp client software.

4 Follow the logon procedure.

5 Upload the file from your computer to the server where your Web pages are stored.

6 Upload the PDF file to the location defined in the URL.

■ The PDF can be opened by clicking the link in the HTML code or by navigating to the URL with a Web browser.

ACCESS A WEB-HOSTED PDF

After a PDF has been uploaded to a Web server, you can open the PDF in your Web browser.

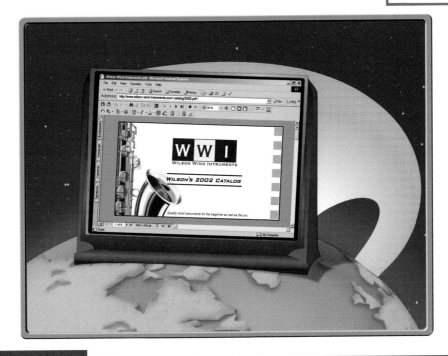

For more on making online comments with PDF documents viewed within Web browsers, see Chapter 6.

ACCESS A WEB-HOSTED PDF

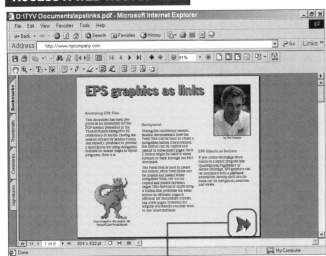

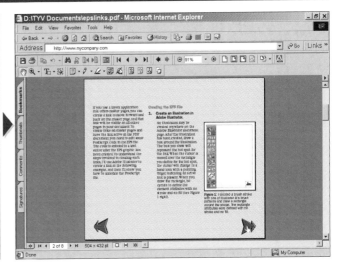

1 Open your Web browser.

2 Enter the URL of the PDF in the Address bar.

3 Press Enter (Windows) or Return (Macintosh).

■ The PDF opens in the Web browser window.

4 Click a link button that navigates to another page.

■ The linked page opens in the Document Pane inside the Web browser window.

Note: Links to external files do not work with Web-hosted PDFs. Links can only be activated to other pages in the currently open PDF.

CREATE A SUBMIT BUTTON

If you create a PDF form for a group of users, you can have the form or the data returned to you. When the data are retrieved, you can import the data into the PDF form. By sending data, you cut down the transmission time a user needs to send a larger file via e-mail.

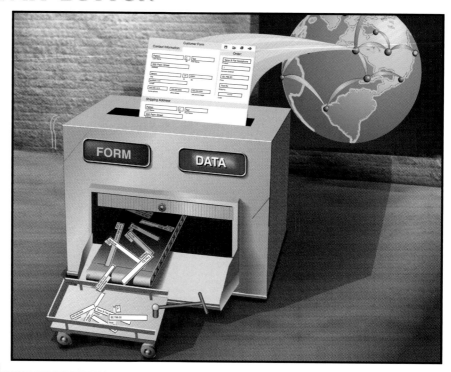

CREATE A SUBMIT BUTTON

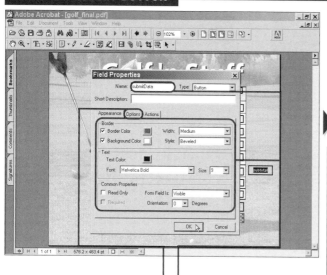

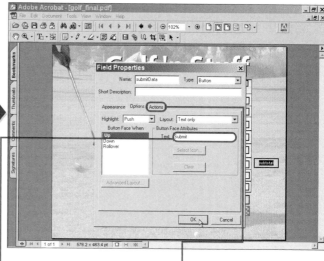

1 Create a button field on a form.

Note: For more information on creating button fields, see Chapter 11.

2 Provide a name and set the appearance to your liking.

3 Click the **Options** tab.

4 Type **Submit** in the Text field.

5 Click the **Actions** tab.

**How do I get the data into a PDF after I
receive it from a user?**

When you receive a data file, follow these
steps to import data into a PDF:

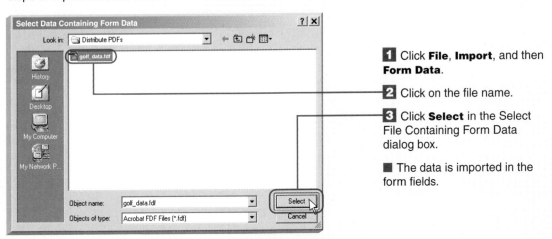

1 Click **File**, **Import**, and then
Form Data.

2 Click on the file name.

3 Click **Select** in the Select
File Containing Form Data
dialog box.

■ The data is imported in the
form fields.

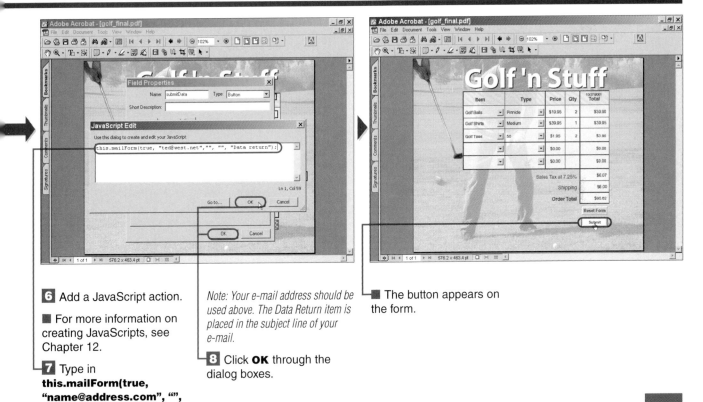

6 Add a JavaScript action.

■ For more information on
creating JavaScripts, see
Chapter 12.

7 Type in
**this.mailForm(true,
"name@address.com", "",
"", "Data Return");**.

*Note: Your e-mail address should be
used above. The Data Return item is
placed in the subject line of your
e-mail.*

8 Click **OK** through the
dialog boxes.

■ The button appears on
the form.

CREATE A CD-ROM ARCHIVE

CD-ROMs can hold many thousands of PDF files. Distributing CDs is often a much more cost-effective solution than sending printed brochures and product catalogs. At less than $1 per CD, you can distribute more information at a fraction of the cost of printed matter.

Before writing CDs of your PDF archives, you need to know a few things about PDFs and storing them on CD-ROMs.

Save with Fast Web View

Before you write a CD, be certain to click **File** and then **Save As** to resave all your PDFs. Check the General Preferences before you save your files to be certain the Allow Fast Web View option is checked. This reduces the size of all your PDF files.

Check Links and Watch Nested Folders

You should test all links, especially those that open files. If you relocate a file outside of its original folder, Acrobat loses track of the location. If you have nested folders, do not move any files outside their folders after you set the links.

Set the Open Options

Decide what view you want the user to see when your PDFs are opened. If you want a Fit in Window view, set the Open Options to **Fit in Window**. See Chapter 2 for more on controlling the opening view.

Make Files Cross Platform

Use a hybrid format when writing to CDs for cross-platform use. Be certain all the filenames are completely written and not truncated. Truncating names render inoperable links among PDF files.

OTHER CD-ROM CONSIDERATIONS

When distributing CDs, you can be certain your CDs will be in circulation longer than the life of some of the files. Keep these tips in mind to produce a quality product and to keep your user constituency updated.

Create a Text File

Not all users will have Acrobat viewers installed on their computers. To be certain that all users can see instructions you want to provide on the CD-ROM, add a plain text file. Create the file in WordPad (Windows) or SimpleText (Macintosh). Name the file ReadMe.

Organize the CD-ROM Contents

On your hard drive, organize all the files to be replicated to a CD-ROM in a single folder. At the root level of the folder, copy the ReadMe text file. All HTML files and Web page graphics can be copied to a single folder nested below the ReadMe file. Add all the PDF files to the folder and check all links before copying the files to a CD-ROM.

Create a Web Page for Updating CD-ROM Files

Create a Web page and save the HTML and supporting images to a folder. Add all the image files used on the Web page and copy them to the same folder. Test the HTML page in a Web browser to be certain all links work properly.

Create Another Web Page with a Link to Adobe's Web Site for the Acrobat Reader Download

Add another Web page and create a hyperlink to http://www.adobe.com/ acrobat. On the Web page, inform users that the Acrobat Reader software can be updated by following the link. You can link this page to the CD update page. Although Adobe Systems has granted permission in the past for distribution of the Reader software as long as licensing information is copied to the CD, rules change. Creating a download link is the safest route. If you do want to distribute the Reader software, check the latest legal restrictions and authorizations by logging on to Adobe's Web site at www.adobe.com and reviewing the most recent documents on "How to Distribute Acrobat Reader."

CREATE DIRECTORY KEYS FOR CD CONTENTS

For personal archiving, you can use Acrobat to help you manage files and find information you retain on archived documents. You can create an index and store all pertinent information regarding the file contents to help you sort through many volumes of CDs. You can also create links to documents located on your CD-ROM from your index PDF file.

CREATE DIRECTORY KEYS FOR CD CONTENTS

1 Open a folder that is to be copied to a CD-ROM.

2 Take a screenshot of the folder.

Note: On Windows, use a utility like Corel Capture or download a screen capture utility from the Internet. On the Macintosh, press ⌘ + Shift + 3 in Mac OS 9 or use the Grab utility in Mac OS X.

3 Click **File**.

4 Click **Open as Adobe PDF**.

5 Click 🔲.

6 Crop the screen to the window size.

Note: See Chapter 8 for more on cropping pages.

How do I know what CD to look for when I am searching for a document?

You can capture the screenshots with Paper Capture (Windows only) and create an index file for all your directory keys. Back up the index and directory keys to a removable cartridge and rebuild the index as new directories are added. For more information on Paper Capture, see Chapter 14. For more information on creating and rebuilding index files, see Chapter 9.

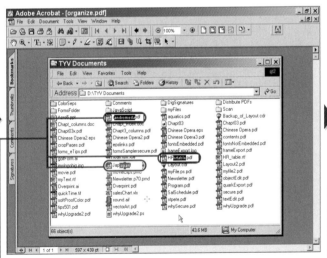

7 Create links to open the files associated with the filenames.

Note: For links to non-PDF documents, use the File Attachment tool.

Note: See Chapter 5 for more on opening files from links. See Chapter 6 for more on creating file attachments.

8 Add comment notes for short descriptions regarding file contents.

Note: See Chapter 6 for more on comment notes.

9 Save the PDF to the folder where the files are copied to the CD reside.

■ When you click a link to a PDF, the document opens in Acrobat. When you double-click a file attachment, the linked file opens in its original program.

GLOSSARY

Accessibility: Documents meeting standards for the vision, hearing, and motion challenged. Accessible documents can be read in logical order by screen readers.

Acrobat: The authoring application. Part of the suite of Adobe Acrobat programs.

Acrobat Approval: A low-cost application less capable than Acrobat, but offering more than Acrobat Reader, such as forms support and digital signatures.

Acrobat Capture: A stand-alone application sold apart from Adobe Acrobat. Used for OCR conversions.

Acrobat Catalog: A plug-in used for creating search index files.

Acrobat Distiller: A stand-alone application sold as part of the Adobe Acrobat suite of software. Used for converting PostScript files to PDF.

Acrobat Reader: A free downloadable program designed to view and print PDF files.

Acrobat Scan: A plug-in permitting scanning from within Acrobat.

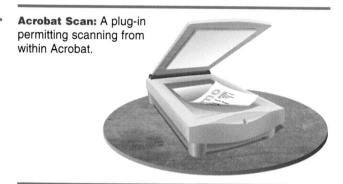

Adobe Acrobat: A suite of software applications, including Acrobat, Distiller, and Catalog.

apf: A file extension used for digital signature profile files.

Articles: Links created in text passages to assist a user's linear movement through a passage.

ASCII: American Standard Code for Information Interchange. A file format for text-only files that preserves no formatting.

Base 14 fonts: Courier, Helvetica, Times, Symbol, and Zapf Dingbat fonts.

bitmap: A graphics file format described in pixels or raster type images.

bookmark: A link to a view, a page, or an action type contained in a palette in Acrobat viewers.

CMYK: Process colors of Cyan, Magenta, Yellow, and Black.

comment: An annotation that can be represented in notes, markups, attachments, sounds, and icons.

CompuServe GIF: A Graphic Image Format created by CompuServe to port image files between mainframes and microcomputers. Today, it is a common file format for Web graphics.

crop: Clipping or trimming edges of an image or PDF page.

destination: Similar to bookmarks, destinations are links to pages and views.

digital signature: An electronic signature that can be validated through a public certificate.

Document Summary: User-supplied information for title, subject, author, and keywords fields.

downsample: Reducing the size of raster images by discarding pixels.

dpi: Dots per inch. A measure of resolution of raster images.

e-book: An electronic book. Often e-books are distributed in Acrobat PDF formats.

Fast Web View: A file compression scheme using pointers to common data in a file. When using Fast Web View, PDF files are compressed in file size.

fdf: Form Data Format. A file format for data exported from Acrobat Forms.

form field: A data entry field, button, combo box, list box, check box, radio button, or signature field used in creating Acrobat forms.

HTML: Hypertext Markup Language. A scripting language used to design Web pages.

GLOSSARY (CONTINUED)

JavaScript: A scripting language developed by Sun Microsystems, commonly used to extend HTML designs.

Job Options: A series of controls used with Acrobat Distiller to assign attributes to the resultant PDF.

JPEG: Joint Photographic Expert Group compression algorithm used for compressing image files.

knockout: When printing color separations, a top color of one element cuts out the underlying element of another color.

link: A hypertext reference used to navigate to the link destination.

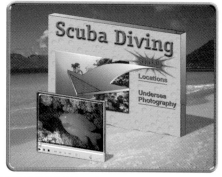

OCR: Optical Character Recognition. Used for converting image scans of text documents to recognizable text that can be edited and searched.

online: Reference to Web-hosted services on the Internet.

overprint: Two overlapping elements of different colors where both colors print.

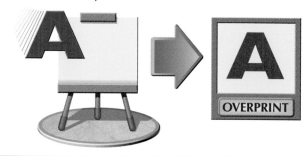

Paper Capture: A plug-in used to perform optical character recognition.

Paper Capture Online: A Web-hosted service from Adobe Systems designed to convert image scans to text on a per-page fee basis.

PCX: A native file format used by Windows applications.

PDF: Portable Document Format. A proprietary file format developed by Adobe Systems to preserve document integrity.

PDFZone: A Web site devoted to distribution of information and advancement of the PDF community. URL: www.pdfzone.com.

pdx: A file extension used for index files created with Acrobat Catalog.

PICT: Picture format native to Macintosh computers.

PlanetPDF: The premier Web site devoted to information and advancement of the PDF community. In addition to the vast library of information files, a PDF store sells virtually all PDF related add-ons and utilities. URL: www.planetpdf.com.

plug-in: A mini-application used to extend the functionality of Acrobat. Many third-party developers distribute plug-ins to suit almost any imaginable need for enhancing Acrobat.

PNG: Portable Network Graphics. A file format for image files commonly used with Web page images.

PostScript: A page description language developed by Adobe Systems to communicate computer-hosted data to PostScript device printers.

raster: An image composition comprised of pixels. Resolution is fixed at the image.

rasterize: The process of converting vector artwork to raster images.

RGB: Red, Green, and Blue. The color model used by computer monitors and Web-hosted graphics.

self-sign: A security mechanism whereby a PDF can be secured against unauthorized viewing. Users who receive public certificates from the document's author can open self-signed files.

server: A computer system in an office or on the Internet where multiple users access files.

submit: In regard to PDFs, form data or documents are delivered to a URL.

TIFF: Tagged Image File Format. A common format among graphic designers for raster images used in layouts and designs.

upsize: Creating more resolution in a document. Through an algorithm, pixels are manufactured artificially.

URL: Uniform Resource Locator. The address where a Web site is found.

vector: An image that uses mathematical formulas to represent an illustration or design. Resolution is dependent on the output device.

watched folder: A folder used with Acrobat Distiller to automatically convert PostScript files to PDFs when files are dropped in the In folder and Acrobat Distiller is running.

Web capture: The process of navigating to a Web page and converting the Web page to a PDF.

Web host: Files stored on servers with Internet access.

INDEX

A

Acrobat (Adobe). *See also specific programs*
  described, 15, 308
  installer, 75
  menus, 18–19
  preferences, 20
  upgrades, 21, 125
  window, 8, 10
Acrobat Approval (Adobe), 12, 195, 308
Acrobat Capture (Adobe), 283, 290–291, 308
Acrobat Catalog (Adobe)
  described, 194–203, 308
  launch, 7, 9, 194–195
  preferences, 194–195, 213
Acrobat Distiller (Adobe). *See also* Job Options
  close, 7
  color separations and, 186–187
  convert EPS files to PDF with, 88–89
  Create Adobe PDF option, 73–74
  create Watched Folders with, 82–83
  described, 78–79, 308
  fonts and, 80–81, 86–87
  Illustrator and, 61
  launch, 7, 9, 70–71
  page size settings, 76
  PPDs and, 187
  preferences, 72
  print with, 57, 68–69, 190
  repurpose PDFs with, 84–85
  security settings, 90–91
  shortcuts/aliases, 71
Acrobat PDF Maker (Adobe), 46–51
Acrobat Reader (Adobe)
  comments and, 145
  described, 8, 308
  download link for, 305
  save PDFs from, 14
  search indexes and, 195
  sound files and, 107
  view PDFs in, 12
  window, 8
Acrobat Scan (Adobe), 282, 286–287, 308
actions. *See also* JavaScript
  check box, 234
  described, 95, 227
  document, 262
Adobe Systems. *See also specific programs*
  Online services, 21
  Web site, 125, 147, 305
AdobePS printers, 68, 73
AIFF (Audio Interleave File Format), 107, 132–133

aliases, 71
annotations. *See* comments
application beep, 250–251
Approval. *See* Acrobat Approval (Adobe)
articles, 59, 95, 100–101, 308
ASCII (American Standard Code for Information Interchange), 45, 71, 308
audio. *See* sounds
audio comments, 122, 132
Audio Interleave File Format (AIFF). *See* AIFF (Audio Interleave File Format)

B

bleeds, 190–191
bookmarks
  convert index entries to, 56
  convert TOC entries to, 54–56
  convert Word headings to, 49
  CorelDraw and, 63
  create, 49–51, 96
  described, 27, 94, 308
  display settings for, 49
  Excel and, 50
  FrameMaker and, 59
  parent/child, 97
  PDF Maker and, 49
  properties of, 98–99, 102
Bookmarks palette, 27, 37, 96, 99
Bookmarks tab, 27, 49
Boolean operators, 214–217
borders
  field, 228
  link, 103
  movie clip, 108
Browse button, 12
Browse for Folder dialog box, 81–82, 87, 147
browsers
  access Adobe Online services with, 21
  access Web-hosted PDFs with, 301
  create links with, 106
  online comments and, 148–149
  save files viewed with, 14
  view Document Summaries with, 201
  view PDFs with, 12–13, 25
Button Appearance dialog box, 111
buttons
  create, 110–111
  duplicate, 114–115
  field, 114–115, 224, 260–261
  icons for, 111
  link, 110–113, 254–255
  radio, 224, 232–233

C

cameras, digital, 283, 288–289
Capture (Acrobat). *See* Acrobat Capture
Catalog (Acrobat). *See* Acrobat Catalog
CD-ROMs, 4, 304–307
check boxes, 225, 234–235
Chooser, 73
color
    border, 108, 228
    calibration, 191
    CMYK, 179, 187–189, 309
    of comments, 128, 133
    knockout, 188–189, 310
    link, 103
    management systems, 76
    overprints, 188–189, 310
    printers, 178, 181, 191
    RGB, 188, 311
    scanners and, 285
    separations, 186–189
    spot, 179
combo boxes, 225, 236–237
Command bar, 6–7, 16
comments
    change position of, 129
    create, 5, 124–125
    described, 122–123, 309
    delete, 129
    filter, 142–143, 145
    Free Text, 130, 122
    graphic, 123, 140
    hidden, 129
    identity settings for, 124–125
    online, 123, 145–149
    note, 112, 126–130, 135, 148
    preferences for, 124–125
    properties of, 128–129, 134–135
    repurpose process and, 85
    spell-check, 150–151
    stamp, 123, 134–139
    summaries of, 144–145
Comments palette, 143
compression, of files, 43, 75
context menus, 34, 115
Continuous Page view, 24–25
conversion to PDF. *See also* export; PDF (Portable Document Format) files
    with CorelDRAW, 62–63
    with the Create Adobe PDF option, 73–74
    described, 64–65
    from EPS format, 88–89
    of HTML, 44, 64

of images, 42–43
with Microsoft Word, 46–47
of multiple files, 43
when opening files, 40, 43
with PDF Maker, 46–51
with the Publish to PDF command, 62
of style sheets, 48–49
of text files, 45
of Web pages, 41, 64–65
Corel Paint, 162
CorelDraw, 62–63, 164–165
crop pages, 154, 172–173, 309

D

destinations
    create, 116–117
    described, 95, 116
    links to, 118–119
Destinations palette, 116
dictionaries, 150–151
digital
    cameras, 283, 288–289
    signatures, 266, 270–273, 278–279, 309
directories. *See* folders
directory keys, 306–307
Distiller (Acrobat). *See* Acrobat Distiller (Adobe)
Document Assembly items, 91
Document menu
    Crop Pages command, 173
    Delete Pages command, 161
    Go to Page command, 29
    Insert Pages command, 160
    Replace Pages command, 159, 161
    Rotate Pages command, 35
Document Pane
    comments and, 126–127
    context menus and, 34
    described, 6
    Go to Page feature and, 29
    help, 19
    links and, 95, 102, 105, 113
    navigate, 7
    open PDFs in, 11
    organize tools in, 16
    Thumbnails tab and, 19
    view options, 24–25, 28–29, 32–33
Document Summaries, 138–139, 200–203, 212–218, 220, 309
Document window, 6–7

E

e-books, 46, 74, 309
Embed All Fonts option, 61, 75, 97

INDEX

Embed Tags in the PDF option, 47
embedded fonts, 53, 74–75, 80–81, 87
encryption, 268. *See also* security
EPS (Encapsulated PostScript) format, 41, 60–61, 76, 88–89. *See also* Acrobat Distiller (Adobe)
Excel (Microsoft), 50, 171
export. *See also* conversion to PDF
    Document Summaries, 201
    form field data, 242
    Job Tickets and, 62–63
    to PDF, 40, 46–49, 55, 57
    styles, 48–49
    table data, 171
    text, 155, 171
expressions, 214–217
Extract Pages dialog box, 158

F

Fast Web View, 304
field buttons, 114–115, 224, 260–261
Field Properties dialog box, 110, 113
fields. *See also* field buttons; form fields
    alignment of, 231, 240
    described, 309
    delete, 115
    JavaScript and, 256–257
    names of, 243
    properties of, 110, 113, 226–228, 230, 235
    resize, 241
    tab order and, 238
    table arrays and, 230–231, 233
    test, 233
    types of, 224
file
    attachments, 123, 131
    compression, 43, 75
    formats, 42, 111
    names, in URLs, 13
    replace existing, 72
    size, 74, 245
film recorders, 179
filter comments, 142–143, 145
Find dialog box, 53
Fit in Window view, 36
folders. *See also* Watched Folders
    browse for, 81, 82, 87, 147
    deleting, 81
    fonts stored in, 80–81, 86, 87
    nested, 304
fonts. *See also* text
    Base 14, 75, 308
    bit-mapped, 183

    for buttons, 110
    color of, 45
    corrupted, 86
    Distiller and, 80–81, 86–87
    embed, 53, 74–75, 80–81, 87
    Illustrator and, 61
    installation of, 75
    preservation of, 53
    printers and, 53, 183
    problems with, correction of, 86–87
    storage of in folders, 80–81, 86, 87
    symbol, 110
    tagged PDFs and, 47
form fields. *See also* fields; forms
    bookmarks and, 98–99
    described, 95
    link buttons in, 110–113
    spell-check feature for, 150–151
forms. *See also* buttons; form fields
    check boxes in, 225, 234–235
    create, 5, 224–225, 242–245
    export data from, 242
    import data to, 242
    list boxes in, 225, 237
    optimize, 245
    populated, 244–245
    repurpose process and, 85
    save, 244–245
    Submit button for, 302
    text fields in, 224, 228–229
    understanding, 224–225
FrameMaker (Adobe), 58–59
Free Text comments, 130, 122
Free Text tool, 130
FreeHand (MacroMedia), 164–165
Freewarefiles.com Web site, 133
Full Screen Mode, 36

G

Go To Page feature, 29
graphic comments, 123, 140
Graphic Markup tools, 140
graphics. *See* images
grayscale images, 43, 75

H

halftone frequency, 179
Hand tool, 103, 113
help, 19, 21, 27, 77, 194
Highlight tool, 141

HTML (HyperText Markup Language)
    conversion of to PDF, 44, 64
    described, 309
    editors, 300
    links, preservation of in PDF documents, 64
hyperlinks. *See* links

I

icons, 111
Illustrator (Adobe), 60–61, 88–89, 164–165
image setters, 179
images
    compression settings for, 43, 75
    convert to PDF, 42–43
    edit, 155, 162–163
    grayscale, 43, 75
    import, 252–253
    JPEG, 43, 289, 310
    layers in, 52
    optimize, 294–295
    resample, 288–289
    save, 163
    scan, 41, 296–297
    vector, 52, 311
import. *See also* export
    form field data, 110–111, 242
    images, 252–253
    public certificates, 274–265
    sounds, 107, 133
    tables, 171
indexes. *See* search indexes
inline views, 12–14, 25
Invisible option, 103, 104

J

JavaScript
    for application beeps, 250–251
    copy/paste, 249
    described, 248–249, 310
    for document actions, 262
    for the import process, 252–253
    for link buttons, 254–255
    for page number generation, 260–261
    repository, 263
    for sales tax calculations, 256–257
    for spawning templates, 258–259
Job Options
    adjust, 76–77
    conversion from EPS and, 89
    described, 74–77, 310
    fonts and, 87
    select, 78–79
    sets of, 77, 83, 85
    settings for, 46
    Watched Folders and, 82–83
Job Tickets, 62–63
JPEG (Joint Photographics Experts Group) images, 43, 289, 310.
    See also images

K

keyboard shortcuts, 7, 11, 19, 31
keywords, 214–217
knockout, 188–189, 310

L

laser printers, 68, 73, 179, 190. *See also* printers
layers, in graphics, 52
layout programs. *See* CorelDRAW; PageMaker (Adobe)
line screen, 179
link buttons, 110–113, 254–255
Link Properties dialog box, 102–105, 118–119
Link tool, 95, 102–104
links. *See also specific types*
    activate, 33
    CD-ROM archives and, 304
    create, 5, 33, 95, 102–107, 175
    described, 310
    properties of, 98–99, 102–103, 118–119
    repurpose process and, 85
    sound, 107
    text, 104–105, 175
    understanding, 94–95
    video, 107–108
list boxes, 225, 237
log files, 72

M

MacUpdate Web site, 133
magnification options, 30–31, 36
Max Fit Visible Zoom option, 101
menu bar, described, 6
menus
    context, 34, 115
    described, 6, 18–19
    sub-, 18
Microsoft Excel. *See* Excel (Microsoft)
Microsoft Office. *See* Office (Microsoft)
Microsoft PowerPoint. *See* PowerPoint (Microsoft)
Microsoft Word. *See* Word (Microsoft)
microphones, 133
monitors, 191
mouse, navigation with, 7
movie
    clips, 95
    links, 107–108
Movie Properties dialog box, 108

INDEX

N

navigation. *See also* Navigation Pane
    buttons, 112–113
    Go to Page feature, 29
    JavaScript for, 254–255
    with the mouse, 7
    tools, 26
Navigation Pane. *See also* navigation
    Bookmarks tab, 27, 49
    described, 6
    display of palettes in, 17
note comments, 112, 126–130, 135, 148
Note Properties dialog box, 128–129
Note tool, 130

O

objects, edit process for, 164–165
OCR (Optical Character Recognition), 282–283, 284, 289, 310
Office (Microsoft), 46–47. *See also* Excel (Microsoft); PowerPoint (Microsoft); Word (Microsoft)
online comments, 123, 145–149
operators, 214–217
Optical Character Recognition (OCR). *See* OCR (Optical Character Recognition)
overprints, 188–189, 310

P

Page Setup dialog box, 180–181
PageMaker (Adobe), 54–55, 186, 190
pages
    add, 154
    add numbers to, 260–261
    copy, 155–156
    crop, 154, 172–173, 309
    delete, 103, 119, 154–155, 161
    extract, 158–159
    go to specific, 29
    insert, 160–161
    optimize, 294–295
    paste, 155–156
    replace, 159
    rotate, 35
    setup settings for, 76, 180–181
    templates for, 136–139, 258–259
palettes
    Bookmarks palette, 27, 37, 96, 99
    Comments palette, 143
    Destinations palette, 116
    groups of, 17
    size settings for, 28
    Thumbnail palette, 28

Paper Capture (Adobe), 282–285, 290–295, 297, 307, 311
Paper Capture Online service, 283, 311
paragraphs, 55, 165–167
passwords, 90–91, 185, 266, 268–269
PDF (Portable Document Format) files. *See also* conversion to PDF
    basic page view settings for, 24–25
    create, 40–41, 46–51
    distribute, 299–307
    filenames for in URLs, 13
    open, 11–12, 40, 42–45
    repurpose, 84–85
    understanding, 10, 311
PDF Maker (Acrobat). *See* Acrobat PDF Maker
PDF Options dialog box, 53, 54
.pfb extension, 87
Photoshop (Adobe), 52–53, 162–163, 288
plate setters, 179
Portable Document Format (PDF) files. *See* PDF (Portable Document Format) files
PostScript files. *See also* Acrobat Distiller (Adobe); EPS (Encapsulated PostScript) format
    color separations and, 186–187
    described, 311
    distill, 78–79
    errors and, 183
    fonts and, 86–87
    repurpose process and, 84–85
    Watched Folders and, 82–83
PowerPoint (Microsoft), 51
PPDs (PostScript Printer Description) files, 187
preferences
    comment, 124–125
    Distiller, 72
    General, 20, 25
    page view, 25
    search index, 210–211
    zoom view, 101
Preserve Illustrator Editing Capabilities option, 61
Press option, 46, 74
print. *See also* printers
    color separations, 186–189
    to Distiller, 57
    to file setting, 69
    Job Option setting, 46, 74
    process, bookmarks which link to, 98–99
    resolution, 53, 179, 184–185
    setup, 180–181
Print dialog box, 68–69, 99, 182–183
Print to File dialog box, 69
printers. *See also* PostScript files; print
    AdobePS, 68, 73
    color, 178, 181, 191

commercial, 84, 178–179, 187, 189–191
control settings for, 182–183
desktop, 178
fonts and, 53
ink-jet, 178
laser, 68, 73, 179, 190
on-demand services, 179
orientation settings, 181
page size settings, 89
photo, 179
security for, 184–185
.prn file extension, 79
proximity, 217
public certificates, 266, 273–277
Publish to PDF dialog box, 62

Q

QuarkXpress, 10, 56–57
QuickTime format, 107

R

radio buttons, 224, 232–233
Reader (Acrobat). *See* Acrobat Reader (Adobe)
relative referencing, 219
repurpose PDFs, 84–85
Resize Page and Center Artwork for EPS files option, 76, 89
resolution, 53, 179, 184–185
RTF (Rich Text Format), 170

S

sales tax, 256–257
save
        as EPS, 88
        with Fast Web View, 304
        forms, 244–245
        images, 153
        Job Option sets, 77
        as PDF, 14, 40
        PDF to PostScript, 86
        search indexes, 197
        stamp files, 138
        RTF (Rich Text Format) files, 170
        view controls, 37
Save As dialog box, 15, 19, 37
Save button, 14, 15
Save dialog box, 105
scan. *See also* Acrobat Scan (Adobe); scanners
        documents, 41, 286–287
        images, 41, 296–297
        process, understanding, 282–283

Scan (Acrobat). *See* Acrobat Scan (Adobe)
scanners. *See also* Acrobat Scan (Adobe); scan
        configure, 283
        drivers for, 286–287
        OCR and, 282–284, 289, 310
        preparation of, 284
        preview feature for, 285
        resolution of, 285, 287
screen setting, 46, 74
screenshots, 306–307
scroll bars, described, 6
search indexes. *See also* Document Summaries
        Boolean operators and, 214–217
        categories for, 214–216
        copy, 195
        create, 5, 196–197
        entries in,
                conversion to bookmarks, 56
        expressions and, 214–217
        files for, relocation of, 221
        FrameMaker and, 58–59
        keywords and, 214–217
        links from, 104–105
        load, 206–207
        optimize for CD-ROMs, 194–195
        perform searches with, 208–213
        preferences for, 210–211
        purge process, 199
        rebuild process, 199
        relative referencing and, 219
        Search dialog box and, 208–211
        select, 206–207
        word options for, restriction of, 198
search keys, 202–203
security
        digital signatures and, 266, 270–273, 277–279
        Distiller settings for, 90–91
        passwords, 90–91, 185, 266, 268–269
        printers and, 184–185
        public certificates and, 266, 273–277
        self-sign, 267, 271, 275–277, 311
        understanding, 266–267
Select Appearance dialog box, 110–111
Select File to Open dialog box, 105
self-sign security, 267, 271, 275–277, 311
servers, 14, 44, 64, 145–149, 311. *See also* Web servers
signatures, digital, 266, 270–273, 278–279, 309
Single Page tool, 25
Single Page view, 24–25
slide shows, 51, 179
soft-proofing devices, 186–189

INDEX

sort
>comments, 143
>destinations, 117
sounds. *See also* audio comments
>application beep, 250–251
>import, 107
>JavaScript for, 250–251
>record, 132–133
spawning templates, 258–259
spell-check feature, 150–151
stamp comments, 123, 134–139
status bar, 6, 25
Story Editor, 55
Strikeout tool, 141
style sheets, 48–49
Submit button, 302
suitcase icon, 87
summaries. *See* Document Summaries
system administrators, 147

T

tab order, 238
table arrays, 230–231, 233
tables, 47, 171, 202–203. *See also* TOC (Table of Contents)
tagged PDFs, 47
Tagged Information File Format (TIFF). *See* TIFF file format
templates, 136–139, 258–259
text. *See also* fonts; text files
>blocks, 174
>copy, 168–169
>edit, 155, 165–167
>export, 171
>fields, 224, 228–229
>formatting, 45, 47–49
>links, 104–105, 175
>markup comments, 123
>paragraphs, 55, 165–167
>paste, 155–156, 169
>position lines of, 167
>scan, 41, 290–295
>style sheets, 48–49
>table-formatted, 171
Text Attributes dialog box, 167
text files. *See also* text
>CD-ROM archives and, 305
>classification of PostScript files as, 71
>convert, to PDF, 45
Text Markup tool, 141
Text Only file format, 45
thumbnails, 19, 28, 94
Thumbnails tab, 19
TIFF file format, 173, 311

tile views, 32
title bar, described, 6
TOC (Table of Contents), 54–56, 58–59, 104–105
toolbars. *See also* tools
>expand, 17
>orientation of, changes to, 16
tools. *See also* specific tools
>appearance of inside browser windows, 13
>described, 8
>launch, 70–71
>organize, 16
>shortcuts/aliases for, 71
TouchUp Object tool, 167
TouchUp Text tool, 166–167, 174, 293
transparency, preservation of, 60
trusted certificates, 274. *See also* public certificates
TWAIN drivers, 286–287

U

Underline tool, 141
updates, 21, 125
URLs (Uniform Resource Locators). *See also* links
>create, 106, 175
>described, 311
>for movie clips, 109
>PDF file names in, 13

V

vector graphics, 52, 311. *See also* images
video
>clips, 95
>links, 107–108
views. *See also* thumbnails
>activated links and, 33
>control of when documents are opened, 36–37
>Document Pane options for, 24–25, 28–29, 32–33
>Fast Web, 304
>Fit in Window, 36
>inline, 12–14, 25
>keyboard shortcuts for, 31
>navigation tools and, 26
>tile, 32
>zoom, 30–31, 34, 37, 101

W

Watched Folders, 82–83, 311
WAV (Windows Audio) file format, 107, 132–133
Web browsers. *See* browsers
Web pages
>conversion of to PDF, 41, 64–65
>repurpose PDF process and, 84
Web servers, 12, 146–149, 301. *See also* servers

Word (Microsoft)
    conversion to PDF with, 46–49
    Distiller and, 68–69
    export styles from, 48–49
    PDF Maker and, 46–47
    PostScript printers and, 68–69
    RTF files and, 170
    table creation in, 202
    tagged PDFs and, 47
    toolbar, 46
workbooks, 51
workgroups, 145–149, 267, 273
World Wide Web. *See also* Web browsers; Web pages
    host PDFs on, 300–301
    links (URLs), 13, 106, 109, 175, 311

Z

Zoom tool, 30–31
zoom view, 34, 37, 101

Read Less – Learn More™

Visual

Simplified®

For visual learners who are brand-new to a topic and want to be shown, not told, how to solve a problem in a friendly, approachable way.

Simply the Easiest Way to Learn

All Simplified® books feature friendly Disk characters who demonstrate and explain the purpose of each task.

Title	ISBN	Price
America Online® Simplified®, 2nd Ed.	0-7645-3433-5	$27.99
America Online® Simplified®, 3rd Ed.	0-7645-3673-7	$24.99
Computers Simplified®, 5th Ed.	0-7645-3524-2	$27.99
Creating Web Pages with HTML Simplified®, 2nd Ed.	0-7645-6067-0	$27.99
Excel 97 Simplified®	0-7645-6022-0	$27.99
Excel 2002 Simplified®	0-7645-3589-7	$27.99
FrontPage® 2000® Simplified®	0-7645-3450-5	$27.99
FrontPage® 2002® Simplified®	0-7645-3612-5	$27.99
Internet and World Wide Web Simplified®, 3rd Ed.	0-7645-3409-2	$27.99
Microsoft® Access 2000 Simplified®	0-7645-6058-1	$27.99
Microsoft® Excel 2000 Simplified®	0-7645-6053-0	$27.99
Microsoft® Office 2000 Simplified®	0-7645-6052-2	$29.99
Microsoft® Word 2000 Simplified®	0-7645-6054-9	$27.99
More Windows® 95 Simplified®	1-56884-689-4	$27.99
More Windows® 98 Simplified®	0-7645-6037-9	$27.99
Office 97 Simplified®	0-7645-6009-3	$29.99
Office XP Simplified®	0-7645-0850-4	$29.99
PC Upgrade and Repair Simplified®, 2nd Ed.	0-7645-3560-9	$27.99
Windows® 95 Simplified®	1-56884-662-2	$27.99
Windows® 98 Simplified®	0-7645-6030-1	$27.99
Windows® 2000 Professional Simplified®	0-7645-3422-X	$27.99
Windows® Me Millennium Edition Simplified®	0-7645-3494-7	$27.99
Windows® XP Simplified®	0-7645-3618-4	$27.99
Word 97 Simplified®	0-7645-6011-5	$27.99
Word 2002 Simplified®	0-7645-3588-9	$27.99

Over 10 million *Visual* books in print!